The Presidential Difference

THE PRESIDENTIAL DIFFERENCE

LEADERSHIP STYLE
FROM FDR TO GEORGE W. BUSH

Second Edition

FRED I. GREENSTEIN

Princeton University Press
Princeton and Oxford

Published by Princeton University Press, 41 William Street,
Princeton, New Jersey 08540
In the United Kingdom: Princeton University Press, 3 Market Place,
Woodstock, Oxfordshire OX20 1SY

First edition published in 2000 by The Free Press
A Division of Simon & Schuster Inc.

First Princeton edition, with a new afterword, 2001

Second edition, 2004

Library of Congress Cataloging-in-Publication Data

Greenstein, Fred I.
The presidential difference : leadership style from FDR to George W. Bush /
Fred I. Greenstein.— 2nd ed.
p.   cm.
Includes bibliographical references and index.
ISBN 0-691-11909-0 (pbk. : alk. paper)
1. Presidents—United States—History.   2. Personality and politics—United
States—History.   3. Political leadership—United States—History.   4. United
States—Politics and government.   I. Title.
JK511.G74 2004
973.92'092'2—dc22   2003066388

British Library Cataloging-in-Publication Data is available

This book has been composed in Sabon

Printed on acid-free paper. ∞

pup.princeton.edu

Printed in the United States of America

3   5   7   9   10   8   6   4

ISBN-13: 978-0-691-11909-0 (pbk.)

ISBN-10: 0-691-11909-0 (pbk.)

To Barbara

CONTENTS

The Presidential Difference

CHAPTER 1

The Presidential Difference

The President is at liberty, both in law and conscience, to be as big a man as he can.

—WOODROW WILSON, 1907

But nowadays he can not be as small as he might like.

—RICHARD E. NEUSTADT, 1960

On April 1, 1954, President Dwight D. Eisenhower convened the National Security Council (NSC) to consider a matter of war or peace. Communist insurgents had encircled key units of the U.S.-backed French forces in Indochina at Dien Bien Phu in northwest Vietnam. Eisenhower's concern was falling dominoes. If Dien Bien Phu fell, French resistance in Indochina was likely to collapse, and other Southeast Asian nations might come under communist control. After the NSC meeting, Eisenhower confided to an associate that he was thinking about ordering an air strike to relieve the French, an action that could have led to a large-scale American military involvement in Indochina. Instead, he decided on a course of diplomatic action that

1

culminated in the partition of Vietnam into a communist North and a noncommunist South.

One member of Eisenhower's administration who disagreed with his decision not to take military action was the official next in the line of presidential succession, Vice President Richard M. Nixon. Would Nixon have committed American military power in Indochina if he had been president? That can never be known with certainty, but it is likely that he would have.

In 1965, President Lyndon B. Johnson faced a similar choice. The American-backed South Vietnam government was in danger of falling to the Vietnamese communists. On January 27, Johnson's top advisers presented him with two options: seek negotiations and "salvage what little can be preserved with no major addition to our present military risks" or "use our military power in the Far East to force a change of communist policy." Johnson opted for military power, first ordering the bombing of North Vietnam and then committing a mounting U.S. ground force to combat in Vietnam. By 1968, a half-million American soldiers were mired in Southeast Asia, at which point Johnson announced that he would halt the military buildup, seek negotiations with the communists, and remove himself from the running for a second elected term.

Again the vice president did not agree with the president's decision. Shortly after the bombing began, Hubert H. Humphrey sent Johnson a confidential memorandum warning of the risk of becoming embroiled in an unpopular war in Vietnam, and urging Johnson to apply his political skills to finding a diplomatic solution. Johnson reprimanded Humphrey for venturing an opinion on the matter and excluded him from meetings on Vietnam until he fell in line behind the administration's military effort. Would a President Humphrey have taken a different course of action than Johnson? The answer is unknowable, but it is probable that he would have.[1]

The United States is said to have a government of laws and institutions rather than individuals, but as these examples remind us, it is one in which the matter of who occupies the nation's highest office can have profound repercussions. That is not everywhere the case. In

Great Britain, with its tradition of collective leadership, for example, the rare Winston Churchill, Margaret Thatcher, or Tony Blair is far outnumbered by the many Stanley Baldwins, Harold Wilsons, and John Majors, whose personal impact on governmental actions is at best limited.

If some higher power had set out to design a democracy in which the individual on top mattered, the result might well resemble the American political system. American chief executives have placed their stamp on the nation's policies since the founding of the Republic, but until the 1930s, Congress typically took the lead in policymaking, and the programs of the federal government were of modest importance for the nation and world.

Then came the emergence of what is commonly called the modern presidency. Under the stimulus of the New Deal, World War II, and the entrepreneurial leadership of Franklin Delano Roosevelt, there was a vast expansion of the scope and influence of the federal government. Meanwhile, the United States became a world and then a nuclear power, and the presidency underwent fundamental changes that increase the likelihood that the personal attributes distinguishing one White House incumbent from another will shape political outcomes.

The chief executive became the principal source of policy initiative, proposing much of the legislation considered by Congress. Presidents began to make an increasing amount of policy independent of the legislature, drawing on their sweeping administrative powers in an era of activist government and global leadership. The president became the most visible landmark in the political landscape, virtually standing for the federal government in the minds of many Americans. And the Executive Office of the President was created, providing the president with the organizational support needed to carry out his— and someday her—obligations.*

The power of modern American presidents manifests itself in its

---

*I use the masculine pronoun throughout to avoid gender-free locutions in discussing an office that has had only male incumbents at the time of writing. It is highly unlikely, however, that the presidency will remain a male bastion.

purest form in the global arena, where their actions as commander in chief can determine the fate of the human race. This was most strikingly evident in the extended nuclear standoff between the United States and the Soviet Union that followed World War II. However, the president's latitude for independent action is even greater in the unstructured post–cold war world than it was during the cold war, when the threat of mutual destruction concentrated minds and constrained actions.

Presidential power is less potentially apocalyptic at home than abroad, but the occupant of the Oval Office is also of critical domestic importance. The power to nullify legislation gives the chief executive the capacity to thwart the will of Congress, unless his veto is overridden by two-thirds of the Senate and House of Representatives. Presidents have wide discretion over the implementation of laws and allocation of expenditures. The president's ability to command public attention and shape the national policy agenda makes him politically potent whatever his support on Capitol Hill. Even when Richard Nixon and Bill Clinton were under consideration for impeachment, they were far from politically inconsequential. They retained their formal powers; their predicaments preempted normal policymaking; and Clinton even scored significant political victories while Congress deliberated on his removal.

All of this would lead one to expect the qualities that bear on a president's leadership to be subjected to the closest possible attention. That is far from the case. To be sure, every president has been the object of a deluge of prose, first during his presidency, then in the memoirs of his associates, and later in studies based on the declassified records of his administration. Yet, much of that outpouring is directed to the ends the president sought rather than the means he used to advance them, and a large portion of it bears on the merits of his policies rather than the attributes that shaped his leadership.

Two important exceptions are Richard E. Neustadt's *Presidential Power: The Politics of Leadership*, which was published during Eisenhower's final presidential year, and James David Barber's *The Presidential Character: Predicting Performance in the White House*, which appeared during Nixon's first term. Neustadt's interest is with the president's ability to win the support of other policymakers by revealing himself to be politically skilled and to possess the support of the public. Barber's preoccupation is with distinguishing presidents whose emotional insecurities spill over into their official actions from those who are secure in their psychic moorings and free to channel their energies into productive leadership.[2] The merit of Neustadt's emphasis on political skill is made evident by the difficulties encountered by Jimmy Carter, whose policy aspirations were thwarted by his failure to adhere to the norms of Washington politics. The value of Barber's attention to the presidential psyche is illustrated by Richard Nixon, whose character flaws led to actions that made it necessary for him to resign from the presidency.*

A president's effectiveness is a function of more than his political prowess and mental health, however, and there is much to be learned by considering the full sweep of the modern presidential experience. My intention is to do precisely that, focusing on the leadership qualities of each of the presidents from FDR to George W. Bush and their significance for the public and the political community.

I devote a chapter to each of my subjects, providing a concise account of his background, political style, and conduct of the presidency. I consider each chief executive on his own terms, out of a conviction that the modern presidents have been too disparate to be usefully pigeonholed. Nevertheless, I am particularly attentive to six qualities that relate to presidential job performance.

The first, which pertains to the outer face of leadership, is the president's proficiency as a *public communicator*. The second, which relates to the inner workings of the presidency, is the president's *organizational capacity*—his ability to rally his colleagues and structure their activities effectively. The third and fourth bear on the president as political operator—his *political skill* and the extent to which it is har-

---

*For a fuller discussion of these books, see the section on Further Reading for this chapter.

nessed to a *vision* of public policy. The fifth is the *cognitive style* with which the president processes the Niagara of advice and information that comes his way. The last is what the German sociologist Max Weber called "the firm taming of the soul" and has come to be referred to as *emotional intelligence*—the president's ability to manage his emotions and turn them to constructive purposes, rather than being dominated by them and allowing them to diminish his leadership.[3]

I embarked on an extended inquiry into the endlessly fascinating occupants of the modern Oval Office early in 1974, when the presidency of Richard Nixon was on the rocks. Why, I wondered, was that politically gifted chief executive, whose first term had resulted in such dramatic achievements as the opening to China and détente with the Soviet Union, succumbing to what was plainly a self-inflicted political disaster? Rather than confining myself to the enigma of Richard Nixon, I decided to examine presidential political psychology broadly, studying the full array of modern chief executives. In the following years, I immersed myself in the literature on the presidents from FDR to Bill Clinton, mined their unpublished papers, and interviewed large numbers of past and current presidential associates. I also have had informative personal encounters with several of the protagonists of my study, three of which help frame what follows.

In 1977, I led a group of undergraduates in an interview with the recently defeated Gerald Ford. Mindful of the personal toll the presidency had taken on Johnson and Nixon, I asked Ford how he dealt with the pressures of his job. His answer bespoke the even-tempered composure of a stolid son of the Midwest:

> I had to have a physical outlet—swimming or some other activity—that burned up those juices that were not normally consumed during the day. . . . But I found that the pressures I had read about were not nearly as severe as I expected, as long as my staff organized them properly.[4]

The second encounter, which was with Jimmy Carter, was marked by anything but equanimity. Carter's first public appearance after stepping down from office in January 1981 was an informal visit to Princeton University during which he met with the students in my presidency course. One of them asked him what he had found most and least rewarding about being president. He replied by excoriating the Democratic party for not rallying behind his policies, mentioning nothing positive about his White House experience.

Another student observed that Carter had initially managed his own White House but had later appointed a chief of staff. Was this, the questioner asked, because he discovered that the demands on a president had become too great for him to administer his own presidency? For reasons that were unclear, Carter took umbrage at the question, denying that he had ever taken the highly publicized action of appointing a chief of staff. By the end of this unexpectedly contentious session, it was not hard to understand why Carter had failed to bond with the rest of the political community.

The third experience was with Bill Clinton, who had barely been in my line of vision until the final months of 1991. My first clear impression of Clinton came via C-Span. In January and February of 1992, Clinton had survived charges of adultery and draft evasion, run a stronger-than-expected race in New Hampshire, swept the southern primaries, and become the front-runner for the Democratic presidential nomination.

In March, I happened on a telecast of Clinton addressing an African American church congregation that could scarcely have been more responsive if Martin Luther King had been in the pulpit. Speaking with ease and self-assurance, Clinton issued a call for policies that would enable citizens to lift themselves by their bootstraps rather than relying on government handouts. Explaining that he was making the same proposal to audiences of whites, Clinton called on all Americans to put aside their differences and recognize their common bonds.[5]

It was an electric performance by a man who seemed on his way to a presidency of great accomplishments. Instead, Clinton went on to preside over one of the most ragged first two years in office of any modern president. He only hit his stride after his party lost control of Congress in the 1994 midterm election, when he made effective use of the veto to seize the political initiative from the Republicans by forcing two government shutdowns.

In the spring of 1996, I had an occasion to observe Clinton in the White House. I had been invited to the signing of the law providing for the line-item veto, an authorization for the president to nullify provisions in appropriation bills. I was ushered into the Oval Office, where I joined a group of good-government advocates chosen to highlight the event. Clinton entered and launched into a prepared statement. At first, he read from cue cards, sounding somewhat mechanical, but within seconds he put the cards down, faced his audience, and addressed it with great fluency and an impressive sense of conviction.[6]

Clinton's remarks were not particularly profound (and the Supreme Court later struck down the line-item veto), but he radiated the aura of a chief executive who had come into his own and was ready to go on to a productive second term. Instead, Clinton went on to a new term marked by modest policy initiatives, the revelation that he had engaged in sexual relations with a White House intern in the presidential office, and a year consumed by his impeachment. In the process, he had provided a reminder that in the absence of emotional intelligence, the presidency is a defective instrument of democratic governance.

The concern of this book is with the leadership of the modern presidents, but it is also impossible not to be impressed by their sheer diversity. One indicator of their variety is their fathers' occupations. Roosevelt's was a Hudson River Valley country gentleman, Truman's a Missouri mule trader, Eisenhower's a Kansas mechanic, Kennedy's a Massachusetts millionaire, Johnson's a Texas politician, Nixon's a California shopkeeper. Ford's stepfather was a Michigan paint manufacturer, Carter's father was a Georgia planter, Reagan's worked in Illinois shoe stores, George H. W.'s was a Wall Street banker and U.S. senator, and Clinton's was an itinerant southern salesman, who died before his son's birth.

A story is told about an airman who escorted Lyndon Johnson across a tarmac in Vietnam, saying, "This is your helicopter, Mr. President." "They are all my helicopters," Johnson replied. When I am asked which president I admire most, I have come to say, "They are all my presidents." Each of the modern presidents is a source of insight, as much for his weaknesses as his strengths. The variation among them provides intellectual leverage, permitting comparisons and expanding our sense of the possible. The presidency is often described as an office that places superhuman demands on its incumbent. In fact, it is a job for flesh-and-blood human beings, who will be better equipped for their responsibilities if they and those who select them do not begin with a blank slate.

In the depths of the Great Depression, Franklin Roosevelt restored faith in a political system that Americans had few reasons to respect. Following Pearl Harbor, he rallied the nation and its allies in an epic conflict in which victory was by no means assured. Both as an inspirational leader and as a master politician, FDR provides a benchmark for later presidents.

(Corbis/Bettmann-UPI)

CHAPTER 2

The Virtuosic Leadership of Franklin D. Roosevelt

This great Nation will endure as it has endured, will revive and will prosper. So, first of all, let me assert my firm belief that the only thing we have to fear is fear itself — nameless, unreasoning, unjustified terror which paralyzes needed efforts to convert retreat into advance. In every dark hour of our national life a leadership of frankness and vigor has met with that understanding and support of the people themselves which is essential to victory. I am convinced that you will again give support to leadership in these critical days.

> —FRANKLIN D. ROOSEVELT,
> FIRST INAUGURAL ADDRESS,
> MARCH 4, 1933

Very often when some matter was being fought out with his advisers, he would bring up the question at dinner and bait me into giving an opinion by stating as his own a point of view with which he knew I would disagree. He would give me all the arguments which had been advanced to him, and I would try vociferously and with heat to refute them. I remember one occasion . . . when I became extremely vehement and irritated. My husband smiled indulgently and repeated all the things that everyone else had said to him. The next day he asked Miss Thompson if she could have tea in the West Hall in the White House for him and Robert Bingham, who was then our Ambassador to London and about to return to his post.

I dutifully served them with tea, fully expecting to sit and listen in silence to a discussion of questions with which I probably would not be in agreement. Instead, to my complete surprise, I heard Franklin telling Ambassador Bingham to act, not according to the arguments that he had given me, but according to the arguments that I had given him! Without giving me the satisfaction of batting an eyelash in my direction, he calmly stated as his own the policies and beliefs he had argued against the night before! To this day I have no idea whether he had simply used me as a sounding board, as he so often did, with the idea of getting the reaction of the person on the outside, or whether my arguments had been needed to fortify his decision and to clarify his own mind.

—ELEANOR ROOSEVELT,
This I Remember, 1949

T he force of nature known as Franklin Delano Roosevelt swept into the presidency on March 4, 1933, and remained there until his death on April 12, 1945, three months into his fourth term. By then the United States had become a world power and a nascent welfare state, and the presidency itself had undergone a fundamental transformation, replacing Congress as the principal energy source of the political system. Roosevelt was not solely responsible for these changes, but without him American history would have been different, not just in its details but in its larger contours.

A RARIFIED UPBRINGING

It is difficult to imagine a more unlikely candidate for the leader of a powerful coalition of blue-collar workers, labor unions, and ethnic minorities than Franklin Roosevelt. He was born on January 30, 1882, and raised on the Hudson River Valley estate of his family in Hyde Park, New York. He was the only child of James Roosevelt, a wealthy landowner who traced his ancestry to seventeenth-century New Amsterdam, and Sara Delano Roosevelt, who came from a moneyed family that went back to the founding of Plymouth Colony in 1621.

Franklin was the center of attention of his adoring parents and their many retainers. He was educated by governesses and tutors and accompanied his parents on their annual stays at leading European watering spots. When the family traveled within the United States, it was in James's private railway car. In some men this would have been a prescription for snobbery and indolence, but that was inconsistent with the Roosevelt family ethos. James Roosevelt was a vestryman of the local Episcopal church, a guiding spirit in the village of Hyde Park, and a benign force in the lives of those in his employ. Franklin's mother reinforced his father's example, holding him to high standards of gentlemanly conduct and civic responsibility.

To this there was added the teachings of Endicott Peabody, the headmaster of Groton preparatory school where Franklin was sent at age fourteen. Peabody considered his calling to be the molding of "manly Christian character," stressing the importance of service to mankind. From Groton, Roosevelt went to Harvard, where he was an indifferent student but exhibited his interest in leadership by staying on an extra year to serve as editor in chief of the student newspaper.

James Roosevelt died during his son's freshman year at Harvard. Following his death, Sara Roosevelt made Franklin her central concern, going so far as to move to Boston for his remaining college years. When Franklin married his distant cousin, Eleanor Roosevelt, in 1905, Sara set the couple up in a house adjacent to hers in New York City, intervening freely in the raising of their children. She maintained control of the family fortune until her death in 1941. Her persistent effort to control her son had the unintended effect of fostering the wiles that became an integral part of his political style, including what one FDR biographer calls his "selective candor" and "creative use of indirection."[1]

AN ILLUSTRIOUS EXEMPLAR

A further stimulus to FDR's political development was the example of his fifth cousin, Theodore Roosevelt, who was on the ascendant in Republican politics during Franklin's formative years. Between 1895 and 1901, TR served as New York City police commissioner, assistant secretary of the navy, commander of a swashbuckling cavalry regiment in the Spanish-American War, governor of New York, and vice president under President William McKinley. McKinley was assassinated six months after taking office for his second term, and on September 14, 1901, the forty-two-year-old Roosevelt became president.

Theodore Roosevelt's career demonstrated to Franklin that a member of the upper classes could thrive in the rough-and-tumble of politics and even suggested a trajectory. After Harvard, FDR dabbled in the law, but he confided to a contemporary that his real interest was in politics, adding that he hoped to replicate TR's experience by winning office in New York and moving on to become assistant secretary of the navy, governor of New York, and president of the United States.

FDR went on to do precisely that, but as a Democrat, perhaps to avoid competition with TR's sons, who were viewed as likely to enter Republican politics. In 1910, Roosevelt ran for the New York State Senate at the behest of the Democratic organization in his home district, which was attracted by his famous name and the hope that he would finance his own campaign. He fought a vigorous election campaign, winning 52 percent of the vote, and continued his activism in the legislature, where he led a revolt against his party's urban bosses. Before long, FDR was the object of national attention as a promising young Democrat carrying on the progressive tradition of his Republican cousin. In 1912, FDR supported New Jersey governor Woodrow Wilson in his campaign for the presidency. When Wilson was elected, he made him assistant secretary of the navy.

CLIMB TO THE PRESIDENCY

In 1920, the Democrats chose the thirty-nine-year-old Roosevelt as their vice-presidential candidate. Apart from being a rising political star, FDR provided regional balance for the presidential candidate, Ohio governor James M. Cox. The Democrats lost the election, but Roosevelt delivered nearly a thousand speeches in thirty-two states, emerging as one of his party's leading figures.

Before FDR could emulate TR and go on to the New York governorship and the White House, two developments came close to ending his political career. In 1918, his wife discovered that he had been having an affair with her social secretary. She proposed a divorce, which would have been politically fatal in that era, but their marriage continued and evolved into their famous political partnership.

In 1921, the political community was shocked to learn that FDR was paralyzed by a severe attack of poliomyelitis. By the norms of the day, such an affliction would have been an insurmountable barrier to public office, but after strenuous physical therapy, Roosevelt regained the use of his upper body and learned to simulate walking with the use of a cane. At the 1924 Democratic convention, he made a dramatic comeback, winning widespread praise for his address nominating New York governor Al Smith as the party's presidential candidate.

Smith did not secure his party's presidential nomination in 1924, but he did in 1928. To strengthen the national ticket in New York State, Smith persuaded FDR to run for governor. Smith lost the general election to Herbert Hoover, but Roosevelt carried New York by a narrow margin. When the Great Depression set in, FDR enhanced his national stature by instituting a series of bold measures to stimulate economic recovery in his state. In 1930, he was reelected by a record 725,000-vote margin, and in 1932, he won the Democratic presidential nomination on the fourth ballot.

Roosevelt campaigned with his characteristic dynamism, calling for a "new deal" for the American people, but saying little about what its content might be. He was elected with 57 percent of the popular vote and 89 percent of the electoral vote, bringing into office with him an overwhelmingly Democratic Congress.

THE POLITICS OF INSPIRATION

The circumstances under which FDR assumed the presidency could scarcely have been more intimidating. The nation was in the fourth year of a disastrous economic crisis. A quarter of the labor force was out of work, the banks had been closed in thirty-eight states, and farmers had begun to resist foreclosures with violence. The very continuation of a democratic political order was in jeopardy.

Roosevelt was unfazed. The ringing affirmations of his inaugural address signaled many of the changes that distinguish the presidency of the final two-thirds of the twentieth century from what had gone before. His assertion that America had "nothing to fear but fear itself" focused the nation's consciousness on its chief executive, eliciting truckloads of White House mail.*[2] His demand that Congress pass "the measures that a stricken nation in the midst of a stricken world may require" marked the emergence of the presidency as the nation's principal agent of policy initiation. Roosevelt's warning that if the legislature failed to act, he would seek executive power "as great as the power that would be given to me if we were in fact invaded by a foreign foe" heralded a quantum increase in autonomous presidential policymaking.

Roosevelt's formal addresses were at the heart of his public leadership. His speeches derived much of their force from the eloquence of his speechwriters: "I see one-third of a nation ill-housed, ill-clad, ill-nourished." "This nation has a rendezvous with destiny." "The American people in their righteous might will win through to absolute victory." But Roosevelt's oratory made poetry of even the least memorable prose.

Another facet of Roosevelt's public leadership was his fireside chats—the low-key, almost conversational radio broadcasts through

---

*The longtime White House executive clerk William Hopkins recollected that "President Roosevelt was getting as much mail in a day as President Hoover received in a week. . . . They couldn't even get the envelopes open."

which he explained his policies. In contrast to presidents who inundate the nation with words, Roosevelt rationed his broadcasts. After delivering four such talks in 1933, he reduced their frequency, remarking that "the public psychology" cannot be "attuned for long periods of time to a constant repetition of the highest note in the scale."[3]

Finally, there was his hold over the mass media. When he was in Washington, Roosevelt met twice a week with the reporters assigned to the White House. His remarks were off the record, but he provided the press with invaluable background information and occasional direct quotations. The tone was set in the first of the nearly one thousand such meetings:

> When the questioning began, the full virtuosity of the new Chief Executive was demonstrated. Cigarette holder in mouth at a jaunty angle, he met the reporters on their own grounds. His answers were swift, positive, and illuminating. He had exact information at his fingertips. He showed an impressive understanding of public problems and administrative methods. . . . He made no effort to conceal his pleasure in the give and take of the situation.[4]

Everything about FDR made for superb copy: his language, appearance, and attractive family. He also was a constant visual presence. His photograph was everywhere, not only in static portraits, but also in the newsreels that were the era's equivalent of television.

A MASTER OF MANEUVER

No other president has been more politically proficient than FDR. He had a sure instinct for when to proceed obliquely and when to go public, a legendary political network, and charm that could melt glaciers. The complexities of Roosevelt's political style are well captured by Arthur Schlesinger, Jr.:

> He was forever weighing questions of personal force, of political timing, of congressional concern, of partisan benefit, of public inter-

est. Situations had to be permitted to develop, to crystallize, to clarify; the competing forces had to vindicate themselves in the actual pull and tug of conflict; public opinion had to face the question, consider it, pronounce upon it—only then, at the long, frazzled end, would the President's intuitions consolidate and precipitate a result.[5]

But the man behind the style was an enigma. Try as his aides did to understand him, the inner man was terra incognita. One adviser referred to the "secrecy of the Roosevelt inner operations chamber." Another complained to Roosevelt that he was "one of the most difficult men to work with that I have ever known. You won't talk frankly even with people who are loyal to you and of whose loyalty you are fully convinced."[6] A third concluded that Roosevelt was inscrutable out of choice:

> He seemed not to want any one person to know the whole story. At times he seemed to delight in having two or more people do different but related parts of a single job that could have been done by one person. . . . It was an inefficient way of doing things and frequently led to duplication of effort, and sometimes to argument and conflict.[7]

Schlesinger purports to find method in Roosevelt's sphinx-like quality and the byzantine White House politics to which it contributed, arguing that FDR adhered to a "competitive theory of administration," geared to keeping decision making in his hands and maximizing his information.[8]* Whether Roosevelt consciously held such a conception is uncertain. His elusiveness and his practice of playing aides off against one another undoubtedly did enhance his influence and information, but at a cost. His practices made for needless rivalries and poor morale. More important, they elevated divining

---

*In the final two years of the war, Roosevelt's organizational idiosyncrasies were tempered by his reliance on strong subordinates, including Harry Hopkins as emissary to the Allied leaders, Admiral William Leahy as his link with the military, and James F. Byrnes as the overall director of the domestic war effort.

FDR's "operations chamber" over reasoned policy deliberation and complicated the jobs of his aides, leaving them uncertain about how he would come down on issues, how vigorously he would advance them, and whether he would suddenly change direction.

A Cascade of Enactments

Of the many instances of Roosevelt's political artistry that would reward the attention of his successors, two of the most impressive were his leadership of Congress during the cascade of lawmaking known as the Hundred Days and his invention of the policy departure to which he gave the name lend-lease.

Between March 9 and June 6, 1933, FDR proposed and Congress disposed of an unprecedented volume of new legislation: banking reform, a government economy act, unemployment relief, agricultural relief, relief of small home owners, railroad reorganization, public construction and taxation legislation, and the acts that created the Tennessee Valley Authority, the Securities and Exchange Commission, and the National Recovery Administration (NRA).[9]

The Hundred Days was an unpremeditated triumph. There had been no plan for it on Roosevelt's part. He had convened Congress to act on a few emergency measures, but on the opening day, the legislature showed a dramatic readiness to act on Roosevelt's bidding. Before the day was over, it had passed the banking bill even though its text was not yet available. Attempts to debate the measure were greeted with cries of "Vote! Vote!" Seizing the occasion, Roosevelt arranged for Congress to remain in session until it enacted the rest of his program.

Roosevelt's hand was evident throughout the Hundred Days. *He* approved policies, set strategies, met with legislators, explained his purposes, and courted the press. His timing was superb. When the pension cuts provided for in the economy bill met the opposition of veterans' groups, Roosevelt deflected criticism by proposing the legalization of beer. He was buoyantly improvisatory, comparing himself to a quarterback who knows "what the next play is going to be," but cannot say what the play after that will be "until the next play is run off." He even recovered his own fumbles. He initially opposed a proposal for bank deposit insurance, considering it unsound, but when it became evident that it would pass, he took credit for it.[10]

INVENTING LEND-LEASE

More advance planning went into lend-lease than the Hundred Days. Roosevelt had viewed Hitler with abhorrence from the time that they both came into power early in 1933, but until the German dictator's meeting with the leaders of Britain and France at Munich in October 1938, he was uncertain about the extent of Hitler's ambitions. The severity of Hitler's demands at Munich and his sheer unreasonableness resolved Roosevelt's doubts. He set out to align the United States with the Western democracies, embarking on a sustained effort to educate his nation to his views and build up its military capacity.

By summer 1940, Germany had overrun Europe, and Britain stood alone, dependent on arms purchases from the United States for its survival. In December, Prime Minister Winston Churchill informed FDR that his nation could no longer pay for American arms. As the balance of forces stood on Capitol Hill, Congress was unlikely to approve a loan to the United Kingdom.

Roosevelt himself devised the solution in what his labor secretary and long-time political ally Frances Perkins called a "flash of almost clairvoyant knowledge and understanding."[11] The United States would send armaments to Britain without charge, asking only that they be returned after the war. He floated the proposal in an off-the-record meeting with reporters in December 1940, employing a homely analogy:

> Suppose my neighbor's home catches fire and I have a length of garden hose four or five hundred feet away. If he can take my garden hose and connect it up with his hydrant, I may help to put out his fire. Now what do I do? I don't say to him before that operation, "Neighbor, my garden hose cost me $15; you have to pay me $15 for it." What is the transaction that goes on? I don't want $15—I want my garden hose back after the fire is over.

The following week, Roosevelt took his creation to the public. He called on the nation to discard the mentality of "business as usual" and become an "arsenal of democracy" and proceed "with the same spirit of patriotism and sacrifice as we would show were we at war." Otherwise, he declared, the "unholy alliance" of Germany, Italy, and Japan would advance toward world domination, and Americans "would be living at the point of the gun." By January, the lend-lease bill, complete with the symbolic designation HR 1776, had been submitted to Congress. In March it was signed into law.[12]

THE PERILS OF GRANDIOSITY

The boldness and aplomb that Roosevelt's aides found awesome could be a prescription for ill-conceived ventures. During FDR's first term, the Supreme Court had struck down numerous New Deal measures. In February 1937, Roosevelt suddenly announced a proposal to add as many as six justices to the Supreme Court. Roosevelt's frustration with the Court was understandable, but the proposal was drastic and it was launched out of the blue. He consulted neither members of Congress nor his closest aides. The resulting tempest consumed political energies that might have been better expended and mobilized a bipartisan conservative coalition that continued to block liberal policy departures long after Roosevelt left the political stage.

Roosevelt was equally capable of acting on untested intuitions in international affairs, as in his overly personalized wartime relations with the Soviet Union.*[13] In 1942, Roosevelt apprised Churchill of his belief that he could "personally handle Stalin better than either your Foreign Office or my State Department."[14] When the two met with the Soviet dictator in November 1943, he acted on that belief, seeking to

---

*There is unlikely ever to be a resolution to the debate over the larger question of whether FDR needlessly sacrificed the interests of the West in his agreements with Stalin late in the war or simply responded to the realities of Soviet power in Eastern Europe. Positions on that issue require unverifiable inferences about complex historical contingencies and depend as much on the values of the disputants as the appeal to evidence.

make a personal connection with Stalin by needling Churchill. The angrier Churchill became, Roosevelt later recalled, the more it amused Stalin: "Finally Stalin broke out into a deep, hearty guffaw. From that time on our relations were personal, and Stalin himself indulged in an occasional witticism. The ice was broken and we talked like men and brothers."[15]

So Roosevelt wanted to think. Six months later, the Yugoslavian communist Milovan Djilas had a conversation with Stalin in which the Soviet dictator commented that FDR was even less trustworthy than Churchill. The latter, Stalin observed, "is the kind who, if you don't watch him, will slip a kopeck out of your pocket," but Roosevelt "dips his hand only for bigger coins."[16]

SIGNIFICANCE

Public Communication   In his communication practices, as in much else, FDR provides a benchmark for his successors. His soaring rhetoric roused imaginations and stirred souls. He restored faith in a political system that Americans had few reasons to respect and rallied the nation and its allies in an epic conflict in which victory was by no means assured. He dominated his times, defining the terms of politics at home and abroad. As a communicator, Roosevelt is to later presidents what Mozart and Beethoven have been to their successors—inimitable but endlessly inspiring. Future presidents are unlikely to equal FDR's eloquence, but they could scarcely do better than to immerse themselves in his record, reading his addresses, listening to recordings of them, and studying his public presentation of self.

Organizational Capacity   Roosevelt's famously chaotic organizational methods are not a promising model for presidents to come. Despite Arthur Schlesinger's praise of his "competitive theory of administration," Roosevelt's practice of playing aides off against one another provoked needless rivalries, sapping the morale of his lieutenants. It also put a premium on wile, making the influence of his advisers a function of their bureaucratic skills rather than the merits of their recommendations. By encouraging his aides to vie with one another, FDR generated sparks. His policies would have profited from steadier illumination.

Roosevelt did make an enduring organizational contribution by creating the cluster of presidential agencies known as the Executive Office of the President (EOP). To constitute the EOP agencies, FDR created the White House Office, an entity that for the first time provided the chief executive with a staff of high-level aides. He also moved a minor treasury department unit called the Bureau of the Budget to the new executive office, where it was to become the nerve center of the federal government. Roosevelt employed his new EOP assistants in much the same freewheeling manner as the many unofficial aides who buzzed around him. Still, he laid the groundwork for the organization-minded Harry Truman to create a cadre of dedicated civil servants who serve the presidency, as well as its incumbent, providing the chief executive with the institutional capacity to shape the nation's policy agenda.[17]

Political Skill   The Roosevelt presidency is laden with insights into how presidents can get results in an often intractable political system. Future presidents might well begin with the beginning, using the Hundred Days as a source of lessons on such matters as setting the agenda for congressional action, timing proposals, and even transforming a defeat into a seeming victory, as Roosevelt did when he took credit for bank deposit insurance. They would be equally advised to study FDR's international maneuvers, especially his patient, step-by-step alignment of the United States with the Western democracies in the period following Munich and his display of political imagination in inventing lend-lease. But Roosevelt's successors should take warning from his failures, many of which stemmed from his reluctance to expose his intuitions to debate within his advisory circle.

Vision   For those who lived through the Great Depression and World War II, it may border on blasphemy to suggest that a leader with Roosevelt's superlative inspirational qualities and sweeping imagination was deficient in vision. Nevertheless, FDR's thinking about policy was intuitive rather than conceptual or analytic. In international affairs, his faith in democracy and instinct for power relations lent coherence to his administration's policies, especially after Munich. In domestic affairs, however, his views were vague and contradictory and his policies were a patchwork. A telling illustration is provided by a member of Roosevelt's legendary Brain Trust, the Columbia University economist Raymond Moley. On an occasion when Roosevelt's advisers were deeply divided on tariff policy, Moley presented him with alternative speech drafts announcing diametrically opposed policies. Roosevelt left Moley "speechless" by instructing him to "weave the two together."[18]

The enactments of the Hundred Days point to the consequences of such indifference to policy content. Some of them were unproductive, because they cancelled one another out; others were even counterproductive. The economy bill, which was deflationary, negated the effect of the relief measures, which were inflationary. The National Recovery Act triggered a boom *in advance* of going into effect, as businesses scrambled to fill orders before price and wage controls were in force. It impeded recovery once it was operational by interfering with market forces.[19] Small wonder that it took the war to bring about recovery.

Cognitive Style   Supreme Court justice Oliver Wendell Holmes famously remarked that FDR had "a second-class intellect" and "a first-class temperament."[20] He was on target in both respects. Roosevelt's intellectual strengths included an exceptional memory, a remarkable ability to synthesize diverse ideas and facts, and the openness to "almost clairvoyant" insights to which Frances Perkins referred. His weaknesses included his insensitivity to abstractions and his inability to identify the contradictions in his policies.

In a revealing episode, one of FDR's associates arranged for him to meet John Maynard Keynes in the hope that the great economist would help provide coherence to the New Deal, but to no avail. Roosevelt did not know what to make of Keynes. "I saw your friend Keynes," he reported to the associate who set up the meeting. "He left a whole rigmarole of figures. He must be a mathematician rather than a political economist."[21] One need not be a Keynesian to recognize that an FDR who was better able to grasp economic abstractions would have been less likely to preside over policies that cancelled one another out.

Emotional Intelligence FDR presents a complex emotional picture. The "selective candor" and "creative use of indirection" he acquired at his mother's knee made for a leadership style that was manipulative and inscrutable, even when circumstances did not warrant it. Roosevelt also had a striking capacity for ignoring disagreeable realities. He showed no compunction about seeking a fourth term, even though he had undergone a severe physical decline, and after being reelected, he left Truman uninformed about the Manhattan Project and what had transpired at Yalta. None of this is the mark of a blemish-free personality.[22]

Yet Roosevelt fully deserved Holmes's encomium. His temperament could scarcely have been better suited for inspiring public confidence. There is no way of knowing whether he himself felt no fear in 1933, when he assured the nation that it need only be afraid of "nameless, unreasoning, unjustified terror," or whether he was as supremely confident as he appeared to be on December 8, 1941, when he declared to the nation that "the American people in their righteous might will win through to absolute victory." Even if the sense of absolute assurance he radiated was only that of a masterful performer, it reveals his singular emotional fitness for the demands of his times.

Harry Truman came to terms with the intimidating requirements of the presidency by working hard and drawing on his previous governmental experience. As a county administrator and member of the Senate Finance Committee, Truman had acquired a close understanding of government finance. As chief executive, he devoted special press conferences to expositions of the federal budget. Truman also worked with the civil servants of the Executive Office of the President to create the institutional underpinnings of the modern presidency.

(Corbis/Bettmann-UPI)

CHAPTER 3

The Uneven Leadership of Harry S. Truman

Boys, if you ever pray, pray for me now. I don't know whether you fellows ever had a bale of hay fall on you, but when they told me yesterday what happened, I felt like the moon, the stars, and all the planets had fallen on me.

—HARRY S. TRUMAN,
REMARK TO REPORTERS,
APRIL 13, 1945

Within the first few months I discovered that being a President is like riding a tiger. A man has to keep on riding or be swallowed. . . . I never felt that I could let up for a single moment.

—HARRY S. TRUMAN,
Years of Trial and Hope, 1956

Declare an emergency and call out the troops. . . . Adjourn Congress and run the country. Get plenty of atomic bombs on hand—drop one on Stalin, put the United Nations to work and eventually set up a free world.

—HARRY S. TRUMAN,
NOTE TO SELF, JUNE 1946

A short time after the new President takes his oath of office, I will be on the train going back to Independence, Missouri. I will once again be a plain, private citizen of this great Republic. . . . It is a good object lesson in democracy. I am very proud of it.

—HARRY S. TRUMAN,
FAREWELL ADDRESS,
JANUARY 15, 1953

W hen the giant who bestrode American politics for over a dozen years was abruptly succeeded by an unimposing "little man" from Missouri, there was every reason to believe that the presidency would move from center stage in American politics to a position closer to the wings. The presidential activism of FDR had been preceded by the assertive leadership of Theodore Roosevelt and Woodrow Wilson, but each of them was succeeded by a far more reactive chief executive under whom the presidency receded to its traditional status.

Whatever his personal limitations, Harry S. Truman had neither William Howard Taft's principled reservations against strong presidential leadership nor Warren G. Harding's back-to-normalcy complacency. Under Truman, the presidency maintained its centrality in the political system, but with a difference. In an evolution marked by what the German political sociologist Max Weber calls the "routinization of charisma," the intensely personal leadership of FDR gave way to collective development of policy by the president and his administration colleagues.[1]

No other American president has been more differently perceived by lay observers and scholars than Harry Truman. During much of his time in office, Truman's public approval ratings were abysmally low. Yet in the same period many students of American history came to hold him in high regard, lauding him for his integrity, liberal domestic program, and decisiveness in standing up to international communism.

By the mid-1970s, positions had reversed. Many scholars came to view Truman critically, characterizing him as a rigid anticommunist, whose confrontational policies toward the Soviet Union were a principal cause of the cold war. Meanwhile, members of the public and the political community reacted to the perceived abuses of power of Presidents Johnson and Nixon by idealizing Truman for his plain-speaking unpretentiousness, elevating him to the status of a presidential paragon. One of President Ford's first actions upon succeeding Richard Nixon was to place Truman's portrait in the Oval Office.[2]

ROOTS

The "real" Harry S. Truman is best understood by beginning with his origins. He was born on May 8, 1884, in the tiny farm village of Lamar, Missouri. In 1896, his family moved to Independence, Missouri, not far from Kansas City. Truman was just two years younger than FDR, and both men were progressive Democrats, but their life experiences were light-years apart.

Roosevelt was the Harvard-educated child of independently wealthy parents. Truman was the son of a Missouri mule trader and the only twentieth-century president not to attend college. For most of the period in which FDR was becoming nationally prominent as a member of the Wilson administration, Truman was a Missouri dirt farmer, working for his father. He was also a bespectacled, book-reading, self-confessed "mama's boy," who had to struggle to win his father's regard in a frontier-like community in which men prized toughness and settled arguments with their fists.

Truman's liberation from the plow did not come until 1917, when the United States entered the war in Europe. As a thirty-three-year-old farmer with bad eyes, Truman was not required to serve in World War I, but he joined the National Guard, memorizing the eye chart to pass the physical. He was made captain of his artillery unit and won the respect of his troops by rallying them under a withering enemy bombardment.

If the war increased Truman's self-esteem, his first postwar endeavor did not. He and a fellow veteran became partners in a haberdashery, but the business failed in 1922, and it took years for Truman to pay off his debts. At thirty-eight, he approached middle age possessed of what his most authoritative biographer deems a "small ego."[3]

Truman returned from the war with a substantial following among the men he commanded in Europe and added to his popularity in the Kansas City area by participating in veterans' affairs. In 1922 he embarked on what proved to be his vocation—that of an elected official. The Kansas City party organization of Thomas Pendergast recognized his promise as a candidate, running him successfully for county judge, a position concerned with the construction and maintenance of roads and public buildings. He held county office for ten of the twelve years between 1922 and 1934, remaining untainted by the corruption of the Pendergast organization and winning recognition for his industry and competence.

A PRESIDENTIAL ACTIVIST IN THE MAKING

Two aspects of Truman's presidential leadership style stemmed from his years as a county administrator. One was his interest in sound budgetary practices. As president, Truman was closely involved in the budgetary process, so much so that he devoted special news conferences to reviewing his budgets, even employing a flip chart and pointer. The other was his commitment to efficient administrative procedure, which led to important contributions on his part to the institutional side of the presidency.

A second influence on Truman's presidential leadership was his uncritical reading of works of popular history. He became a self-taught adherent of the great man theory of leadership. Truman's conviction that leaders are the driving force in history is evident in a speech he gave at an ROTC summer camp during FDR's first year in the White House:

From the Magna Charta to the Declaration of Independence and the American Constitution is a space of some 560 years and every step forward is the result of the ideals and self-sacrifice of some great leader. We have an idealist in the White House now, the first we've had since Woodrow Wilson, and he's going to show us how to pull ourselves out of our present woes.[4]

Truman's reading led him to form an expansive view of the prerogatives of the chief executive. It imbued him with a reverence for the presidency that enabled him to transcend his sense of his own limitations. It was to provide him with the rationale for such bold presidential actions as relieving Douglas MacArthur as commander in Korea in 1951 and placing the steel industry under federal control in the face of a threatened strike in 1952.

In 1934, Pendergast tapped Truman to run for the U.S. Senate, turning to him after several other potential candidates proved unavailable. Riding the year's powerful Democratic electoral tide, Truman defeated his state's anti–New Deal Republican senator. In Washington, he became a hard-working member of the Appropriations Committee, living down his initial image as the "Senator from Pendergast."

During World War II, Truman's sense of responsibility and capacity for hard work earned him favorable recognition. Building on his experience as a county administrator, he chaired a Senate investigating committee that conducted a much-praised probe of waste and fraud in the defense industry. In 1944, when the Democrats nominated FDR for a fourth term, the party split on its choice of a vice-presidential candidate. Vice President Henry A. Wallace was too far to the left for the party's moderates and conservatives. The other major contender, former South Carolina senator James Byrnes, was too far to the right for its liberals and for labor. Truman was an uncontroversial compromise choice.

After Roosevelt's reelection, Truman found himself next in line to an obviously ailing Roosevelt for the grave responsibilities of the wartime presidency. During his eighty-two days in that status, he had virtually no one-to-one contact with FDR, who left him uninformed about his negotiations with Stalin and the ongoing effort to develop nuclear weapons. Then, on April 12, 1945, Roosevelt died, and Truman was thrust into a presidency he had never sought.

31

A FAVORABLE FIRST YEAR

Truman became president under politically advantageous circumstances. The war in Europe was drawing to a close, Japan was in retreat, and there was a rush to rally around the man who had the burden of succeeding the larger-than-life FDR. Truman's initial Gallup poll rating of 87 percent was surely as much an expression of sympathy as an assessment of how he was carrying out a job he had barely assumed. An account in *Time* of Truman's first ten days in office praised "the small, trim man behind the big mahogany desk," describing Truman as a vigorous, determined "product of rural Missouri" with "a talent for working hard without getting confused or losing his temper."[5]

As it happened, Truman also was a practical politician with an undoctrinaire mindset. One of his earliest presidential acts was to enlist his similarly pragmatic former Senate colleague James Byrnes as his chief foreign policy adviser, later elevating him to secretary of state. In spite of the claim of revisionist historians that Truman and Byrnes willfully abandoned Roosevelt's policy of seeking a modus vivendi with the Soviet Union, they are better understood as practical politicians maneuvering in an imperfectly understood environment.

In the weeks before FDR's death, the Soviets installed a communist-controlled government in Poland. Truman sent Roosevelt's former alter ego Harry Hopkins to negotiate with Stalin, knowing Hopkins to be sympathetic to the Soviet desire for secure borders. When Hopkins secured token noncommunist representation in the Polish government, Truman recorded his pleasure in his diary, wryly remarking that he would be content if the balloting in Eastern Europe was as free as the notoriously corrupt elections conducted by the Pendergast organization in Kansas City.[6]

Truman and Byrnes approached their meeting with the leaders of Great Britain and the Soviet Union at Potsdam in the summer of 1945 in the tradition of political horse traders, revealing no ideological agenda. Truman was more wary of Churchill than of Stalin, noting that the former gave him "a lot of hooey about how great my country is," whereas the latter struck him as honest and "smart as hell."[7]

Truman's critics claim that he used the atom bomb more to intimidate the Soviet Union than to defeat Japan, but the record reveals that he was going along with policies he inherited from Roosevelt. Roosevelt's advisers differed about how to use the bomb, but not over whether to use it. As the head of the Manhattan Project put it, to the extent that any decision of Truman's led to the use of nuclear weapons, it was "not to upset the existing plans."[8]

A STUMBLING SECOND YEAR

By mid-1946, Truman was faltering. The underlying source of his problems is captured in a chapter title in Robert Donovan's book on Truman's first term: "Peace Is Hell."[9] The abrupt ending of the war in August 1945 was like the breach of the flood walls of a swollen river. It released an outpouring of demands for wage and price increases. Unemployment soared, and there were shortages of consumer goods and demands for the immediate return of overseas troops. The politics of postwar reconversion would have been daunting even for FDR.

Truman, however, was no Roosevelt, and he brought many of his problems on himself. He allowed Byrnes to make foreign policy pronouncements with little White House consultation. He communicated no vision to the nation of how he proposed to address its domestic woes. His addresses lacked dramatic flair, his delivery was halting, and his flat Missouri accent contrasted painfully with Roosevelt's rich sonority.

Truman made matters worse by being distinctly blunder prone. Most damaging was the way he parted company with the more liberal holdovers from FDR, particularly Henry Wallace. After Wallace was denied renomination as vice president, Roosevelt had made him secretary of commerce. In 1946, Wallace began to take issue with Byrnes's stiff stand against the installation by the Soviet Union of communist regimes in Eastern Europe. Late in the summer, Wallace showed Truman the draft of a speech calling on the United States to exhibit greater understanding of the Soviet desire for a sphere of interest in Eastern Europe. Truman signed off on it, apparently without reading it closely.

When reporters obtained the advance text and asked Truman if Wallace's remarks conformed with his policies, Truman insisted they did. The speech was greeted with a storm of criticism for its accommodating stance toward the Soviet Union; Truman countered with the unconvincing claim that he had only approved Wallace's *right* to give it. Compounding the perception that he was out of his depth, Truman then fired Wallace, giving in to Byrnes's threat to resign if he did not.[10] Before long, he was the object of the taunt, "To err is Truman."

By September 1946, Truman's approval rating was down to 32 percent. His difficulties were made worse by a severe meat shortage in the weeks leading up to the 1946 congressional election. The Republicans campaigned with the slogan, "Had enough?" Evidently the voters had. In the resulting landslide, the Democrats lost fifty-five seats in the House and twelve in the Senate. The GOP assumed control of Congress for the first time since 1930.

GLOBAL STATESMANSHIP

After the Republican midterm victory, Truman was widely viewed by political commentators as a presidential lame duck who would be able to do little more than bide his time until his inevitable electoral defeat. Before long, however, his political standing was enhanced by international developments that cast him as a statesman-like defender of the national interest.

In February 1947, Great Britain let it be known that it no longer had the financial wherewithal to defend Greece and Turkey, both of which were in danger of falling under Soviet control. By then General George C. Marshall, the much-admired World War II army chief of staff, had become secretary of state. Truman and Marshall concluded that the United States should pick up where Britain had left off.

Truman engaged in careful negotiations with leaders of both parties. Having prepared the way, he addressed a joint session of Congress on March 12, calling for $400 million in aid to Greece and Turkey. Within two months, Congress acted, approving what the press labeled the Truman Doctrine. On June 5, the Truman administration made the even more ambitious proposal that the United States provide billions of dollars of foreign aid to the economically struggling democracies of Western Europe.

Truman's approach to persuading the Republican-led Congress to approve what came to be called the Marshall Plan was intentionally self-denying. He insisted that it bear Marshall's name rather than his own, and he enlisted the support of the leading Republican congressional internationalist, Michigan senator Arthur Vandenberg, allowing Vandenberg to take much of the credit for it. Despite his deference to Marshall and Vandenberg, Truman's international leadership enhanced his public standing. On the four occasions in 1947 when Gallup asked the public to evaluate his performance, his ratings were consistently high, ranging from 54 percent to 60 percent.

SETBACK AND RECOVERY

By late 1947 Truman was back in the depths. In December, Henry Wallace declared that he would run for president as a third-party candidate, charging that Truman had needlessly antagonized the Soviet Union, risking a third world war. Wallace also promulgated a strongly liberal domestic program, placing particular emphasis on the need for federal guarantees of the rights of African Americans.

Early in 1948, Truman announced his own civil rights program, but the move alienated his party's influential southern wing. Before long an unlikely combination of Democratic liberals and conservatives was working to deny Truman the Democratic nomination. In spite of approval levels of only 36 percent in April and 39 percent in May, Truman won his party's nomination, but he went into the presidential campaign very much an underdog. Truman's Republican opponent was New York governor Thomas E. Dewey, who had run a strong race against FDR in 1944. Making Truman's plight worse, he also had to contend with a pair of third-party candidates who drained the support of important Democratic constituencies—Henry Wallace, who had a following among left-leaning liberals, and South Carolina governor Strom Thurmond, whose appeal was to southern segregationists.

Mounting a fighting campaign, Truman replaced his prepared addresses with fiery ad-lib stump speeches and announced a strikingly liberal program. He called for passage of his civil rights proposal, repeal of the labor-curbing Taft-Hartley Act, universal health insurance, aid to education, income support for farmers, tax credits for low-income groups, and taxes on corporate profits. Following the Democratic convention, he made the Republican-led Congress his foil, calling it back into session with a challenge to enact his program. When it failed to do so, he crisscrossed the nation in a campaign train, castigating the "do nothing 80th Congress."

Truman's "give 'em Hell" speeches made for lively press coverage, but his campaign was widely assumed to be a prelude to defeat. Then, in an upset that appears to have surprised everyone but the man in the White House, he triumphed over his three adversaries, winning 49.5 percent of the popular vote and 57 percent of the electoral vote. Crowning Truman's achievement was the return of Congress to Democratic control.

A DISPIRITING SECOND TERM

After the victory celebrations, Truman and his staff repaired to Key West for their annual winter respite of poker playing and bonhomie. By their return, conservatives of both parties had coalesced in opposition to the domestic program Truman came to call the Fair Deal. Business groups put their all into blocking the repeal of the Taft-Hartley Act, and the American Medical Association spent huge sums of money to defeat Truman's health plan. The new Congress was not completely unresponsive to Truman. It passed his slum clearance and public housing proposals, and increased the minimum wage and social security benefits, but his other major proposals were killed in committee or defeated on the floor of Congress.

In late 1949, the Truman administration received a pair of body blows. In September, the Soviet Union was revealed to have developed nuclear weapons. The next month, mainland China came under communist control, fueling a venomous public debate over whether the Truman administration had "lost China" and was "soft on communism." On June 25, 1950, there was still another politically damaging development: the invasion of South Korea by communist North Korea.

Five months earlier, Secretary of State Dean Acheson had declared the Korean peninsula to be outside the strategic perimeter the United States was committed to defend.[11] In the face of an actual invasion, Truman and his associates concluded that they could not allow a communist takeover of South Korea. The communist invaders had nearly driven the defenders of the South into the sea, when U.S. and U.N. field commander General Douglas MacArthur executed a daring amphibious landing near the line dividing the two Koreas, scattering the North Korean forces. Now it was the turn of the North to be driven deep into its own territory.

There followed a copybook example of snatching defeat from the jaws of victory. With Truman's tacit approval, MacArthur sought to occupy all of North Korea and eliminate its communist regime. He ignored instructions from Washington to exercise extreme caution as his troops approached the border between Korea and China. In October, the Chinese army unexpectedly crossed that border, routing MacArthur's forces.

MacArthur then began to make public demands that the war be extended to China, using Republican members of Congress to advance his cause. On April 11, 1951, Truman responded to MacArthur's insubordination by relieving him from command, triggering a huge domestic uproar. Truman was vilified by the conservatives for whom MacArthur was an icon. There were demands for his impeachment, and his public support plunged to the lowest levels of his presidency, remaining in the 20 to 30 percent range for the rest of his time in the White House.

The final period of the Truman presidency was marked by stalemate in Korea, the revelation that a number of Truman's aides had engaged in influence peddling, and the ascendancy of the monumentally irresponsible Wisconsin senator Joseph McCarthy, who specialized in issuing unsubstantiated allegations that the Truman administration was riddled with subversives. For all practical purposes, the Truman presidency became a holding operation. Early in 1952, Truman announced that he would not seek the second elected term for which he was eligible. If he had entered the running, he almost certainly would have been defeated.

A DIVIDED PSYCHE

For all of his lack of public support, Truman was beloved by his aides for his good cheer, spunk, and seeming imperviousness to the attacks that were showered on him. Their impression of Truman's ebulliently positive personality is well captured by Dean Acheson:

> Mr. Truman could work, reading and absorbing endless papers, and at times play, until well past midnight and be up at six o'clock with hardy Secret Service men and reporters. He slept, so he told us, as soon as his head touched the pillow, never worrying, because he could not stay awake long enough to do so.

Like everyone else in Truman's political universe, Acheson was also aware of the "peppery, sometimes belligerent, often didactic" Harry Truman—the Truman who is remembered for firing off a scathing letter to a music critic who presumed to criticize the singing of his daughter, Margaret. To Acheson, that was "the public figure," whereas the Truman he and others in the administration "knew and loved" was "the patient, modest, considerate, and appreciative boss, helpful and understanding in all official matters, affectionate and sympathetic in any private worry or sorrow."[12]

What Acheson did not know was the extent to which Truman suffered from the heat in the political kitchen. Many years after Truman's death, it became known that while in the Senate, he was hospitalized for work-related exhaustion, complaining to his doctors of the invective that marked his 1940 reelection campaign. Truman's thin-skinned tendencies continued in the White House, taking the form of intemperate letters, memoranda, and speech drafts that he composed in private but sensibly consigned to his files.

Included were a caustic missive to Senator McCarthy and a self-pitying 1949 speech draft alleging that in the previous year's campaign, he was subjected to "a campaign of vilification, misrepresentation and falsehood" that was "unequaled in the history of the world." He even entertained thoughts about the unthinkable, as in this 1952 unsent broadside:

> This means all-out war. It means that Moscow, St. Petersburg, Mukden, Vladivostok, Peking, Shanghai, Port Arthur, Dairen, Odessa, Stalingrad, and every manufacturing plant in China and the Soviet Union will be eliminated. This is the final chance for the Soviet Government to decide whether it desires to survive or not.[13]

Yet far from risking Armageddon, Truman incurred severe political costs by refusing to extend the Korean conflict to China. The day after his fantasized declaration of hostilities, he proceeded with business as usual, urging Congress to authorize the St. Lawrence Seaway. In short, Truman was not insensible to anger, but he was endowed with a healthy capacity to manage his bellicose impulses. He blew off steam in private, but acted cautiously in his public capacity.

SIGNIFICANCE

Public Communication   As a public communicator, Truman is instructive mainly as a source of warnings. Although he and his aides devoted great effort to writing his addresses, Truman was unable to transform them into effective public discourse. He did much better when he spoke off the cuff, but an unscripted Harry Truman was an invitation to political embarrassment. It was in a stump speech that Truman drew fire by remarking that he was fond of Joseph Stalin and in a press conference that he called the Alger Hiss case a "red herring." In another press conference, he conveyed the false impression that he was contemplating the use of nuclear weapons in Korea, forcing the British prime minister to rush to Washington to repair the damage.

There were ways in which Truman's personal strengths might have been better communicated. On one occasion, he hosted a televised tour of the White House, commenting with charm and thoughtfulness about its history and occupants. In Truman's time, the White House press office did little more than issue news releases and attend to the logistical needs of the reporters who covered the presidency. It would not have been necessary for the Truman White House to use public relations gimmicks to place the redoubtable Harry Truman in a more favorable light. It would have been sufficient to devise ways of highlighting the personal qualities that endeared him to his colleagues.

Organizational Capacity   Just as he had rallied his troops in combat, Truman inspired and energized his White House staff. Meeting with his aides in the Oval Office six mornings a week, he fostered camaraderie and esprit, despite as adverse a political climate as any administration has encountered. When it came to team selection, however, he was less impressive. His administration included some outstanding public servants of their time, but he also tolerated mediocrity and even venality, stubbornly retaining associates who were better suited for Kansas City than the nation's capital.

Truman also made enduring contributions to the institutional presidency. Working closely with the civil servants of the Bureau of the Budget, he brought about a quiet revolution in presidential procedures. During his time in office, the bureau initiated the practice of reviewing the policies for which funds were requested to determine their "consistency with the program of the president" and took on the responsibility of recommending whether congressional enactments be signed or vetoed. The result was a set of operating procedures that make presidential leadership of Congress automatic rather than a function of the individual who happens to occupy the White House.[14]

Political Skill   After his first two years, it became decreasingly true that to err was Truman, but his performance remained uneven to the end of his time in office. His most impressive lessons are in the realm of persuasion. In his memoirs, he explains how he cultivated the art of getting along with others: "I used to watch my father and mother closely to learn what I could do to please them, just as I did with my schoolteachers and playmates. Because of my efforts to get along with my associates I usually was able to get what I wanted."[15]

Truman's success in convincing a heavily isolationist Republican Congress to pass the Marshall Plan warrants the attention of any future president. His readiness to give the credit for his achievement to Marshall and Vandenberg provides support for the aphorism that you can accomplish a great deal in politics if you give others the credit.

Vision   Like other presidential pragmatists, Truman's leadership was fundamentally reactive. He was what the philosopher Sidney Hook calls an "eventful" leader, whose actions are determined by external influences, rather than an "event-making" leader who molds his political environment to his purposes. Truman's lack of a broad policy perspective was especially costly in the case of Korea. A president with more of a policy blueprint would have been less likely to allow his secretary of state to exclude Korea from the U.S. defensive perimeter or permit MacArthur to advance to the border of China.[16]

Cognitive Style   Truman's diaries and correspondence reveal him as a less-than-ideal cognitive prototype. His political universe was informed by simplistic categories, and he used questionable historical analogies, especially in an effort to make sense of the Soviet Union. In the Potsdam period, he compared Stalin to the political bosses he had known in Kansas City, making the false assumption that Stalin was another Pendergast and could be trusted once he made a deal. When that proved not to be the case, Truman concluded that Soviet imperialism was an extension of a Russian imperialism that had been mandated in the will of Peter the Great, an apocryphal historical forgery that figured in a work of popular history he had read.[17]

Emotional Intelligence   The emotional qualities that Truman's associates most prized in him were courage and decisiveness. In the light of his private fulminations, he now seems most noteworthy for his sturdy self-restraint. As a presidential Walter Mitty, Truman entertained fantasies about leveling the Soviet Union. Yet the real-world Harry Truman was judicious and measured, revealing a capacity for self-discipline that establishes a standard for the other inevitably flawed mortals who take up residence at 1600 Pennsylvania Avenue.

CAN NATIONAL CONVENTION

By the end of World War II, Eisenhower had become one of his nation's most popular figures. The public's love affair with the likeable Ike continued after he entered politics. He was elected president by an overwhelming majority in 1952, and reelected by an even greater margin four years later. During his time in office and for the next two decades most students of the presidency had a distinctly negative view of Eisenhower as a leader, holding him to have been little more than the front man of his subordinates. He is now known to have been a sophisticated political operator who exercised political power by indirection, delegating the most divisive of his administration's actions to associates.

(Courtesy Dwight D. Eisenhower Library)

CHAPTER 4

The Unexpected Eisenhower

With respect to the draft of your speech to the United Nations, my chief comment is one of a rather general character. . . . I had the impression that the speech is intended as a new indictment of the Bolshevik Party, the USSR, and the Communist governments in the world. . . . I rather feel that it would be well to state flatly in the beginning that you have no intention of producing a Philippic—that your purpose is to advance the cause of conciliation and understanding and not to be concerned merely with excoriation. The recital, therefore, of past misdeeds, including broken faith, calumny, or anything else would be made . . . regretfully and only to establish the basis for proceeding more constructively in the future.

—MEMORANDUM FROM
PRESIDENT DWIGHT D. EISENHOWER TO
SECRETARY OF STATE JOHN FOSTER DULLES,
SEPTEMBER 8, 1953

The President called [Treasury Secretary George] Humphrey and asked him to speak to [Texas oil magnate] Sid Richardson, who was really the angel for Lyndon Johnson when he came in. Ask him what it is that Texas wants. [Johnson] tells Sid he is supporting us, then comes up here and disproves it.

Perhaps Sid could get him into right channel, or threaten to get [Texas governor Allen] Shivers into a primary and beat him for Senate.

— NOTES ON A TELEPHONE CONVERSATION
OF EISENHOWER WITH HUMPHREY,
MARCH 19, 1954

In the spring of 1955, when I was president of Penn State, Ike was the commencement speaker. As the time for the outdoor ceremony approached, storm clouds formed. I was distressed at the possibility of moving the commencement to an indoor facility that was too small to accommodate all of the guests. When I asked my brother for advice, he said, "Milton, I haven't worried about the weather since June 6, 1944."

— ANECDOTE TOLD BY MILTON EISENHOWER

Dwight David Eisenhower is the most misunderstood of the modern presidents. He was enormously popular with the American people from the period of his service as supreme allied commander in Europe in World War II to his death in 1969, but it was long held by students of American politics that his performance as chief executive was largely a nonperformance. It was widely assumed that the policies of the Eisenhower administration were made not by the amiable Ike but by his less-than-amiable secretary of state, John Foster Dulles, and his stony-faced White House chief of staff, Sherman Adams.

A poll of specialists on the presidency conducted immediately after he left office relegated Eisenhower to the rank of such nineteenth-century nonentities as Chester Arthur, but within two decades a transformation of his reputation had begun.[1] As the inner records of his presidency came into the public domain, an Eisenhower emerged who was wholly unlike the seeming political innocent who spawned the

1950s joke that while it would be terrible if Eisenhower died and Vice President Nixon became president, it would be worse if Sherman Adams died and *Eisenhower* became president.

The Eisenhower of the declassified record *was* president. He was a keen political operator who engaged in the kinds of persuasion and bargaining many believed he had left to subordinates. Most interesting for students of presidential leadership, Eisenhower proved to have a nonstandard but remarkably effective approach to carrying out his responsibilities—one in which he advanced his purposes by indirection, concealing those of his moves that were inconsistent with his apolitical exterior. Indeed, Eisenhower proves to have initiated a number of the actions that had been attributed to his subordinates.

ANTECEDENTS

Eisenhower was born in Denison, Texas, on October 14, 1890, and raised in the farm community of Abilene, Kansas, not far from the geographical center of gravity of the lower forty-eight states. His father was a mechanic in the local creamery, and his parents were members of a pietist Pennsylvania Dutch sect that migrated to Kansas in the nineteenth century in search of cheap land.

Eisenhower was an outgoing, popular youth and an enthusiastic athlete who did well in those high school subjects that interested him. After graduating from high school, he worked in the creamery where his father was employed. He then competed successfully for admission to the U.S. Military Academy at West Point, New York, which he attended in order to play football and get a free college education.

At West Point, Eisenhower revealed a greater interest in sports than academic matters, graduating sixty-first in a class of 164. His intellect was awakened while serving under General Fox Conner in the Panama Canal Zone in the early 1920s. Conner, who was a legendary military intellectual, sensed Eisenhower's intelligence and introduced him to such works as Clausewitz's *On War*, the classic statement of the intrinsically political nature of war.

Conner, who was well connected in the informal networks of the military, arranged for Eisenhower to attend the army's prestigious Command and General Staff School at Fort Leavenworth, Kansas. Eisenhower graduated first in his class in 1926 and for the next decade and a half was singled out for important staff assignments. From 1929 to 1935, he served in the War Department in Washington, D.C., where he acquired an insider's understanding of Washington's political folkways. Between 1935 and 1939, he served in the Philippines as assistant to the highly political General Douglas MacArthur, helping that nation in its preparations for independence.

Eisenhower's rise to global prominence began five days after Pearl Harbor. Army Chief of Staff George C. Marshall, who had spent the interwar years identifying the army's most promising young officers, summoned Eisenhower to Washington as chief of the Army War Plans Division. He so impressed Marshall that six months later, he was made commander of the U.S. military forces in Europe. Eisenhower's talents as a strategist had led Marshall to send him to Europe, but his superiors quickly recognized that he also had a radiant public manner and a gift for coordinating collective endeavors. In January 1944, he was appointed supreme commander of the Allied military effort in Europe, and in that capacity he led one of the most complex collective endeavors in human history: the invasion of France and the campaign in Europe that culminated with the defeat of Nazi Germany in May 1945.

FROM SUPREME COMMANDER TO COMMANDER IN CHIEF

After the war, President Truman prevailed on Eisenhower to serve as chief of staff of the army, which he did until early 1948. Eisenhower then retired from active duty and became president of Columbia University. As the most popular military figure to emerge from World War II, he received overtures to run for the presidency from both parties in 1948 but rejected them. In 1950, Truman called Eisenhower back to active duty to serve as the first military commander of the North Atlantic Treaty Organization (NATO).

By the time Eisenhower assumed his NATO post, he had made a number of public statements that revealed him to be an economic conservative. It was evident that any political future he might have would be as a Republican. While he was at NATO, a number of leading Republican internationalists appealed to him to become their party's 1952 candidate. Eisenhower's diary entries for the period make it evident that he would not have run if the likely Republican nominee could have been counted on to maintain the nation's commitment to NATO. Instead, the almost certain GOP choice was Ohio's isolationist-leaning Senator Robert A. Taft.

Early in 1952, Eisenhower supporters entered his name in the New Hampshire Republican presidential primary. Although he was not a declared candidate, he defeated Taft handily. That testified to his vote-getting power, but the bulk of Republican delegates were to be chosen by pro-Taft party organizations. Eisenhower then returned home to seek the nomination personally.

After a hotly contested convention, he won the nomination and embarked on a vigorous campaign against the Democratic candidate, Illinois governor Adlai E. Stevenson. Eisenhower promised that if elected he would go to Korea, implying that he would do what was necessary to end the stalemated war. Even without such a pledge by the architect of victory in Europe, Eisenhower's triumph was a foregone conclusion. He defeated Stevenson by six million votes, bringing a narrowly Republican Congress into office with him.

A COVERT PRIME MINISTER

Eisenhower's presidential leadership style stood on its head the recommendation of such analysts of presidential leadership as Richard E. Neustadt, who counsel chief executives to enhance their influence with fellow policymakers by engaging in visible displays of political skill. In rejecting that advice, Eisenhower devised a unique solution to a dilemma the founding fathers embedded in the presidency.[2]

The Constitution obliges the president to balance roles that in most democracies are divided between a head of state and a prime minister. In the first capacity, the chief executive is a national unifying figure, much like the British monarch. In the second, he has the intrinsically divisive responsibility of mobilizing a governing coalition. Eisenhower resolved this contradiction by highlighting his status as head of state and masking his prime ministerial actions. By avoiding partisan stances, he maintained a broad base of public support and an average of 64 percent approval over his eight years in the White House.

One of Eisenhower's methods of distancing himself from his administration's more controversial policies was to hide his hand in actions that were inconsistent with his nonpolitical image. During the sequence of events that led to the political demise of Wisconsin senator Joseph McCarthy, for example, Eisenhower took the public position that it was up to the Senate to discipline McCarthy, but privately he played a central part in the campaign that led to McCarthy's censure by the Senate in December 1954.

Other of Eisenhower's covert prime ministerial practices included avoiding public fights and farming out controversial actions to his aides. When his allies urged him to confront McCarthy head on, he told them that it would help McCarthy's cause if the president of the United States tangled with that political gutter fighter. When the occasion arose for a member of the Eisenhower administration to speak out publicly against McCarthy, Eisenhower delegated the task to Vice President Richard Nixon.[3]

Eisenhower further advanced his purposes by employing a layered communication style. In his public addresses, he used rhetoric that was at once simple and elevated. He was informal, colloquial, and often deliberately obscure in press conferences, contributing to the impression that he was removed from the specifics of his administration's policies. Nevertheless, he was a prolific writer of crisply analytic private letters and memoranda, advancing complicated arguments in a lucid prose that belies the notion that his policies were determined by his aides.

A Studied Head of State

Eisenhower's low-profile political methods were complemented by his studied means of fulfilling his obligations as head of state. The winning Eisenhower smile and magnetic crowd appeal seemed wholly spontaneous, but Eisenhower's chemistry with the public was not free of calculation. He revealed his views in a document he did not intend to see the light of day—a discarded introduction to his World War II memoirs in which he recalled the tense days that he spent in November 1942, awaiting the intelligence he needed to order the invasion of North Africa.

"During those anxious hours," he wrote, "I first realized how inexorably and inescapably strain and tension wear away at the leader's endurance, his judgment and his confidence. The pressure becomes more acute because of the duty of a staff constantly to present to the commander the worst side of any eventuality." Realizing that the commander has the double burden of "preserving optimism in himself and in his command" and that "optimism and pessimism are infectious and they spread more rapidly from the head down than in any direction," Eisenhower made the following resolution:

> I firmly determined that my mannerisms and speech in public would always reflect the cheerful certainty of victory—that any pessimism and discouragement I might ever feel would be reserved for my pillow. To translate this conviction into tangible results, I adopted a policy of circulating through the whole force to the full limit imposed by physical considerations. I did my best to meet everyone from general to private with a smile, a pat on the back and a definite interest in his problems.[4]

President Eisenhower was as committed to instilling morale as General Eisenhower had been. In his final year in office, the sixty-nine-year-old Eisenhower embarked on a series of global goodwill tours, subjecting himself to an exhausting regimen of motorcades and official meetings. His concern with public leadership extended to giving tips on self-presentation to the politicians with whom he appeared at campaign events. "Now here's what you do," he would declare. "Get out there. Don't look so serious. Smile! When the people are waving at you wave your arms and move your lips, so you look like you're talking to them."[5]

A SEAMLESS TRANSITION

Some leaders are primarily concerned with maneuver; others are most attentive to policy. Eisenhower falls into the latter category. As a veteran strategist, his characteristic response to an emerging problem was to reach for a governing principle. A second legacy of Eisenhower's military career was his preoccupation with organization. Both were evident in his seamless steps to constitute his administration and formulate its stance in the area of his greatest concern: national security.

On election night, Eisenhower named his White House chief of staff and budget director. He then promptly selected his cabinet appointees and in late November embarked on his promised visit to Korea. The official reason for the trip was military, but Eisenhower made it do double duty as a team-building exercise. Arranging for his future aides to join him on his return, he presided over several days of discussion of his administration's proposed policies on a navy cruiser steaming from Wake Island to Honolulu. He went on to convene a second meeting with his aides-to-be in New York early in January.[6]

The issues that most concerned Eisenhower bore on establishing a long-term posture for waging the cold war. The twin pillars of that stance were deterrence of the Soviet Union and maintenance of a thriving American economy. As he put it in a 1951 diary entry, what the nation needed was to "reexamine our whole philosophy of defense in its foreign and domestic aspects" and develop a strategy that would achieve "security without paying the price of national bankruptcy."[7]

Once he was in the White House, Eisenhower enlisted his aides in a year-long deliberation that culminated in the creation of a national security policy designed to accomplish those ends. Its centerpiece was a planning exercise in which three groups of experienced national security analysts were charged with working out alternative national security strategies. One team spelled out what in effect was the Fortress America strategy of Republican isolationists. A second framed a plan reflecting the views of those who favored "liberating" the nations under communist control. A third perfected the containment strategy that had informed Truman's postwar national security policy. The seriousness of the review is indicated by Eisenhower's choice of a chairman for the third review: the veteran Foreign Service officer George F. Kennan, who had formulated the original doctrine of containment.

The task forces met for six weeks, presenting their findings to the National Security Council in mid-July. Following the presentation, Eisenhower took over, summarizing the findings and spelling out his view of their significance. His comments, according to Kennan, were impressive for their "mastery of subject matter, thoughtfulness, and penetration."[8] Shortly thereafter, the Eisenhower administration formalized its strategy, which came to be called the "New Look," a term derived from a postwar women's clothing fashion.

Eisenhower used the rationale of the New Look to make major cuts in the proposed military budget of the outgoing Truman administration.[9] That was the beginning of a controversy that continued throughout his presidency in which representatives of the armed forces and hawkish members of the political community argued that Eisenhower was allowing the nation to fall behind the Soviet Union in its military capacity. Such was Eisenhower's credibility on matters of national security that he was largely successful in holding down military and other spending.

THE NEW LOOK AND INDOCHINA

Eisenhower's performance in the crisis occasioned by the imminent collapse of French resistance to the Indochinese communists in 1954 provides an excellent illustration of his conceptually driven leadership.[10] The United States had been providing aid to France in its effort to maintain control of Indochina since 1950, when the outbreak of fighting in Korea led to a sudden intensification of the cold war in Asia. Throughout Eisenhower's first year in office, the French reported progress, but there was no end to the tunnel.

Then came a drastic turn for the worse. In the opening days of 1954, the communists encircled a major French force at the remote village of Dien Bien Phu in northern Vietnam. It soon became evident that the defenders were in deep peril and that if Dien Bien Phu fell, France was likely to abandon its effort to maintain a noncommunist Indochina. The members of Eisenhower's national security team were split. Joint Chiefs of Staff chairman Admiral Arthur Radford and Vice President Nixon were the most vociferous proponents of U.S. military intervention to relieve Dien Bien Phu's defenders. Treasury Secretary George Humphrey led the opponents of that course of action.

Eisenhower and his aides grappled with the situation in Indochina from early January to late July, when the parties to the conflict agreed to a truce and the partition of Vietnam at the seventeenth parallel. Eisenhower's oblique political style was in evidence throughout. He employed hidden-hand leadership early in April, absenting himself from a crucial conference of Secretary of State Dulles and Admiral Radford with congressional leaders on whether Congress would be willing to pass a resolution authorizing him to intervene in Indochina if he deemed it necessary. Instead, he carefully briefed his aides in advance of the meeting and debriefed them afterward. He was also artful in his use of language, first employing his famous domino metaphor to refer to the need to prevent Indochina from falling and later changing its meaning to refer to the need to shore up its neighbors when it became evident that Indochina might fall.

Eisenhower made his most important contributions to his administration's Indochina decision making at the strategic level. In the first NSC meeting to address the crisis, for example, the director of the Central Intelligence Agency had barely completed his briefing when Eisenhower interjected with an assessment of the situation, forcefully declaring, "This war in Indochina would absorb our troops by the divisions!"[11] In the months that followed, Eisenhower drew on the strategic framework of the New Look, insisting that it would be foolish to squander the nation's resources on a peripheral conflict, when its real adversaries were China and the Soviet Union.

THE NOT-SO-BULLY PULPIT

Eisenhower's ostensibly nonpolitical leadership style helped him maintain a high level of public support, providing him political cover for holding down spending and engaging in international crisis management. It would be a mistake, however, to suggest that his unconventional approach to leadership was without weaknesses. His flat-footed actions in the missile gap controversy point to a fundamental limitation of a presidential style that underplays the role of the chief executive as an enunciator of policies and educator of the public.

Assertions that the United States trailed the Soviet Union in missile development were first made in the mid-1950s. The missile gap controversy was of modest proportions until the Soviet launching of the earth satellite *Sputnik* on October 4, 1957. The shock of the launching can be compared only to that of Pearl Harbor or the acts of terrorism of September 11, 2001. What was worrisome was not that the ostensibly backward Soviet Union had orbited a satellite but that its ability to do so implied the capacity to project nuclear warheads to the American heartland. Suddenly a tempest in a teapot became a maelstrom.[12]

Eisenhower's reaction to *Sputnik* was to stand pat. His administration's first statement was by his press secretary and the secretary of state, who minimized the Soviet accomplishment, declaring that the United States had never intended to engage in a space race with the Soviet Union. Other Eisenhower aides were even more dismissive of the Soviet achievement. Secretary of Defense Charles E. Wilson called it a "nice scientific trick," and White House chief of staff Sherman Adams referred to it as an "outer space basketball game."[13]

Eisenhower's first public response was in his October 9 press conference. It was a lackluster performance. His responses to reporters' questions were digressive, and his effort to convey a sense of calmness came across as complacency. At one point he seemed to disparage the Soviet feat, calling *Sputnik* "one small ball in the air." Eisenhower went on to make several rather general speeches designed to reassure the nation. They failed to do the job. Claims that there was a missile gap continued to the end of the Eisenhower presidency, figuring prominently in the 1960 presidential campaign.

As it happens, Eisenhower knew from the findings of highly secret U-2 spy plane flights over the Soviet Union that there was no missile gap. He did not make the U-2 findings public in part because he did not want to whip up cold war tensions. He also had a more fundamental reason for holding the line on missile development, which remained valid after the Soviets shot down a U-2 plane in May 1960 and the overflight program was halted. In Eisenhower's conception of national security, the United States did not need to equal the Soviet Union in all areas of military endeavor. What it needed was sufficient retaliatory power to deter the Soviets from aggression. Eisenhower's corollary was that excessive military expenditures *reduced* national security by weakening the economy. This thesis was eminently suited for public enunciation by a respected former supreme commander, but persuading the nation of its validity called for the bully pulpit, not the hidden hand.

SIGNIFICANCE

Public Communication   Of all of Eisenhower's qualities, his political communication style has least to commend it to future chief executives. The preexisting public support the popular Ike carried over into the White House made it unnecessary for him to sell himself; his propensity to get results by indirection reduced his interest in public persuasion; and his wartime achievements left him with no need to use his presidency to establish a place in history. He put serious effort into his addresses, commenting on the drafts of his writers, but he seemed to view speeches more as state documents than as a means of galvanizing his audiences.[14]

To the extent that Eisenhower's communication style is a source of lessons, it is as a warning of the costs of inattention to presidential pedagogy. Eisenhower's failure to refute the claim that there was a missile gap had unhappy consequences. His successor entered the White House pledged to bring about a major increase in the nation's missile capacity. Kennedy did just that, triggering an arms race between the Soviet Union and the United States that continued throughout the cold war. The upshot is a post-cold war world burdened by stockpiles of nuclear warheads that could destroy life on the planet many times over, an eventuality Eisenhower would have viewed with horror.[15]

Organizational Capacity   When we turn to the internal face of presidential leadership, Eisenhower deserves the closest of attention. No other chief executive has entered the White House with his organizational experience, and none has put comparable effort into structuring his presidency. Eisenhower gave careful thought to finding the right incumbents for the right roles. Once his aides were in place, he observed their performance carefully, adjusting their responsibilities accordingly.

Eisenhower also was an institutional innovator. He created the first White House chief of staff, the first congressional relations office, and the first presidential assistant for national security affairs, a post that has come to be called the national security adviser.* The crown jewel of Eisenhower's advisory system was the institutional machinery associated with the weekly meetings of the National Security Council.

Eisenhower viewed the NSC as a mechanism for engaging his national security team in sharply focused debate on issues bearing on the nation's global policies. To that end, he instituted a procedure in which the top planners of each of the national security agencies met throughout the week to flush out policy disagreements within the administration and frame them clearly for NSC debate. The result was an impressively rigorous process of deliberation and team building that can be commended to any chief executive who wants to make effective use of the intellectual resources of the executive branch.

---

*Eisenhower enjoined his national security assistant to be a coordinator of foreign affairs decision making, insisting that he not compromise his neutrality by putting his own gloss on the advice and information that reached the Oval Office.

Because Eisenhower's main interests were in foreign and national security policy, his procedures for analyzing and debating domestic policy were not as elaborate as those of his NSC. Still, he met weekly with the cabinet to discuss domestic policy, and the cabinet's debates were informed by discussion papers that were prepared during the week by a formal agenda- setting body known as the cabinet secretariat. He also met at length with his domestic aides in December 1953, agreeing on a program of "moderate Republicanism" that expanded incrementally on such New Deal measures as social security.*

Political Skill   Any president would profit from an understanding of how Eisenhower operated in a variety of circumstances, including many of those reviewed in this chapter. Of particular interest is his smooth orchestration of the transition between his election and inauguration and the systematic manner in which he formulated his administration's policies and rallied his associates around them.

Eisenhower's indirect leadership style cannot be directly emulated today. It is better suited for a national icon than a garden variety politician. Behind-the-scenes political activity is also more likely to become public in the goldfish bowl of contemporary Washington than in Eisenhower's time. Hidden-hand leadership is also is not well suited for presidents with more ambitious domestic goals than Eisenhower's. Still, it can be employed in modified form. Presidents who emphasize the ecumenical side of their job and play down their political machinations may well experience a payoff in the form of public respect and approval.

Vision   Much of what made Eisenhower effective was the explicitness and clarity of his goals. Of all of the presidents considered in these pages, only Nixon compares to Eisenhower in the extent to which his

---

*He also led the way in projects to improve the nation's infrastructure, most notably the St. Lawrence Seaway and the interstate highway system. Another domestic development during the Eisenhower presidency was the enactment of the first civil rights act since Reconstruction, albeit one that lacked enforcement provisions.

leadership was informed by clearly defined policies. Eisenhower also had an impressive aptitude for policy analysis. The importance of that capacity is underscored by the experience of Lyndon Johnson. In 1965, Johnson transformed the American advisory presence in Vietnam into a full-scale military involvement. He accomplished that with utter skill, managing not to arouse significant controversy, but in doing so, he failed to establish a clear set of goals for the intervention, or analyze its probable duration and troop requirements. Three years later, a half million American military personnel were enmeshed in Vietnam, and the Johnson presidency was in shambles.

Cognitive Style Eisenhower was not one to flaunt his intelligence, but it was impressive. He had a retentive memory, a rich vocabulary, and a gift for lucid written expression that was at variance with the jumbled syntax of his press conferences. He also had a capacity to cut through to the core of problems and an ability to arrive at what one of his aides referred to as unusually persuasive "net judgments" about complex problems.[16] Many of Eisenhower's aides were more articulate than their boss, but in the end it typically was Eisenhower who resolved debates—not just because of his official authority, but also because his aides viewed him as a consistent source of wisdom and sound judgment.

Emotional Intelligence Eisenhower's aides witnessed an emotional intensity on his part that was not publicly evident. A standard jibe in the 1950s was that in the Eisenhower administration, "the bland led the bland," but there was nothing pallid about the behind-the-scenes Eisenhower. He had a temper that could burst forth like a summer thunderstorm, though it subsided just as rapidly. What is striking is not his lack of passion, but the freedom of his public actions from extraneous emotion. As the ever-observant Richard Nixon later put it, when it came to decision making, Eisenhower was the "most unemotional and analytical man in the world."[17]

Kennedy's incisiveness and wit in news conferences seemed wholly spontaneous. In fact, he prepared carefully for these televised events, making sure to be well rested before them and warming up by fielding hypothetical questions from his aides. Kennedy's mastery of public communication helps account for his success in maintaining a high level of public support, despite his administration's limited accomplishments and such negative developments as the failed effort to land anti-Castro guerrillas at Cuba's Bay of Pigs.

(John F. Kennedy Library)

CHAPTER 5

Coming to Terms with Kennedy

Let every nation know, whether it wishes us well or ill, that we shall pay any price, bear any burden, meet any hardship, support any friend, oppose any foe to assure the survival and the success of liberty.

—JOHN F. KENNEDY,
INAUGURAL ADDRESS,
JANUARY 20, 1961

Kennedy was a study in irony. He had his life style which was deeply hedonistic. All those girls! And yet in politics he was quite different, all discipline, all rationality.

—KENNEDY WHITE HOUSE AIDE
INTERVIEWED BY DAVID HALBERSTAM,
NOVEMBER 4, 1969

I have chosen this time and this place to discuss a topic on which ignorance too often abounds and the truth is too rarely perceived—yet it is the most important topic on earth: world peace. . . . I speak of peace because of the new face of war . . . in an age when a single nuclear weapon contains almost ten times the explosive force delivered by all of the allied air forces in the Second World War . . . an age when the deadly poisons produced by a nuclear exchange would be carried by wind and water and seed to the far corners of the globe and to generations yet unborn. I speak of peace, therefore, as the necessary rational end of rational men.

—JOHN F. KENNEDY,
COMMENCEMENT ADDRESS,
AMERICAN UNIVERSITY,
JUNE 10, 1963

QUESTION: Mr. President, in the 1960 campaign you used to say that it was time for America to get moving again. Do you think it is moving, and if so, how and where? The reason I ask you the question, Mr. President, is that the Republican National Committee recently adopted a resolution saying you were pretty much a failure.

THE PRESIDENT: I am sure it was passed unanimously. (Laughter)

—JOHN F. KENNEDY,
PRESS CONFERENCE,
JULY 17, 1963

The modern American presidency is constituted so as to ensure that the personal predispositions of its incumbent will leave an imprint on national and international events. This is most decisively so where the stakes are greatest—on matters of war and peace. President John F. Kennedy, who presided over a confrontation with the Soviet Union that brought the world close to the nuclear abyss, was an imprudent risk-taker in his private life. Does it follow that he was a risk-taker in his capacity as president? An answer is to be found in a close examination of the man and his presidential actions.

GROWING UP A KENNEDY

John Fitzgerald Kennedy was born on May 29, 1917, in Brookline, Massachusetts. He was the second of the nine children of Joseph P. Kennedy, a self-made millionaire and early supporter of FDR. His mother was the deeply religious Rose Fitzgerald Kennedy. His paternal grandfather, Patrick J. Kennedy, was a saloonkeeper and Massachusetts state legislator. His maternal grandfather, John F. ("Honey Fitz") Fitzgerald, was a professional politician and sometime mayor of Boston.

In 1934, Roosevelt made Joseph Kennedy the first chairman of the Securities and Exchange Commission, and in 1937 he named him ambassador to Great Britain. Kennedy served in that capacity until 1940, but his support of Prime Minister Neville Chamberlain's accommodating policies toward Nazi Germany and increasing conservatism led to a falling out between the two men.

Kennedy groomed his sons for public service, setting up trust funds that made them independently wealthy. Political issues of the day were debated intensely at the family dinner table, and the Kennedy boys were provided with opportunities to become politically informed. Kennedy's expectation was that his oldest son would become the family's principal aspirant for high electoral office; Jack inherited that status when his brother was killed in the war.

As a child and young man, JFK had repeated illnesses, but he lived up to the intensely competitive ethos of his family, participating actively in sports and engaging in a spirited social life. He was educated in private schools, graduating from Choate Academy in 1935. His father then sent him to England for a summer of study at the London School of Economics, but he was forced to return because of an attack of jaundice. He entered Princeton in the fall but dropped out after a recurrence of the same illness. He entered Harvard in the fall of 1936, graduating cum laude in 1940. His undergraduate honors thesis, entitled "Appeasement in Europe," was published as *Why England Slept*.[1]

Like his brothers and father, JFK moved easily between the eastern upper classes and Hollywood, where his father had business and personal connections. Like them he also had numerous romances and sexual liaisons, before and during his marriage.*[2] In 1940, Kennedy enlisted in the navy and went on to command a torpedo boat in the South Pacific. In 1943, a Japanese destroyer rammed his ship, killing two crew members. Kennedy swam with the survivors to a deserted island several miles away, towing a badly burned crewman to safety. After a brief postwar foray in journalism, Kennedy was elected to the House of Representatives in 1946 from a safely Democratic Boston district, serving there until his election to the Senate in 1952.

PREPRESIDENTIAL TRAJECTORY

Kennedy evinced little clear direction during his time in the House. His occasional public declarations, such as a 1949 attack on Truman's China policy, revealed him less as an independent political thinker than as the inheritor of his conservative father's views. Even after he achieved national recognition by withstanding the 1952 Republican sweep and winning election to the Senate, Kennedy's political purposes remained unclear. His prominence came less from policy stands than his family connections, war record, and much-publicized society wedding to the glamorous Jacqueline Bouvier.

To the extent that Kennedy had a political persona, it was as a dynamic young public official who conveyed a sense of idealism without seeming soft-minded or impractical. Kennedy's attractive personal and political qualities were very much in evidence in his spirited effort to win the 1956 Democratic vice-presidential nomination. His reputation was enhanced a year later when his book *Profiles in Courage* was awarded the Pulitzer Prize.[3]

---

*The extent of Kennedy's promiscuity is probably exaggerated in the supermarket tabloids that vie with one another to present accounts of his amorous exploits, but there is unambiguous evidence of the most notorious of his affairs in White House gate logs in the Kennedy Library. These document repeated visits to the Executive Mansion by Judith Campbell Exner, who later reported having simultaneous affairs with JFK and mafia don Sam Giancana.

None of this mattered to such Democratic liberals as Eleanor Roosevelt, who viewed JFK as little more than a cosmetically improved version of his father. They faulted him for failing to take a stand on the 1954 Senate censure of Wisconsin senator Joseph McCarthy and his equivocal position on the enforcement provisions of the Civil Rights Act of 1958. The quip of the day was that the handsome JFK needed to show less profile and more courage.

Between 1956 and 1960, Kennedy was engaged in near nonstop pursuit of the Democratic presidential nomination. He increasingly took liberal positions on domestic issues, but his principal emphasis was on foreign affairs. He played a leading part in enunciating the claim of Democratic foreign policy hawks that the Eisenhower administration had been lax in military preparedness, allowing a missile gap to develop.

In 1960, Kennedy became his party's nominee and defeated Vice President Richard Nixon in the general election, but his victory margin was a mere half a percent, and the Democrats lost twenty seats in the House and two in the Senate. In the face of this distinct nonmandate, Kennedy put his more progressive campaign promises on hold, narrowing his focus to such achievable goals as tax reduction, redevelopment of economically depressed localities, and tariff liberalization. Only as events on the streets in the South forced his hand in the final year of his presidency did he act on the civil rights pledges of his campaign, speaking for racial justice and sending a civil rights bill to Congress.

A CONTESTED LEGACY

When Kennedy arrived in Dallas on the day of his assassination, he was in something of a slump. His approval ratings had declined by 19 percentage points over the previous eighteen months. His belated civil rights activism had cost him support in the South, his domestic program was stalemated in Congress, and there was widespread skepticism about his capacity to exert sustained, effective leadership. His approval level remained at a respectable 58 percent, but a continuing erosion of support would have made his reelection problematic.

Then came his posthumous apotheosis. For three days the nation was transfixed as the rituals of national mourning were observed, culminating with the drama and poignancy of Kennedy's state funeral. The public immediately added him to the ranks of presidential greats. As long after his death as 1991, when a cross-section of Americans was asked to name the three greatest presidents, Kennedy tied Lincoln for first place.[4]

During the first several years after Kennedy's death, large numbers of authorities on American politics also held favorable views of him, but within a decade there was a wave of scholarly Kennedy revisionism. Two quite different kinds of critical writings on JFK bear on whether he took unwarranted political risks: one ideological, the other psychological. Those who criticize Kennedy on ideological grounds depict him as a virulent cold warrior whose anticommunism led him to be needlessly antagonistic toward the communist world.[5] Kennedy's psychological critics stress his father's efforts to prod his sons to ever-higher political achievement and inculcate a fierce sense of competitiveness in his children. The effect of the overbearing Joseph Kennedy on JFK, according to such interpreters, was to imbue him with an ethos of personal and political machismo.[6]

THE SOVIET UNION AS A TEST CASE

Writings that invoke Kennedy's libido to explain his prosecution of the cold war share a flaw with those that stress his ideology: they fail to test their claims against his actions. An obvious way of establishing whether Kennedy took needless risks in his presidential capacity is to examine his conduct in the cold war. The 1,037 days of the Kennedy presidency were marked by intense, potentially lethal confrontation between the United States and the Soviet Union. But the sources of that conflict prove to be misperceptions on the part of Kennedy and Soviet Communist party general secretary Nikita Khrushchev and the tendency of both leaders to placate their domestic hard-liners, not Kennedy's ideology or need to display his manliness.[7]

The irony is that Kennedy was alert to the danger of misperception in relations between the United States and the Soviet Union. Despite his public use of anticommunist rhetoric, Kennedy's private beliefs about the Soviet Union were remarkably dispassionate. In a 1959 interview with biographer James MacGregor Burns, for example, Kennedy compared the United States and the Soviet Union to a pair of individuals "who are both of good will, but neither of whom can communicate because of a language difference."[8]

It was just such a lack of mutual understanding that led to the spiral of conflict and confrontation between the United States and the Soviet Union during the Kennedy years. Twelve days before Kennedy's inauguration, Khrushchev addressed a private conclave of Communist party activists, speaking out in favor of "wars of liberation" in the Third World. Kennedy took Khrushchev's declaration to be the prelude to a period of Soviet expansionism, failing to realize that it was an effort on the Soviet leader's part to counter criticism by China of his moderate domestic and global policies.

Kennedy distributed Khrushchev's statement to his aides, telling them he viewed it as a key to Soviet intentions. His inaugural address was already drafted at the time, and he did not revise it. He responded to the Soviet leader's speech by calling for a major increase in U.S. military spending on January 30 in his State of the Union address, couching his request in terms that Soviet leaders were bound to find alarming:

> Each day, we draw nearer to the hour of maximum danger, as weapons spread and hostile forces grow stronger. I feel I must inform the Congress that our analyses over the last ten days make it clear that, in each of the principal areas of crisis, the tide of events has been running out.[9]

There is no evidence that Kennedy or his principal speechwriter, Theodore Sorensen, pondered the possible effect of Kennedy's words on the men in the Kremlin. In fact, the address was viewed with alarm in the Soviet Union. *Izvestia* declared that it evoked "irksome echoes of the Cold War," and Khrushchev began to reconsider his assumption that the Kennedy administration would be more congenial than Eisenhower's had been.[10]

Then, eighty-nine days into the new presidency, the Kennedy administration landed a brigade of Cuban exiles on the coast of Cuba. The invasion was fatally ill conceived, and the landing force was promptly overwhelmed. The Bay of Pigs was doubly counterproductive for relations with the Soviet Union. In authorizing the invasion, Kennedy left the impression in Moscow that his administration had hostile intentions toward the Soviet Union and its allies. In failing to bring the invasion to a successful conclusion, the young president seemed to reveal a lack of political will that could be exploited by the Soviet Union.

Seeking to intimidate Kennedy, Khrushchev bullied him on the issue of Berlin at their June 1961 meeting in Vienna, threatening to turn the divided city over to communist East Germany. Before the year was over, Kennedy had become so convinced that the Soviet Union was underestimating the military strength and political determination of the United States that he authorized an administration spokesman to make public the vast strategic advantage of the United States. Khrushchev responded to this politically embarrassing evidence of Soviet weakness by surreptitiously deploying missiles in Cuba. The upshot was the October 1962 nuclear face-off that came to be called the Cuban missile crisis.

AN UPWARD LEARNING CURVE

If Kennedy had made better use of the sources of advice and information available to him in the executive branch, it is possible that the first two years of his presidency would have been marked by reasonably amicable relations between the two nuclear superpowers. He failed to do so in large part because of his administration's haphazard operating procedures. Upon taking office, Kennedy had scrapped the deliberative machinery of the Eisenhower presidency, putting nothing in its place. He eliminated the practice of holding regular official meetings in which top administrative officials argued out their policy disagreements. Instead, he relied on ad hoc consultations, meeting with his aides when he deemed it appropriate. Such was the informality of his procedures that he did not seek the counsel of his administration's specialists on the Soviet Union until after his stern "hour of maximum danger" address.*[11]

Kennedy's reluctance to institute a formal advisory system was partly a function of his background on Capitol Hill, where legislators tend to be independent political operators, and partly a result of reading the books of two of his academic advisers: Arthur Schlesinger, Jr., and Richard E. Neustadt. Schlesinger, in his 1959 *The Coming of the New Deal*, extolled FDR's practice of encouraging his advisers to compete for his ear. Neustadt in his 1960 *Presidential Power* advanced the more general thesis that fluid advisory procedures serve presidents better than structured arrangements by exposing them to a wide range of views and preserving them from becoming the captives of their advisers.[12]

The Bay of Pigs provided Kennedy with a high-decibel wake-up call. His consulting procedures in the run-up to that debacle were notably disorderly. At no point did he convene the members of his administration for a thorough debate. Planning for an invasion of Cuba had originated during the Eisenhower administration and had been headed by Douglas Dillon, who had become Kennedy's treasury secretary, but there was no consultation with Dillon. The views of aides who doubted the wisdom of the venture were kept from Kennedy. The invasion site had been shifted from its original location to the Bay of Pigs, where the swampy terrain made a planned retreat into the mountains an impossibility, but no one explored the military implications of the change.

Kennedy responded to the Bay of Pigs with a capacity for self-correction that has not always been manifested by American presidents.

*The meeting, which was on February 11, 1961, was with Kennedy's ambassador to the Soviet Union, Llewellyn Thompson, and former ambassadors Averell Harriman, George Kennan, and Charles Bohlen.

Although he did not institute a structured advisory system, he created a partial equivalent of one by ordering his two closest advisers, Robert Kennedy and Theodore Sorensen, to scrutinize proposed national security decisions, watching for insufficiently examined assumptions. He also moved his national security adviser, McGeorge Bundy, from the Executive Office Building to the White House, so he could more readily avail himself of Bundy's incisive intellect.

The value of these changes became evident in the missile crisis. As soon as it became known that the Soviet Union had placed offensive missiles in Cuba, Kennedy constituted an ad hoc committee known as Ex Com, instructing its members to assess the situation and develop options. The discussion in Ex Com was uninhibited, sometimes occurring in Kennedy's presence and sometimes in his absence so as not to constrain debate.

From the start, Kennedy ruled out allowing the missiles to remain in Cuba, as much on political as strategic grounds, but the debate on how to remove them was extended and searching. After leaning toward an air strike, the group devised a less provocative option: a blockade of Soviet ships supplying missiles to Cuba. Kennedy finally resolved the crisis personally by secretly assuring the Soviets that he would remove the American missiles from Greece and Turkey, not informing the Ex Com conferees he had done so. Still, his aides' deliberations were highly significant. The extended give-and-take of Ex Com had prevented premature closure on an air strike. If that had not occurred, the result might well have been a nuclear exchange between the United States and the Soviet Union.

KENNEDY THE COMMUNICATOR

The audiovisual archives of the Kennedy Library contain instructive film footage of television interviews given by JFK shortly after his election to the House of Representatives. The diffident, soft-spoken young man they reveal bears little resemblance to the soaring orator who on January 20, 1961, put the world on notice that "the torch has been passed to a new generation of Americans—born in this century, tempered by war, disciplined by a hard and bitter peace, proud of our ancient heritage."

The high oratory of the latter-day JFK was a product of his collaboration with Theodore Sorensen, who joined his staff after he entered the Senate. Kennedy's speechmaking helped him transform his razor-thin election victory into the highest average public support for any twentieth-century modern chief executive. Kennedy won the presidency with 49.9 percent of the popular vote. In the first Gallup poll after he entered the White House, he was positively evaluated by 72 percent of the public. As it happened, that was his lowest approval level of his first year. (His highest was 83 percent.) His approval level declined to 61 percent in 1962 after he dispatched federal troops to Mississippi to enforce a racial integration order, but it surged to 76 percent with the resolution of the missile crisis and did not dip below 60 percent until the final three months of his life.

One source of Kennedy's stratospheric ratings was the oratory into which he and Sorensen put so much effort. Among their more memorable efforts were his stirring inaugural address, his 1962 Rice University speech on the challenge of placing a man on the moon, the eloquent condemnation of racism in his 1963 civil rights message, and his dramatic affirmation to the people of Berlin that in the "world of freedom" of the day, "the proudest boast is 'Ich bin ein Berliner.'"[13]

Kennedy's popularity was furthered by his innovative use of live television. On the day of his twice-a-month news conferences, Kennedy prepared like an athlete in training, taking a long nap in the afternoon of the news conference, fielding trial questions from aides, and strapping on his back brace. He then strode easily into the amphitheater, where he met with reporters, fielding questions with a crispness and wit that transformed a commonplace routine into a prime-time media event, winning support for him and, by extension, his policies.

Kennedy was assiduous in his attention to individual journalists, remembering their names, commenting on their writing, and exposing them to his charm. He disarmed them by poking fun at his own high-flown locutions. He even parodied the grandiloquence of his inaugural address, declaring that the Democratic party's campaign debt would not be paid off "in the next hundred days," or "the first one thousand days," or "the life of this administration."[14]

Students of public opinion have done better at measuring presidential approval than determining its wellsprings. Kennedy's political appeal clearly had many sources: his manner, his wife and children, the glitter of his White House, the ambiance of the New Frontier. It seems to have been as much the attraction of a celebrity as of a conventional political figure. Whatever its underpinnings, Kennedy's bond with the public served his presidency well, contributing to a political climate marked by optimism and good cheer—qualities that have been in short supply in later decades.

SIGNIFICANCE

Public Communication On the positive side of Kennedy's approach to public communication is the eloquence of his oratory and his intelligent and stylish performance in press conferences. Kennedy's public performance and the attractive ambiance of his presidency won him impressive levels of public approval, despite such negative developments as the Bay of Pigs and the erection of the Berlin Wall. Public support does not in and of itself buy policymaking success, and Kennedy was constrained in what he could accomplish by the existence of a powerful coalition of conservative Republicans and southern Democrats on Capitol Hill. A less popular Kennedy would have had difficulties even with such undramatic achievements as the 1962 tariff liberalization act. Future chief executives can scarcely go wrong by attending to Kennedy's communication practices.

On the minus side of Kennedy's performance as a public communicator is his inattention to the signals his oratory conveyed to the Soviet Union. Kennedy's declarations about the "long twilight struggle" the United States faced with the forces of totalitarianism helped immunize him from charges that he was not up to leading his nation in the cold war. Nevertheless, the Kennedy years would have been safer if he had followed the practice of Eisenhower and allowed his policy pronouncements to be toned down by his national security team.[15]

Organizational Capacity Kennedy's organizational legacy is also two-sided. He excelled at team building and at rallying his aides. It is not a complete idealization to refer to the New Frontiersmen as the best and the brightest. If only because plodders bored him, JFK surrounded himself with talented compatriots, inspiring a spirit of colleagueship and dedication that can serve as a model for any White House incumbent.

When it comes to the more mundane matter of White House organization, Kennedy is mainly a source of cautionary tales. Upon taking office, he abolished the policy analysis machinery of the organization-minded Eisenhower, going on to evolve his own unstructured method of stimulating closely joined debate. The deliberate informality of the Kennedy White House was lauded in his time, but few of today's students of the presidency would recommend that a president personally coordinate his own White House. Kennedy did tighten his operating procedures following the Bay of Pigs, but as late as the final month of his life, there was a chaotic deliberation in which his team signed off on the profoundly destabilizing coup in South Vietnam that resulted in the assassination of President Ngo Dinh Diem.

Political Skill JFK was never a Capitol Hill insider, but he came from a highly political family and was a political professional with more than a dozen years of legislative experience. Moreover, he surrounded himself with politically experienced aides. Not surprisingly, his presidency provides many examples of political skill. He began his presidency with a successful all-out campaign to break the stranglehold of the conservative Rules Committee over what legislation could be voted on by the House of Representatives. Among other examples, it would serve any president well to examine Kennedy's carefully managed campaign to bring about tariff liberalization in order to advance his administration's economic program. What is missing in Kennedy's leadership is skill harnessed to a larger view of public policy, a gap that leads us to the topic of vision.

Vision   It might seem self-evident that a president famed for inspirational addresses was not deficient in vision, but in fact Kennedy had little in the way of an overarching perspective. This was of slight moment in the domestic realm, where he lacked grand aspirations and was limited in what he could accomplish by the balance of forces in Congress. But it was of grave consequence in the relationship with the Soviet Union, which culminated in the near disaster of October 1962. Kennedy showed an impressive capacity to empathize with his Soviet counterpart once that confrontation was underway. A clearer sense of direction might have made it unnecessary to put his crisis management skills to use.

Cognitive Style   Kennedy's cognitive qualities have much to commend them. Despite his reputation today as a presidential playboy, Kennedy did not confine his spare time to carnal indulgences. He left for his family estate on Cape Cod on weekends with vast amounts of official reading and showed every sign of having mastered its essentials. He was a speed-reader and a quick study, whose wit was an indication of a supple mind. Moreover, he did not confine his reading to official memoranda. At the time of the missile crisis, he was reading Barbara Tuchman's *The Guns of August,* an account of the role of miscalculation and escalation of conflict in the origins of World War I. His comment to his brother Robert was that he would not follow a course that would lead a future historian to write a comparable book on the missiles of October. "If anyone is going to write after this, they are going to understand that every effort was made to find peace and every effort to give our adversary room to move."[16]

Emotional Intelligence   The seeming compulsiveness of Kennedy's sexual activity suggests that at some level he was in the thrall of his emotions. (According to his friend LeMoyne Billings, Kennedy treated "each day as if it were his last, demanding of life constant intensity, adventure, and pleasure," because he had repeatedly come close to death in the war and in surgery and believed that he would die at an early age from Addison's disease.)[17] Kennedy's philandering also was a threat to his presidency, even in a period when public officials were accorded more privacy than they are now. Nevertheless, in his public capacity, the famously detached JFK showed little sign of the unsettled emotions that suffused the leadership of Johnson and Nixon. In that he provides a reminder that a president's actions are a function not only of the intensity of his passions, but also of his capacity to channel them and prevent them from confounding his official responsibilities.

Lyndon Johnson ranks with Henry Clay as one of the most gifted practitioners of the art of the possible in American history. Here he is seen in a nose-to-nose exercise in political persuasion with Rhode Island senator Theodore F. Green. Johnson's political prowess was not coupled to a disposition to assess the feasibility of his policies. In 1965, he led the United States into a military intervention in Vietnam without exploring its costs and probable consequences. By 1968, there were a half-million American troops in Vietnam, and the Johnson presidency was on the ropes.

(George Tames/NYT Pictures, The New York Times Company)

CHAPTER 6

Lyndon B. Johnson and the Primacy of Politics

All I have I would have given gladly not to be standing here today. The greatest leader of our time has been struck down by the foulest deed of our time. Today John Fitzgerald Kennedy lives on in the immortal words and works that he left behind.

—LYNDON B. JOHNSON, ADDRESS BEFORE
A JOINT SESSION OF CONGRESS,
NOVEMBER 27, 1963

Let this session of Congress be known as the session which did more for civil rights than the last hundred sessions combined; as the session which declared an all-out war on human poverty; as the session which finally recognized the health needs of all our older citizens; as the session which helped to build more homes, more schools, more libraries, and more hospitals than any single session of Congress in the history of our Republic.

—LYNDON B. JOHNSON,
STATE OF THE UNION ADDRESS,
JANUARY 8, 1964

I have today ordered to Vietnam the Airmobile Division and certain other forces which will raise our fighting strength from

75,000 to 125,000 men almost immediately. Additional forces
will be needed later and they will be sent as requested.

—LYNDON B. JOHNSON,
NEWS CONFERENCE,
JULY 28, 1965

With American sons in the fields far away, with America's
future under challenge right here at home, with our hopes and
the world's hopes for peace in the balance every day, I do not
believe that I should devote an hour or a day of my time to any
personal partisan causes or to any duties other than the awesome duties of this office—the Presidency of your country.
Accordingly, I shall not seek, and I will not accept, the nomination of my party for another term as your president.

—LYNDON B. JOHNSON,
ADDRESS, MARCH 31, 1968

If a president's ability to fulfill his responsibilities depended only on
his command of the rules of Washington politics and ability to use
them to good effect, the presidency of Lyndon Baines Johnson would
have been an unqualified success. Yet by almost any standard, Johnson's tenure in the White House was marked by phenomenal failures
as well as towering achievements.

Lyndon Johnson was one of the most gifted practitioners in American history of the art of coaxing decisions out of a political system
that makes it easier to block policy initiatives than bring them to
fruition. In 1965, Johnson initiated an open-ended military intervention in Vietnam while presiding over the enactment of a sweeping program of domestic policy innovation. Doing so was a short-run tour de
force, but he undertook the intervention without carefully assessing its

likely costs and consequences. In the longer run it crippled his presidency and left lasting scars on the body politic.

POLITICAL INCUBATION

Johnson was born on August 27, 1908, in rural south-central Texas and raised in Johnson City, which was founded by his grandfather. He was the son of Sam Ealy Johnson, Jr., and Rebekah Baines Johnson. Both his father and maternal grandfather served in the Texas legislature. Johnson's father was a roughhewn, hard-drinking, poor provider. His mother was a genteel contrast to her husband—a schoolteacher who had worked her way through Baylor College in Belton, Texas, and was drawn to literary pursuits. Not surprisingly, their marriage was fraught with strains and incompatibilities.

Johnson's family was the incubator of his political proclivities in two respects. The legislative experience of his father and grandfather inspired him to make politics his career. At a deeper level, he acquired the instinct for maneuver that undergirded his actions in the political arena by negotiating his way through the minefield of family tensions.

Under the tutelage of a mother who rivaled Sara Roosevelt in her psychic investment in her son, Johnson was pushed in school, learning to read at four and graduating from high school at age sixteen. His early experiences included accompanying his father on political campaigns and on the floor of the state legislature. After high school, Johnson ran away from home, doing odd jobs in California and returning broke and hungry. At age nineteen, he succumbed to parental pressure and entered Southwest Texas Teachers College, where he cut a swathe as a campus politician.

In 1931, the twenty-three-year-old Johnson went to Washington as the secretary of a newly elected Texas congressman. He quickly learned the ropes in Washington, earning the reputation of a political operator with the ability of a seasoned Washington hand. In 1935, Johnson returned to Texas to administer a New Deal relief agency. In 1937, the congressman in Johnson's home district died, and Johnson won the seat in a special election. He served five and a half terms in the House, before going on to the Senate in 1948.

A LEGISLATIVE WIZARD

Johnson rapidly rose to the leadership ranks of the Senate. In 1951, he was named whip, and two years later was chosen as party leader. When the Democrats gained control of Congress in 1954, Johnson became the youngest majority leader in Senate history. He promptly expanded the resources of that office, acquiring the power to name senators to committees and making himself the dispenser of such perquisites as office space and authorizations to conduct investigations. Wielding his resources with great effect, he transformed the Senate from a graveyard for policy proposals to a productive law-making body.

It would be difficult to imagine anyone better equipped for legislative leadership than LBJ. He had an unerring sense of the preoccupations of his colleagues and a genius for linking the provisions of proposed laws to the interests of sufficient numbers of legislators to enact them. His indifference to the merits of specific policy provisions left him with wide latitude for action, enabling him to reserve his own stand until he had found a position on which a majority of lawmakers could unite.

The goals Johnson advanced during his years in Congress were highly variable. In the 1930s, when he represented a pro-Roosevelt congressional district, he was a liberal Democrat, ingratiating himself with FDR and the New Dealers of his circle. In the 1940s, when his constituency became the entire state of Texas, he veered to the right, joining forces with conservative southern segregationists to block civil rights legislation. In the 1950s, when he became a presidential hopeful, he shifted to a centrist, cautiously pro-civil rights stance.

The constant was the man. Johnson was unforgettable, beginning with his appearance. "At six feet three and a half inches, with long arms, big ears, a prominent nose, and outsized personality to match, LBJ left a lasting impression on everyone he met." Behind the exterior was a bewilderingly contradictory human being. One associate described him as "brave and brutal, compassionate and cruel, incredibly intelligent, and infuriatingly insensitive"; another as "generous and selfish, kind and cruel, earthy and incredibly charming"; still another as "driven, tyrannical, crude, insensitive, humorless, and petty, but also empathic, shy, sophisticated, self-critical, witty, and magnanimous."[1]

Johnson's assets included his energy, shrewdness, and extraordinary capacity to broker coalitions. His pyrotechnic exercises of political persuasion were legendary, and he had a powerful personal magnetism, but he also had outsized liabilities. He was self-centered, suspicious, and sensitive to real and perceived slights, and his effectiveness with face-to-face groups was not matched by a consistent ability to communicate effectively with the public. In short, he was a brilliant behind-the-scenes politician and a complex and flawed human being.

Johnson had barely become majority leader when there was speculation that his success in taming the Senate might be transferable to the Oval Office. He sought the Democratic presidential nomination in 1960, but he was handily defeated by his Senate colleague John F. Kennedy. Accepting Kennedy's offer to be his running mate, Johnson campaigned energetically for the Democratic ticket and went on to the vice presidency. Although Johnson played only a marginal role in the New Frontier, he and Kennedy were in the same motorcade in Dallas at the time of Kennedy's assassination.

A FLAWLESS ACCESSION

Kennedy was pronounced dead at Parkland Hospital, Dallas, on Friday, November 22, 1963, at 1 P.M. An hour and a half later, Johnson took the oath of office in the cabin of *Air Force One* on the runway of the Dallas airport. When the presidential jet arrived in Washington, Johnson declared, "We have suffered a loss that cannot be weighed. I ask for your help and God's."

In the days that followed, Johnson was the personification of gravity and humility. He refused to move into the executive residence until Mrs. Kennedy vacated it and carried out his duties in his vice-presidential office until the Oval Office was emptied of Kennedy's possessions. He met with Kennedy's cabinet, asking its members to stay on. He made the same request of Kennedy's White House aides, telling them, "I need you even more than he did."

Meanwhile, he was a whir of behind-the-scenes action. Recordings of his telephone calls show him building bridges to leaders of his party's core constituencies and consulting with a multitude of Washington insiders. His almost obsequious entreaties for backing from Democratic constituency groups contrast with his crisply professional enunciation of his priorities to the leaders of Congress.

On Wednesday, November 27, Johnson addressed a joint session of Congress. Speaking with great solemnity, he noted his long service on Capitol Hill, voicing his pride in the ability of Congress "to meet any crisis" and "distill from our differences strong programs of national action." It was up to the lawmakers, he declared, to "do away with uncertainty and doubt and delay" and demonstrate that "from the brutal loss of our leader we will derive not weakness, but strength."

There had been no way of knowing what to expect of a chief executive who at various times had aligned himself with New Deal liberals, conservative southern Democrats, and middle-of-the-road moderates. Liberals and blacks were particularly uneasy about what it might mean to have a sometime southern conservative in the White House. Johnson instantly did away with any uncertainty about what his administration would stand for, declaring that "no memorial oration or eulogy could more eloquently honor President Kennedy's memory than the earliest passage of the civil rights bill for which he fought so long." The country had "talked for one hundred years or more" about equal rights, he continued. "It is time now to write the next chapter, and to write it in the books of law."[2]

TOWARD A GREAT SOCIETY

In December, Gallup asked the public to evaluate the new president's performance. His approval level was 79 percent—21 points higher than Kennedy's of the previous month. Early in January, Johnson revealed the specifics of the program he began to call the "Great Society." In addition to pressing for action on Kennedy's civil rights bill, he advanced a second Kennedy administration proposal: a tax cut intended to serve as an economic stimulus. To impose his own brand on the program, he seized on an antipoverty program that was still in the planning stage and placed it at the top of his agenda, increasing its budget and giving it the arresting title "The War on Poverty."[3]

In advancing his program, Johnson went out of his way to remind his fellow policymakers of his skill and determination. In December 1963, he kept Congress in session until the day before Christmas to defeat a Republican attempt to gut a provision in a Kennedy bill on grain exports. His reason, he later explained, was more to establish his credibility than out of a concern for the measure. Similarly, in April of the following year, he took personal control of negotiations over a threatened rail strike, arranging for a favorable tax ruling to the railroads in exchange for a wage increase for the rail workers.[4]

Johnson's approval level remained in the 70 percent range in the months leading up to the 1964 presidential campaign, a period that saw the passage of the tax stimulus, the legislation authorizing the War on Poverty, and the first civil rights act with enforcement provisions since Reconstruction. Running against the defiantly conservative Barry Goldwater, Johnson appropriated the middle ground and was swept into office with 61 percent of the popular vote and 90 percent of the electoral vote, carrying with him the largest congressional majority of any other president since FDR in 1936.

Johnson began 1965 riding high. *Time* named him "Man of the Year" in its New Year's Day issue, publishing a cartoon of a beaming, pajama-clad LBJ greeting the morning sun from his bedroom window with the declaration: "I am up, world—ready or not!"[5] On January 4, he addressed a joint session of the just-elected Eighty-Ninth Congress. After a passing reference to Vietnam, he outlined a far-reaching list of domestic proposals, some of which had been blocked for over two decades by the coalition of conservatives that had dominated Congress since 1938.

By the end of the year, the bulk of Johnson's program had become law. Included were major breakthroughs in voting rights for African Americans, medical care for the poor and aged, and aid to primary and secondary schools. Especially notable was Johnson's success in sidestepping the church-and-state issue that had doomed previous aid to education bills. In what one of the participants in the deliberations described as a "fantastically skilled breakthrough," the bill was structured to provide funds to pupils rather than their schools, making it possible to provide aid to parochial school children.[6] The first session of the Eighty-Ninth Congress passed more landmark legislation than any legislative session since 1933.

Before most of Johnson's domestic initiatives were signed into law, he had presided over still another departure: a major military commitment in Vietnam. Astonishingly, the records of decision making on the Great Society contain little reference to Vietnam, and those on Vietnam barely allude to domestic matters. Johnson's ability to confine these policy streams to their own channels is yet another illustration of his tactical proficiency, but it was a "success" that was a prelude to failure.

INTO A MORASS

The event that triggered the use of U.S. combat forces in Vietnam was a February 5, 1965, surprise Vietcong attack on the American base at Pleiku in which 6 American military advisers were killed and 116 wounded. Johnson then instituted a two-step contingency plan his aides had prepared several months earlier. Step 1 was to respond to a specific act of communist aggression in South Vietnam with a retaliatory air strike against North Vietnam. Step 2 was to commence sustained bombing of the North, intensifying the air war until the communists abandoned their efforts to prevail in the South. By March, sustained bombing was underway.

There followed a third step that was in no way envisaged in the blueprint prepared by Johnson's aides. Once the bombing was underway, American air bases in South Vietnam became prime targets for communist reprisal. The American commander in Vietnam, General William Westmoreland, requested that marines be dispatched to South Vietnam to guard the American air base at Da Nang. Johnson approved the request. When the marine force encountered stiff resistance, Westmoreland asked for and received additional reinforcements.

By June, the number of American troops in Vietnam exceeded 60,000. Late that month, South Vietnam suffered a series of devastating military reverses which prompted Westmoreland to recommend that his forces be increased to 125,000, adding that he would soon need an additional 50,000 troops. On July 20, Johnson convened eight days of high-level meetings within his administration about what to do next, letting it be known that these deliberations were underway. On July 28, Johnson announced his approval of Westmoreland's request at a midday news conference in an almost routine manner.

Because the public had been led by Johnson's aides to believe that he might call up the civilian reserves and place the nation on a wartime footing, his statement was received as an act of moderation. Few commentators made much of the passage in his statement that best predicted what was to come: his assertion that General Westmoreland had told him "what more he needs to meet this mounting aggression" and that "we will meet his needs."[7]

THE UNMAKING OF A PRESIDENCY

In his January 1966 State of the Union message, Johnson insisted that "this nation is mighty enough, its society is healthy enough, its people are strong enough to pursue our goals in the rest of the world while still building the Great Society here at home."[8] His affirmation seemed plausible at the time. Congress was overwhelmingly Democratic. Opposition to the war was confined to a narrow segment of the public and the political community, and Johnson's approval level was a still-substantial 61 percent.

By August 1966, Johnson's approval level had declined to 47 percent, and with only two exceptions it remained in the forties with occasional dips into the thirties for the remainder of his presidency. Johnson's approval level never descended to the depths of Truman's after he relieved General MacArthur or Nixon's during Watergate, but opposition to his policies was highly visible because of the intensity of antiwar protests. By the final period of his presidency, demonstrations against the war made him a near-prisoner in the White House.

As the war heated up, the Great Society floundered. The 1966 session of the Eighty-Ninth Congress saw no domestic enactments that approximated the importance of Medicare, aid to education, and voting rights. Many lesser bills were passed, but to achieve them, Johnson was forced to make major concessions, and he suffered defeats on key bills barring racial discrimination in housing and forbidding states to pass union-curbing laws.

By 1968, the troop level in Vietnam had reached 535,000. The United States had dropped a greater tonnage of bombs on Vietnam than it had during all of World War II, and the war was costing $2 billion a month. Vietnam had become Johnson's obsession. He haunted the White House situation room. When an American force was besieged in a South Vietnamese stronghold at Khe Sanh, Johnson had a scale model of the battlefield erected in the White House and followed the siege as closely as if he had been the field commander. Johnson became so troubled by the war that he broke into tears when he met privately with his mentor, Georgia senator Richard Russell.*⁹

On January 30, 1968, during the traditional cease-fire to observe the Vietnamese lunar New Year, the communists launched a surprise assault on a large number of population centers in South Vietnam. The Americans and South Vietnamese inflicted terrible casualties on the attackers. The offensive was a tactical defeat for the communists but a strategic victory. It produced a dramatic decline in support for the war in the United States. Opinion leaders, including such respected figures as television anchorman Walter Cronkite, began to come out against continued involvement in Vietnam.

By then the exhausted defense secretary, Robert McNamara, had stepped down. Johnson replaced him with the veteran Washington insider, Clark Clifford, expecting Clifford to back the war. Instead, Clifford concluded that the war was a losing proposition and led a

---

*Late in Johnson's time in office, Russell told his press secretary, Richard Allen Moore, that he now avoided visiting the White House alone because he was so troubled by Johnson's displays of emotion.

determined effort within the Johnson administration to halt the war's escalation and seek a political solution.

On the final day of March, the efforts of Clifford and those associated with him came to fruition. In an address to the nation from the Oval Office, Johnson announced that he was ordering a fundamental redirection of the nation's Vietnam policy. He declared that he was sharply reducing the bombing of North Vietnam and that his administration was now prepared "to discuss the means of bringing this ugly war to an end." In the concluding moments of his address, he shocked even his closest aides by announcing that he would neither seek nor accept his party's nomination for another term.[10]

A FLAWED DECISION-MAKING PROCESS

It is sometimes argued that the American military intervention in Vietnam was the inevitable consequence of the cold war political climate and the unwillingness of the nation's leaders to risk the political costs of allowing portions of the "free world" to fall under communist domination.[11] In fact there were so many possible American strategic options in Southeast Asia in early 1965 that it is unlikely that any two presidents would have proceeded identically. The choice was not simply between intervention and nonintervention. Johnson could have sought only to defend the most populous areas of South Vietnam, he could have intervened even more decisively, or he could have chosen some other course of action.

To the extent that the political climate provided Johnson with guidance on Vietnam in January 1965, it pointed toward a political solution. An Associated Press survey of the Senate reported on January 7, 1965, revealed that most members favored a negotiated outcome. Public opinion polls indicated that the bulk of the nation shared the same view. Indeed, Johnson had just won a landslide election victory after repeatedly making such statements as, "We don't want our American boys to do the fighting for Asian boys."[12]

Johnson did not lack advisers who warned against becoming enmeshed in an Asian war. Vice President Hubert Humphrey privately urged him to employ his "unrivalled talents as a politician" to avoid becoming mired in Vietnam. CIA director John McCone and Treasury Secretary Douglas Dillon advanced the hawkish position that intervention was in principle appropriate, but the United States should not commit its forces in Vietnam unless it was prepared to engage in an immediate, comprehensive assault on the North. Under Secretary of State George Ball took the dovish stance that the United States should not intervene at all lest it duplicate the disastrous French experience in 1954.

Johnson's response to such warnings was fundamentally political. He ignored McCone and Dillon, who expressed their views just before their scheduled departures from his administration. He dressed down Humphrey for venturing an opinion and froze him out of deliberations on Vietnam until he fell into line. He responded to Ball by praising him for the thoughtfulness of a memorandum in which he expressed his views, revealing a detailed mastery of its content. What he failed to do was commission a rigorous examination of the options in Vietnam.

Throughout the escalating military commitment, Johnson worked with the same national security aides as Kennedy: Secretary of Defense Robert S. McNamara, Secretary of State Dean Rusk, and national security adviser McGeorge Bundy. Under Kennedy, these men had been part of a process of vigorous policy debate. Under Johnson, deliberation and decision making had a quite different quality. He turned meetings called to examine substantive matters into forums for inveighing against his critics and devising public relations measures to address their objections. He also operated in a manner that was even more ad hoc than Kennedy's. He met with the NSC several times in some months and not at all in others, making many of his most crucial decisions on Vietnam with a handful of top aides at luncheon meetings in which no note-takers were present.

SIGNIFICANCE

Public Communication   The highly eventful presidency of Lyndon B. Johnson is fraught with implications, a high proportion of which are cautionary. When he was at his most effective as a communicator, Johnson's addresses conveyed a powerful sense of conviction. Examples include his moving address to Congress in the aftermath of Kennedy's assassination and his speech proposing the voting rights bill of 1965, which included a dramatic invocation of the anthem of the civil rights movement, "We Shall Overcome." More often than not, however, Johnson's oratory came across as bombastic and long-winded.

One might have expected Johnson to excel in news conferences, displaying his colorful persona and impressive command of facts to telling effect. Instead he was stiff and defensive in his encounters with reporters, revealing little of the vividness that made him memorable in less formal settings. As his aide Jack Valenti put it:

> In a small room with a hundred people or ten people, Johnson was magnificent—the most persuasive man I ever met. But when he went on television something happened. He took on a presidential air, he fused a kind of new Johnson, which wasn't the real Johnson. He became . . . stiff and foreboding.[13]

A rare exception was a November 1967 news conference in which Johnson employed a portable microphone, pacing easily on the stage as he answered questions. But he took offense when admiring commentators pronounced his performance to be Kennedy-like, and he refused to repeat the experiment.[14]

Organizational Capacity A second area in which Johnson is a source of warnings is organization. He surrounded himself with able aides, pumping them for political intelligence and bombarding them with instructions. But Johnson inherited a free-form White House from Kennedy and made no effort to institute rigorous procedures for assessing policy options. Kennedy's alertness and interest in policy enabled him to make the most of his fluid advisory system, but its lack of built-in structure made it ill suited for Johnson, who was erratic about calling meetings and dominated those he did convene.

Nothing in Johnson's legislative career had provided him with a conception of how to organize the presidency. For precisely that reason, if he had inherited well-designed policy planning arrangements, he might have taken them as a given and employed them. Such procedures were sorely needed in connection with Vietnam. On a number of occasions in 1964, Johnson voiced private concern that Vietnam would become "another Korea." As he put it in a telephone call to McGeorge Bundy, "It just worries the hell out of me. I don't see that we ever can get out of there once we're committed. . . . I don't think it's worth fighting for. . . . It's just the biggest damned mess that I ever saw."[15] If a forum had been available to him for airing such concerns, it is possible that he would have found a way to avoid the disaster that enveloped his presidency and the nation.

Political Skill   Johnson's actions in instituting his domestic program constitute a textbook on how to wrest results from an intractable political system. Taking to heart the prophet Isaiah's injunction, "Come let us reason together,"[16] Johnson engaged in countless acts of political persuasion, many of which are captured in secret tape recordings of his telephone conversations that became available in the 1990s. He was particularly adept at cutting political Gordian knots, as he did in devising the formula that permitted federal aid to education while preserving separation of church and state.

Vision   Johnson provides a reminder of the limitations of political dexterity when it is not informed by policy vision. He led the nation into a ground war in the jungles of Asia, doing so by responding to events as they arose and splitting the difference among his advisers' recommendations. At no point did he address such questions as what precise outcome he was seeking to achieve, whether that outcome was feasible, and, if so, whether it was worth the cost.

The Great Society *was* informed by a broad affinity for progressive policy innovations on Johnson's part, which went back to his time as an acolyte of FDR. However, in his early years in the Senate, Johnson had been anything but liberal, aligning himself with southern segregationists on issues relating to civil rights. Moreover, many of his domestic presidential programs were vitiated by his insensitivity to the content of policies. The War on Poverty is a case in point. Despite massive expenditures, it never found a formula for breaking the poverty cycle. Johnson's effort to combat poverty also had unanticipated political costs. It empowered new local political activists, who mobilized against the established urban officials who were an integral part of Johnson's political base.

Cognitive Style Johnson provides a compelling reminder of the importance of presidential political psychology. Few politicians have exceeded him in the capacity to absorb information and put it to short-term use. Johnson once explained to a friend that he could read an official report and "fix it in his mind so well that if you gave him a sentence from it, he could paraphrase the whole page and everything that followed." But once the political struggle for which he performed that feat was over, "he wouldn't remember the contents or even the name of the report."[17]

Emotional Intelligence Johnson's impressive cognitive strengths were subverted not only by his lack of interest in policy but also by his emotional deficiencies. His sense of his own educational shortcomings made him unduly deferential to the views of the aides he inherited from Kennedy. By browbeating his aides, he impaired his already defective advisory system. He also was susceptible to mood swings of near-clinical proportions. So great were they that on the eve of the 1964 Democratic convention, Johnson telephoned press secretary George Reedy, declaring that he was withdrawing his candidacy. "I don't want this power of the Bomb," he told Reedy. "I just don't want these decisions I'm being required to make. I don't want the conniving that's required. I don't want the disloyalty that's around." It took the calming influence of Lady Bird Johnson to get him back on track.[18]

Lyndon Johnson is one of an alarmingly large number of chief executives whose emotional flaws impeded the conduct of their responsibilities. Johnson's deficiencies were magnified for the nation because his presidency was followed by that of another figure whose darker impulses suffused his political actions: Richard Milhous Nixon.

By the end of his first term, Richard Nixon had extricated the United States from the Vietnam War and transformed his nation's relations with China and the Soviet Union. A year and a half into his second term, he was forced to resign from office after it became known that he had covered up his administration's complicity in the 1972 Watergate break-in, lying even to his supporters about having done so. Here Nixon is shown on the final morning of his presidency, boarding the helicopter that took him from the White House grounds on the first leg of his trip to his California home.

(National Archives)

CHAPTER 7

The Paradox of Richard Nixon

The greatest honor history can bestow is the title of peace-maker. This honor now beckons America—the chance to lead the world at last out of the valley of turmoil and onto that high ground of peace that man has dreamed of since the dawn of civilization.

—RICHARD M. NIXON,
INAUGURAL ADDRESS,
JANUARY 20, 1969

Let us in these next five days start a long march together. Not in lockstep, but on different roads leading to the same goal: the goal of building a world structure in which all may stand together with equal dignity and in which each nation, large or small, has a right to determine its own form of government free of outside interference or domination.

—RICHARD M. NIXON,
TOAST AT BANQUET IN THE
GREAT HALL OF THE PEOPLE,
BEIJING, CHINA,
FEBRUARY 21, 1972

I want the most comprehensive notes on all those who tried to do us in. They didn't have to do it. If we had a very close election and they were playing the other side, I would understand this. No—they were doing this quite deliberately, and they are asking for it, and they are going to get it. We have not used the power in this first four years. . . . We have not used the [FBI] and we have not used the Justice Department, but things are going to change now.

—RICHARD M. NIXON,
WHITE HOUSE TAPE,
SEPTEMBER 15, 1972

Throughout the long and difficult period of Watergate, I have felt it was my duty to persevere, to make every possible effort to complete the term of office to which you elected me. In the past few days, however, it has become evident to me that I no longer have a strong enough political base in the Congress to justify continuing that effort. . . . To leave office before my term is completed is abhorrent to every instinct in my body. But as President, I must put the interests of America first. . . . Therefore I shall resign the presidency effective noon tomorrow.

—RICHARD M. NIXON,
ADDRESS TO THE NATION ANNOUNCING
HIS DECISION TO RESIGN THE OFFICE OF
PRESIDENT OF THE UNITED STATES,
AUGUST 8, 1974

For the near half-century from his emergence as a communist-hunting member of Congress in 1947 to his death in 1994, Richard Milhous Nixon was an intensely controversial presence on the American political scene. In six years, he rose from freshman congressman to vice president of the United States. Thereafter, he underwent such an unlikely succession of political ascents, near demises, and rehabilitations that it scarcely seemed out of the ordinary that a eulogy was delivered at his funeral by President Bill Clinton, who had been a protester against his Vietnam policy and whose wife had served on the staff of the congressional committee that recommended his impeachment.

Nixon was a source of mystification even to his closest associates. The puzzle resulted from his highly private nature, the coexistence in his political personality of a corrosive cynicism and a desire to bring about constructive achievements, and the paradox that a political figure with so many strengths could take actions that were so self-destructive.

Nixon's Jekyll-and-Hyde nature is a consistent theme in his associates' accounts of him. As veteran Republican operative Bryce Harlow observed, Nixon's intelligence and political acumen were exceptional. "He seems to remember everything. He is an ambulatory computer. He retains it all, correlates it all." Yet in spite of his brilliance, Nixon seemed to bring troubles on himself. Perhaps, Harlow speculated, "my gifted friend somewhere in his youth got badly hurt by someone he cared for very deeply or trusted. From then on he could not trust people."[1]

ORIGINS

As it happens, a great deal is known about the young Richard Nixon. He was born in the tiny farming hamlet of Yorba Linda, California, on January 9, 1913, and brought up in the nearby town of Whittier, a community settled by Indiana Quakers in the mid-nineteenth century. Long before he reached the White House, a procession of journalists made their way to Whittier in search of clues to the "real" Richard Nixon, interviewing his family, teachers, and neighbors. Although they found no support for Harlow's surmise that Nixon had experienced a single overwhelming psychic wound, they turned up abundant evidence of a stress-laden childhood.

One source of strain was economic. As the proprietors of a struggling neighborhood grocery store, Nixon's parents and their sons were engaged in a constant battle to provide the essentials of life. Beyond that, the family was haunted by illness and death. When Nixon was ten, his younger brother, Arthur, suddenly became ill and died. When he was twenty, his older brother, Harold, died following a prolonged illness that drained the family's finances.

There were other tensions. As many of Nixon's biographers have remarked, his father and mother presented diametrically opposite role models. The irascible, chronically irate Frank Nixon was the product of a broken family, a grade school dropout, and a failure in a succession of manual occupations. He was a practitioner of corporal punishment and a devotee of what has been called "the paranoid style in American politics," viewing the nation's woes as the result of the machinations of corrupt politicians.[2]

Nixon's mother, Hannah, came from a solidly middle-class Quaker family and had completed two years of college. She was a compassionate, deeply pious woman, who was well known in her community for her good works. When Nixon referred to her as "a saint" in his tearful remarks on the final morning of his presidency, he was echoing the consensus of her neighbors.

Accounts of the young Nixon reveal many traits that were prominent in the man, including inwardness, intelligence, and a sense of melancholy and vulnerability. The latter are exhibited in a strange pair of documents Nixon's mother passed on to a sympathetic biographer in the 1950s—a letter he wrote when he was ten and an essay he composed for a college English class. The ostensible author of the letter is a dog who has been left in the care of two boys. They abuse him, he bites them, is painfully stung by a swarm of insects, and implores his master to return. The composition is a poignant account of the death of his younger brother in which Nixon concludes by saying that when he is "tired and worried" and "almost ready to quit trying to live as I should," he thinks of Arthur, and it restores his spirits.[3]

One response to a troubled childhood is to sink into passivity. Nixon's was to become a superachiever. He received outstanding grades in high school and college and was active in debating and dramatics, while also helping in the family business. His high school grades earned him a tuition scholarship to Harvard, but his family could not afford the necessary travel and living expenses, so he attended Whittier College in his home town. His college grades won him a scholarship to Duke Law School, where he made ends meet by living in an unheated shack and doing odd jobs.

Nixon graduated from law school in 1937 and returned to Whittier, where he practiced law. When the war broke out he took a position with the emergency agency that regulated prices during the war. In June 1942, the navy put out an offer of direct commissions to attorneys. Nixon availed himself of it, serving as a supply officer in the South Pacific. He proved to be resourceful in obtaining provisions for his service mates. He also learned to play poker, accumulating winnings that covered much of the initial cost of his 1946 congressional campaign.

NIXON ON THE RISE

Nixon's political career began fortuitously. Just as his military service was drawing to a close, he was contacted by a group of Republicans from his home congressional district. They were seeking a strong candidate to run against the district's longtime Democratic incumbent, Jerry Voorhis. At their suggestion, Nixon returned to California, won the nomination, and embarked on what he promised would be a "rocking, socking" campaign.[4]

He delivered with a vengeance. Making softness on communism his prime issue, Nixon pored over Voorhis's voting record until he knew it better than the congressman did, criticizing him for those votes that happened to coincide with the Communist party line and putting him on the defensive in a series of debates. Nixon was swept into office on the powerful Republican tide in the nation in 1946, joining the Republican-controlled Eightieth Congress.

Nixon's campaign did not draw national attention. His name appeared only once in the *New York Times* in 1946, and an article in

Time on the newly elected GOP Congress inaccurately reported that Nixon had "politely avoided attacks on his opponent."[5] As an experienced attorney and a veteran, Nixon was viewed by the Republican House leadership as one of the party's most promising freshmen. They assigned him to the House Committee on Un-American Activities (HUAC) and named him to a blue-ribbon panel that traveled to Europe to assess the need for the Marshall Plan, the Truman administration's proposed aid program to rebuild the economies of war-ravaged Europe.

Nixon studied the situation in Europe, concluded that the Marshall Plan was in the national interest, and strongly endorsed it. When it became evident that a large proportion of the voters in his district opposed the plan, Nixon returned to his district for the better part of a month to defend it. However, it was not his early global statesmanship that was to catapult him to prominence.

In 1948, HUAC heard testimony that Alger Hiss, a respected foreign policy aide in the Roosevelt administration, had spied for the Soviet Union in the 1930s. Although Hiss's accuser, the ex-communist journalist Whittaker Chambers, had anything but impeccable credentials, Nixon examined Chambers's claims. When Chambers proved to possess compelling evidence, Nixon backed him up. After a convoluted sequence of events in which Hiss sued Chambers for slander, Hiss was convicted of perjury and sentenced to five years in prison. The Hiss case made Nixon a national celebrity and a hero to the American right.

In 1950, Nixon capitalized on his newfound prominence and won his party's nomination to represent California in the Senate. Again his opponent was a liberal Democrat—Representative Helen Gahagan Douglas. Again Nixon impugned his opponent's patriotism, declaring that Douglas was "pink down to her underwear." And again he won. By then he had become the anathema of liberals, acquiring such sobriquets as "Tricky Dick" and "Joe McCarthy in a white shirt." But he had also acquired a fervent conservative following.

THE NEW NIXON

When the 1952 Republican convention nominated Dwight D. Eisenhower as its presidential candidate, it chose the thirty-seven-year-old Nixon as his running mate. Living up to his reputation for aggressive campaigning, Nixon called Eisenhower's opponent, Adlai Stevenson, "a weakling, a waster, and a small-caliber Truman." He accused Stevenson of holding "a Ph.D. degree" from Secretary of State Dean Acheson's "College of Cowardly Communist Containment," and declared Truman and Stevenson "traitors to the high principles in which many of the nation's Democrats believe."

Once in office, Nixon assumed a much more moderate stance, coming to be perceived by many Americans as a mature and responsible public servant who only occasionally reverted to slashing partisanship. The "new Nixon" comported himself with discretion when Eisenhower was incapacitated with a heart attack and engaged in high-profile overseas travels that cast him in a positive light. In 1958, Nixon and his wife, Pat, behaved courageously when a mob attacked their car in Caracas, Venezuela. In 1959, he received accolades for a spirited exchange with Soviet premier Nikita Khrushchev about the merits of communism and capitalism. In 1960, he handily won the Republican presidential nomination.

The 1960 election was Nixon's to lose. He was second in command to one of the most admired presidents in American history. His eight years as vice president had given him extensive executive branch experience. His opponent, John F. Kennedy, was a Roman Catholic at a time when anti-Catholic prejudice was common. In the view of many Republican activists, Nixon dissipated these advantages by insisting on managing the campaign himself, driving himself to the point of exhaustion, and performing indifferently in his televised debates with Kennedy.

After losing one of the closest presidential elections in American history, Nixon sought to restore his political fortunes by running for governor of California in 1962. Again he was defeated. When it became clear that he had lost, Nixon initially refused to concede. Then he strode into a news briefing and launched a tirade against the press for giving him the "shaft." His tongue lashing ended with a show of mock concern for the plight of the journalists: "Just think how much you are going to be missing. You won't have Nixon to kick around anymore, because, gentlemen, this is my last press conference."

It was widely assumed that Nixon had written his political obituary. He moved to New York, became a successful Wall Street lawyer, and comported himself in a balanced manner that led many commentators to conclude that he had finally exorcised his inner demons. As speculation began to mount about Nixon's chances of a 1968 presidential rerun, he declared a six-month moratorium on deciding about his political future and embarked on an extensive round of world travels, visiting Vietnam, Europe, the Middle East, Latin America, and Africa.

Upon his return, Nixon published a closely reasoned article, entitled "Asia After Viet Nam," in the prestigious journal *Foreign Affairs,* spelling out what were to become the premises of his administration's foreign policy. The article's title anticipated his policy of removing American combat forces from Vietnam. Its acknowledgment that the United States and the Soviet Union had reached nuclear parity presaged his quest for détente. Its assertion that "we simply cannot afford to leave China forever outside the family of nations" foreshadowed his administration's opening to China.[6]

In 1968, Nixon again became the Republican presidential nominee. As usual, he fought a vigorous campaign. Declaring that he was proud of serving in the administration that ended the Korean War, Nixon implied that he had a secret plan for extricating the United States from Vietnam. He also stated that he favored a "lowering of voices" in American politics, vowing to constitute his administration on "the broadest possible base." With the Democrats riven by Vietnam and Alabama governor George C. Wallace running as a third-party candidate, Nixon won the election with 43 percent of the popular vote.

THE MAN AND HIS WHITE HOUSE

It would take a Dostoyevsky to capture Richard Nixon fully, but his principal political qualities are no mystery. His strengths included great intelligence, unbounded willingness to invest effort in advancing his purposes, and an encyclopedic knowledge of politics. He had a shrewd sense of power relations, keen insight into the psychology of others, and an instinctive capacity to discern the possibilities for action in particular situations. He delighted in making bold political moves and had a fascination with international affairs.

Nixon's weaknesses arose from his deep-seated anger and feelings of persecution. Much of his iron self-discipline went into masking his hostile tendencies, but they periodically erupted, particularly when he was in the company of like-minded aides. He also had a set of qualities that made him an anomaly in the world of politics: he was highly introverted and socially awkward.

In the 1968 campaign, Nixon called for "an administration of open doors, open eyes, and open minds." True to his word, he signed on the liberal Democrat Daniel Patrick Moynihan as a domestic adviser and the staunchly conservative Arthur Burns as an economic counselor. Nixon spent numerous hours listening to Moynihan and Burns and mediating their demands. Then he shifted to a highly structured staff system that insulated him from such contacts. Nixon named his campaign director H. R. (Bob) Haldeman White House chief of staff, a position that assumed great importance in his administration.

Nixon also centralized the foreign policy process in the White House. He drew on the Eisenhower experience to strengthen the machinery of the National Security Council, but his decision-making style contrasted sharply with that of Eisenhower, who thrived on the give-and-take of debate. Nixon's practice was to work long hours, laboring in solitude and making his administration's key foreign policy decisions in concert with his special assistant for national security, the Harvard international relations scholar, Henry Kissinger. He also differed from Eisenhower, whose principal foreign policy adviser was

Secretary of State John Foster Dulles. Secretary of State William Rogers was not even informed in advance of some of the Nixon administration's most important initiatives.

Nixon's staff found ways to compensate for his discomfort in social situations, scripting his personal encounters so that they demanded a minimum of spontaneity. Another function of his aides was protecting Nixon from himself. As speechwriter Raymond Price put it, "Those of us who have worked with Nixon over the years often refer to his 'light side' and his 'dark side.' A lot of us routinely conspired to keep the darker side in check—and he was a conscious participant in that conspiracy."[7] But unfortunately for the fate of his presidency, Nixon was also a participant in more ominous conspiracies, using as his instruments the no-holds-barred political operatives whose covert domestic actions were to prove fatal to his presidency.

PEACE MAKING AND CONFRONTATION

The Nixon presidency was as laden with complications as the man. In his inaugural address, Nixon declared that the time had come for the nation "to lead the world at last out of the valley of turmoil and onto that high ground of peace." In his first week in office, he reached out to the Soviet Union, stating that the superpowers should maintain "sufficient" forces to defend themselves rather than competing for superiority. Four months later, he informed South Vietnamese president Nguyen Van Thieu that the United States would be removing its combat forces from Vietnam, while mounting a crash program to prepare South Vietnam to defend itself.

Nixon gradually enunciated what historian John Lewis Gaddis characterizes as a "complex, subtle, and closely interwoven" foreign policy. Included was a reduction of the nation's global commitments, an effort to arrive at agreements with the Soviet Union, and the normalization of relations with China. Of the last, Gaddis comments, "It is difficult to think of anything the Nixon administration could have done that would have produced a more dramatic shift in world power relationships of greater benefit to the United States at less cost."[8]

On November 3, 1969, Nixon made an address in which he announced a program of "Vietnamizing" the war. He went on to lash out against antiwar demonstrators, declaring that his administration would not give in to their demands for immediate withdrawal from Vietnam. He concluded by calling on "the great silent majority of Americans" to back him in his effort to achieve a "just and lasting peace."[9]

The Nixon White House was flooded with favorable responses to his silent majority address. As one of his biographers puts it, he "was doing what the doves wanted," but he appealed to the hawks for support.[10] In the aftermath of the speech, the peace movement became quiescent, but in April 1970 a Nixon action dramatically resurrected it. He ordered an incursion by American troops into Cambodia, which the communists were using as a safe haven to supply their forces in South Vietnam.

Ignoring Kissinger's advice to report the action from the Pentagon as a matter of military routine, Nixon announced it personally from the Oval Office, declaring that the communists should take it as evidence that he would not accept a humiliating defeat in Vietnam. The next morning he made an even more confrontational assertion, contrasting the American soldiers fighting in Cambodia with the "bums blowing up the college campuses."

There was a nation-wide paroxysm of student protest, including a demonstration at Ohio's Kent State University in which national guard troops killed four students. In response to Kent State virtually every college and university in the nation shut down, and a huge antiwar rally was convened in Washington. On its eve, Nixon softened his rhetoric and declared that he agreed with most of the protesters' goals, pointing out that he had withdrawn 115,000 troops from Vietnam and ordered the removal of an additional 150,000.

He then negated the calming effect of his statement by leaving the White House in the company of his valet in the early morning hours and delivering a monologue on his good intentions to a startled group of student protesters camped at the Lincoln Memorial. This overwrought performance belied the impression cultivated by the White

House of an unflappable statesman calmly devising solutions to the problems of the nation and world.

Nixon's comportment in the 1970 midterm election was a throwback to the old Nixon. He railed against his adversaries rather than defending his administration's policies. He broadcast an election eve stump speech excoriating the "violent thugs" who had stoned one of his motorcades. Nixon's preelection speech presented a sharp contrast to a thoughtful, dignified Democratic preelection broadcast by Senator Edmund Muskie of Maine, who began to be mentioned as a strong prospect for unseating Nixon in 1972.

DÉTENTE AND WATERGATE

On July 15, 1971, Nixon announced that he planned to make a state visit to the People's Republic of China. He was the immediate recipient of a bipartisan outpouring of praise. It was widely declared that only the staunchly anticommunist Nixon could have reversed the decades-old policy of not engaging in official relations with the world's most populous nation. A September 1971 Gallup poll showed Nixon leading all of his potential 1972 Democratic rivals, including Muskie.

The year of 1971 was also marked by behind-the-scenes developments that were to prove fatal to the Nixon presidency. Early that year, Nixon had a secret, voice-activated taping system installed in the Oval Office, the Cabinet Room, and his private office in the Executive Office Building. His aim was to have a better record of his private discussions. Later in the year, Nixon responded to the unauthorized publication of the Johnson administration's classified *Pentagon Papers* study of the origins of the Vietnam War by establishing a covert operations group. The assignment of the group (which Nixon and his aides dubbed the plumbers) was to prevent leaks of classified information and harass perceived enemies of the Nixon administration.

In February 1972, Nixon made his visit to China, much of which was televised live in the United States. Three months later, he crowned his global statesmanship with a summit meeting in the Soviet Union, signing treaties limiting offensive missile launchers and restricting both sides from establishing antiballistic missile systems. A few weeks after Nixon's return from the Soviet Union, a security guard at Washington's Watergate office complex arrested four men who had broken into the headquarters of the Democratic National Committee. One of them was on the presidential reelection staff.

Nixon condemned the break-in, declaring that "the White House has no involvement whatever in this particular incident." The Democrats attempted unsuccessfully to make Watergate a campaign issue. Instead, they insured Nixon's reelection by choosing South Dakota senator George McGovern as their nominee. McGovern's demands for nearly immediate withdrawal from Vietnam, amnesty for draft avoiders, and extensive welfare expenditures placed him far to the left of most of the electorate. Nixon was reelected with 61 percent of the popular vote, but the Democrats retained control of Congress.

THWARTED ASPIRATIONS

Three days after Nixon was sworn in for his second term, a settlement was finally reached in Vietnam. It secured the release of American prisoners held by the communists and permitted the United States to remove its remaining troops, leaving the Thieu government in power for the moment. A Gallup poll conducted shortly after found that 67 percent of the public approved of Nixon's conduct of the presidency, a tie with his record approval level following the silent majority address.

Although Nixon's domestic programs were overshadowed by Cambodia, Kent State, and the summits in China and the Soviet Union, his first term had witnessed many legislative enactments. Included were an extension of the Voting Rights Act, clean air and water quality legislation, a major expansion of social security, and the Occupational Safety and Health Act. None of these measures bore Nixon's personal stamp, however. After his reelection, Nixon informed his staff that he wanted to burnish his record with a small number of domestic accomplishments that he could call his own. "What we must do," he explained, is "seize upon three, or at most four, major programs and put the PR emphasis on them virtually to the exclusion of others so that the Administration will be remembered for at least doing something *very* well rather than being forgotten because we did a number of things *pretty* well."[11]

That was not to come to pass. The unraveling of the Nixon presidency commenced with the conviction of the Watergate burglars in January 1973. Several of them implicated Nixon associates in testimony before a special Senate committee charged with investigating "illegal, improper, or unethical activities" in the 1972 campaign. The committee discovered that the Watergate break-in was one of many acts of political espionage and sabotage carried out by the Nixon administration.

Haldeman and Nixon's domestic policy adviser, John Ehrlichman, were forced to resign in order to defend themselves against charges of complicity in criminal acts. Declaring that he intended to get to the bottom of Watergate, Nixon appointed the highly respected Elliot Richardson as attorney general. Richardson appointed Archibald Cox, the former Kennedy administration solicitor general, to investigate the case. Before long, the Senate committee discovered the existence of Nixon's secret taping system.

Cox and the committee demanded all tapes, but Nixon insisted that the tapes were protected by the principle of separation of powers. In a sudden frenzy of weekend actions, Nixon ordered Richardson to dismiss Cox. Richardson and his deputy resigned rather than execute the order, making it necessary for Robert Bork, the third-ranking official in the Justice Department, to carry out Nixon's order. The "Saturday Night Massacre" sparked a huge public outcry. Nixon responded by releasing transcripts of many of the contested tapes, but his concession was self-defeating. The tapes proved to contain detailed discussions between Nixon and his aides of how to silence the convicted felons and otherwise limit the damage of Watergate. They were additionally damaging because they were laced with hostile and contemptuous characterizations of other members of the political community and were shot through with profanity, which was conspicuously indicated in the transcripts by the phrase "expletive deleted."

COUNTDOWN TO RESIGNATION

Early in 1974, the House Judiciary Committee began to deliberate on Nixon's impeachment. By then there had been a succession of damaging disclosures, including revelations that the Nixon administration had engaged in extensive domestic wire-tapping (extending to one of Nixon's brothers) and that Nixon had taken questionable tax deductions, paying almost no federal income taxes the previous year.

The Judiciary Committee voted three articles of impeachment against Nixon (the equivalent of indictments), but even if the House went along with the committee, it was presumed unlikely that two-thirds of the Senate would vote to remove him from office. Then came the ultimate revelation. On July 24, in the landmark case *United States v. Nixon,* the Supreme Court ordered Nixon to make available several tapes that he had withheld when he released the original transcripts. These contained the long-sought "smoking gun," which consisted of the tape of a meeting in which Nixon was informed of the involvement of Republican operatives in Watergate. His response was to order a cover-up, in which the FBI was falsely informed that the Watergate burglars had been engaged in a CIA operation.

Nixon's shocked supporters on the Judiciary Committee announced that if they had it to do over again, they would vote for impeachment. His backing on Capitol Hill evaporated, and it became evident that if he did not leave office of his own volition, he would be impeached, convicted, and removed from office. On August 8, 1974, Nixon addressed the nation from the Oval Office for the final time, announcing his resignation effective the next day. On the morning of August 9, Nixon helicoptered to Andrews Air Force Base and departed for California. At noon, Chief Justice Warren Burger administered the presidential oath to Vice President Ford.

In the final report of the Judiciary Committee, the members who had supported Nixon until it came out that he had lied to them and the country issued a statement that distills much of what makes Richard Nixon so problematic:

It is striking that such an able, experienced and perceptive man, whose ability to grasp the global implication of events little noticed by others may well have been unsurpassed by any of his predecessors, should fail to comprehend the damage that accrued daily to himself, his administration, and the nation, as day after day, month after month, he suppressed the truth about his role in the Watergate cover-up so long and so tightly within the solitude of his Oval Office that it could not be unleashed without destroying his presidency.[12]

SIGNIFICANCE

Public Communication   In the domain of public communication, Nixon provides a reminder that presidents can rise above their limitations by dint of sustained effort. He was a far from natural public speaker, no doubt in part because of his need to censor his spontaneous impulses. He was patently ill at ease in press conferences, and his formal addresses came across as strained and stilted. Undeterred, he invested thought and effort in reaching the public, employing a team of speechwriters that covered a wide spectrum of political persuasions the better to position himself on issues. When the occasion seemed important enough, Nixon took over in the drafting process. In preparing the October 1969 address that bought him time for extricating American forces from Vietnam, he sequestered himself at Camp David for an extended period. Working around the clock, he came up with the phrase "silent majority" in a late-night writing session.[13]

Organizational Capacity   In the realm of organization, the Nixon White House provides evidence of how staff arrangements need to be tailored to the occupant of the Oval Office. The deeply introverted Nixon would have been ill served by an advisory system that relied on the president's interpersonal skills. Contemporary political observers viewed Haldeman and Ehrlichman as a "Berlin Wall," implying that by limiting access to the president, they impeded his effectiveness.

In fact, Nixon's aides adapted themselves to their boss, minimizing the need for him to engage in face-to-face relations and providing him time for strategic planning. Haldeman and Ehrlichman also protected Nixon from himself. As Ehrlichman noted, Nixon sometimes fired off orders in the heat of the moment. His principal aides had "built in a delayed reaction . . . to make sure he really wanted to do them." But there were limits to what they could accomplish, Ehrlichman acknowledged. Nixon sometimes turned to aides with fewer inhibitions, such as Charles Colson, who prided himself on his ruthlessness. "If Nixon said 'Go blow up the Capitol,'" Ehrlichman remarked, "Colson would salute and buy a load of dynamite."[14]

Nixon's staff system worked best in the area of his greatest concern: foreign affairs. In the view of a senior foreign service officer who served every president from Kennedy to Carter, Nixon had the most effective foreign policy team of any of the five presidents for whom he worked, because of the quality of Kissinger's policy analysis and because Nixon insisted that "genuine alternatives be placed before him," rather than "one real choice and several artificially constructed options."[15] In domestic policy, Nixon gave his White House aides broad leeway, encouraging them to provide him with policies consistent with his self-image as a Disraeli-style enlightened conservative.

Political Skill   Despite his personal limitations, Nixon was an agile and adept politician. His skill was a function of his sensitivity to power relations, his grasp of the intricacies of domestic and international politics, and his readiness to devote his waking hours to his job. Nixon's strengths as a politician owed little to the face-to-face persuasion that is second nature to most politicians and much to his ability to establish goals for himself and envisage strategies for bringing them into being.

Vision   In contrast to most modern presidents, Nixon's political efforts were guided—and advanced—by an explicit policy vision, especially in international relations. At one point during the period between his defeat for the California governorship in 1962 and his presidential nomination in 1968, Nixon commented on the roots of his fascination with international politics to his New York law partner Leonard Garment:

> This man, so fiercely determined to stay in the political life for which he was in so many ways so ill-suited, told me that he felt himself driven to do so not by the rivalries or ideological commitments of domestic politics but by his pacifist mother's idealism and the profound importance of foreign affairs. . . . Nixon said he would do anything, make any sacrifice, to be able to continue to use his talents and his experience in making foreign policy.[16]

Cognitive Style   Nixon provides a striking demonstration that cognitive intelligence need not be accompanied by emotional intelligence. Almost to a person, Nixon's associates were awed by his intellectual strengths and mystified by what they referred to as his dark side. Comments abound on Nixon's powers of thought and concentration. "He thinks all the time. I don't think there is a time when his brain is ever idle." "He is so thoroughly informed, it's staggering." "He soaked up information like a sponge."[17] Yet Nixon's cognitive powers were periodically negated by the passions he battled to control.

Emotional Intelligence   No one was a closer observer of Nixon's insecurities than Haldeman, who was in his presence for untold hours every day. What struck Haldeman was the rigidity with which Nixon steeled himself to avoid mistakes. "That self-discipline was so tight it was *unnatural*," Haldeman commented. "When it burst the effects were devastating."[18] Nixon could not have gone as far as he did in American politics if he had not possessed exceptional strengths. In the end, however, his abilities could not prevent him from destroying his own presidency. One shudders at the thought of what other damage might have been done by a chronically suspicious custodian of the huge nuclear arsenal of the United States who had imperfect control of his emotions.

Upon taking office, Gerald Ford was viewed as a refreshing contrast to the hyper-political, emotionally roiled Lyndon Johnson and Richard Nixon. One month into his presidency, Ford announced a "full, free and absolute pardon" of Richard Nixon, triggering a firestorm of criticism and a precipitous decline in his approval ratings. Ford showed no sign of being embittered. He attacked his responsibilities thoughtfully and responsibly, providing a variety of lessons for future chief executives.

(Gerald Ford Presidential Library)

CHAPTER 8

The Instructive Presidency of Gerald Ford

Our long national nightmare is over.

— GERALD R. FORD, REMARKS ON
TAKING THE OATH OF OFFICE,
AUGUST 9, 1975

I'm not one to be tortured by self-doubt, and I had no doubt
about my ability to function well in the office.

— GERALD R. FORD,
A Time to Heal

I, Gerald R. Ford, president of the United States . . . do grant a
full, free, and absolute pardon unto Richard Nixon for all
offenses against the United States which he . . . has committed
or may have committed.

— GERALD R. FORD, REMARKS ON
SIGNING A PROCLAMATION GRANTING
PARDON TO RICHARD NIXON,
SEPTEMBER 8, 1975

The president . . . wants to thank all those thousands of people
who worked so hard on his behalf and the millions who sup-

ported him with their votes. It has been the greatest honor of my husband's life to have served his fellow Americans during two of the most difficult years in our history.

—BETTY FORD,
NOVEMBER 3, 1976

The 895-day presidency of Gerald R. Ford is generally viewed as an interregnum, but it offers valuable insights into the problems of presidential leadership, if only because Ford had to respond to the challenge of being the first chief executive who was elected neither president nor vice president. Ford's sturdy, if less than masterful, leadership style and his solid personal qualities were well suited for governing without an electoral mandate. His presidency is also worth examining for the organizational structures Ford created after initially trying to manage his own White House.

Unlike Harry Truman and Lyndon Johnson, whose first task was to establish continuity with the popular presidents they succeeded, Ford needed to distance himself from a discredited predecessor. Like them, he benefited from the impulse of Americans to idealize those suddenly thrust into the nation's highest office. In the weeks following his abrupt elevation to the presidency, Ford was showered with praise, much of it for attributes that in another context would have marked him as pedestrian. He was seen as an uncomplicated personification of such virtues as integrity, decency, and steadiness—an invigorating contrast to the emotionally convoluted Johnson and Nixon.

THE MAN FROM GRAND RAPIDS

The recipient of this warm reception was born on July 14, 1913, in Omaha, Nebraska. His parents were divorced in 1916, and his mother returned to her home in Grand Rapids, Michigan, where she married

Gerald Rudolf Ford, who adopted her son and gave him his own name. The elder Ford was a paint salesman, who went on to become a manufacturer of paints and varnishes. To keep his business going during the Depression, he moved his family into a rented home and took the same five-dollar-a-week salary he provided his employees.

Only in his teens did Ford discover that the man he had known as his father was actually his stepfather. In spring 1930, Ford's biological father sought him out, took him to lunch, and gave him twenty-five dollars. Ford reports his distress when he realized that his father had little continuing interest in him, but he moved on with his life free of signs of psychic damage from the encounter.

Ford's mature political persona was consistent with his life story. He was a model of hard work and responsibility: an Eagle Scout, high school football player, and honors student. He went to the University of Michigan on an athletic scholarship, which he supplemented by waiting on tables and selling his blood to a local hospital. He rejected an offer to play professional football because it "wouldn't lead me anywhere," and found employment at Yale as a coach. He attended Yale Law School, graduated in 1941, and set himself up as an attorney in Grand Rapids.[1]

In the 1930s, Ford was opposed to U.S. overseas involvements, but in the 1940 presidential campaign, he became a supporter of the Republican internationalist Wendell Willkie and abandoned his isolationism. During the war, Ford served as a naval officer in the Pacific, returning to his Grand Rapids law practice after his discharge. In 1948, he entered the Republican primary in his heavily GOP district, defeated the isolationist incumbent, and went on to win in the general election. He was reelected twelve times by majorities ranging from 61 to 67 percent, but he never represented a broader constituency than Michigan's Fifth Congressional District.

A CAPITOL HILL CAREER

In the House of Representatives of Ford's time, preferment came from seniority, hard work on specialized committee assignments, and recognition by one's peers for competence and effectiveness. The aphorism of the day was "those who go along get along." Ford quickly learned the ropes, attending to his constituents' needs, securing a seat on the powerful Appropriations Committee, and developing a broad acquaintance among his fellow legislators.

As an internationalist in foreign policy and a conservative in domestic affairs, Ford occupied a centrist position in the Republican party of his time. One of his principal assets was his personal popularity, which extended to both sides of the aisle. As he liked to put it, he had no enemies—only adversaries. In 1961, Ford received the American Political Science Association's distinguished public service award. The citation described him as "a congressman's congressman."

Ford's rise to House leadership was propelled by circumstance, although he positioned himself so that opportunity might knock. During the 1950s, he was friendly with a faction of Young Turks in his party which held that the House GOP leadership had become too complacent and was too uncompromisingly conservative. In 1963, the group ousted a second-level party leader and replaced him with Ford. In 1965, it ran him for the party's top position in the House: minority leader. Ford promised to "communicate the image of a fighting, forward-looking party seeking responsible and constructive solutions to national problems," and he was elected.[2]

Ford's legislative leadership was distinctly non-Machiavellian. He was the model of a trusted legislative broker. One observer described him as "an open tactician" who "doesn't look for clever ways to sneak behind you." Another noted that Ford was more disposed to play the negotiator than the "heated partisan or trailblazing innovator." Indeed, his colleagues were said to hold him in such esteem that they sometimes would give him their votes "just to help an old pal."[3]

Ford's highest aspiration was to become Speaker of the House, but the GOP remained in the minority on Capitol Hill throughout his tenure as party leader. With Richard Nixon's election in 1968, Ford finally had a Republican president to work with, even though the House remained in Democratic hands. When Nixon's 1972 reelection failed to bring the GOP into power in Congress, Ford abandoned the thought of becoming Speaker and made plans to retire.

Then the unexpected occurred. Vice President Spiro Agnew resigned to avoid being prosecuted on corruption charges. On October 12, 1973, Nixon nominated Ford to succeed Agnew under the provisions of the Twenty-Fifth Amendment. During Ford's nine months as vice president, he distanced himself from the unfolding Watergate scandal, spending most of his time speaking at party events outside of Washington.

A HEALING TRANSITION

On August 1, 1974, White House chief of staff Alexander Haig notified Ford of the imminent release of White House tapes documenting Nixon's complicity in the Watergate cover-up. On August 8, Nixon announced his resignation, and at noon the following day Ford became the thirty-eighth president of the United States. Upon taking the oath, he vowed that "in all my private and public acts as your president, I expect to follow my instincts of openness and candor with full confidence that honesty is always the best policy in the end." He went on to make a statement that was all the more effective for being plain-spoken:

> My fellow Americans, our long national nightmare is over. Our Constitution works. Our great republic is a government of laws and not of men. Here, the people rule. . . . As we bind up the internal wounds of Watergate, more painful and more poisonous than those of foreign wars, let us restore the Golden Rule to our political process, and let brotherly love purge our hearts of suspicion and of hate.[4]

Continuing in a healing mode, Ford addressed a joint session of Congress on August 12, asserting that his watchword with the legislature would be "communication, conciliation, compromise and cooperation." He declared the state of the nation to be good, but the state of its economy to be problematic. Therefore, he planned to convene the "best brains from labor, industry, and agriculture" to address the nation's economic ills.

Meanwhile, Ford sought to reduce the pomp of the presidency, substituting the playing of the rallying song of the University of Michigan football team for "Hail to the Chief." He also replaced portraits of Theodore Roosevelt and Woodrow Wilson in the Cabinet Room with ones of Abraham Lincoln and Harry Truman, two presidential symbols of the common man.[5] On August 19, Ford announced that he favored creating a way for men who had evaded the draft or deserted from the military during the Vietnam War to rehabilitate themselves.

The next day Ford nominated his party's most prominent moderate—former New York governor Nelson Rockefeller—as his vice president. His amnesty proposal and choice of Rockefeller signaled his intent to build an administration that appealed broadly to the American people rather than to his party's conservative wing. In mid-August, the Gallup organization conducted its first poll on Ford's presidential performance. Seventy-one percent of the respondents expressed approval of the way he was doing his job; only 3 percent expressed disapproval. The comparable figures for Nixon at the beginning of the month had been 24 percent approval and 66 percent disapproval.[6]

AN ILL-ADVISED ACTION

On Sunday, September 8, a month to the day after Nixon announced his resignation, Ford addressed the nation from the Oval Office, announcing a "full, free and absolute pardon" to Richard Nixon for any crimes he might have committed as president. There had been no public preparation for this thunderbolt. Indeed, in a press conference only ten days earlier, Ford had declared it premature even to speculate on his using the pardon power until it was decided whether Nixon would be charged with a federal crime.

The era of good feelings was over. Ford's own press secretary resigned in protest, declaring that he could not defend an absolute pardon for Nixon "but only a conditional pardon for young men who had fled to Canada to escape Vietnam as an act of conscience." Congressional leaders were scathing in their reactions. Senate majority leader Mike Mansfield declared that "all men are equal before the law" and "that includes presidents and plumbers." A poll conducted by the *New York Times* immediately after the pardon found only 32 percent of the public saying Ford was doing a good job. When Gallup canvassed the public later in the month, it found that Ford's approval level had declined from its initial 71 percent to 50 percent.[7]

Ford's decision was not without merit. He had became convinced that while Nixon's fate remained unsettled, he would be unable to devote his undivided attention to such pressing issues as the declining state of the economy. The disposition of Nixon's White House tapes and records was itself consuming an inordinate amount of presidential time. In addition, the media showed no sign of moving on. Ford was distressed at the number of questions bearing on Nixon at his initial press conference. As he later put it, "I had to get the monkey off my back."[8]

There was much to be said for freeing the political system and Gerald Ford of further preoccupation with Richard Nixon. As Ford noted in announcing the pardon, many years would intervene before Nixon could be brought to trial, and during that "long period of delay and potential litigation" the nation would remain mired in Watergate. There is little to be said for Ford's handling of the decision, however. He failed to consult on Capitol Hill and did not inform his press secretary before announcing the pardon. He even failed to seek the advice of his still inchoate White House staff.

Ford did meet with his most senior White House aides several days before his action, but he did not ask their opinions. Instead, he informed them that he was distressed at the attention paid to Nixon at a recent press conference and was inclined to remove the former president from the national agenda by pardoning him. As one of the aides put it, "There was deafening silence" in the room:

Outwardly, nobody was wildly enthusiastic, but neither did anybody violently object. . . . It was pretty clear the odds of changing his mind were close to zero. The President paid us the compliment of his confidence not because he needed our *opinions* but because he needed our *help* to execute his decision and to build a solid front among his senior aides before riding out the expected storm. The meeting broke up with all of us in a state of semi-shock.[9]

Ford's abrupt pardon of Nixon was a body blow to his presidency, but a more thoughtfully orchestrated pardon might have had the opposite effect. Ford could have quietly let it be known to key national opinion makers that the old business of attending to Richard Nixon's fate was impeding the urgent new business of addressing the nation's economic problems. It is likely that there would have been numerous editorials and other public statements calling for Nixon's pardon. Ford then would have been able to accede gracefully to the groundswell. That, however, would have been the action of a political machinator such as FDR or LBJ, not an open tactician like Gerald Ford.

ORGANIZATIONAL ADAPTATIONS

A more self-important individual than Gerald Ford might have blamed the uproar over the Nixon pardon on his critics and persisted in unproductive ways of conducting his presidency. Instead, Ford responded flexibly. In his first news conference, he had announced that he planned to avoid isolation by being his own chief of staff. In the aftermath of the mismanaged Nixon pardon, Ford concluded that "without a strong decision-maker who could help me set my priorities," he "wouldn't have time to reflect on the basic strategy or the fundamental direction of my Presidency."[10] He appointed his former House colleague Donald Rumsfeld to the position. It cannot be said that Rumsfeld magically transformed the Ford White House into a smoothly operating mechanism, but he and his successor, Richard Cheney, lent order to an insufficiently structured White House.

It was not in the cards that a Ford White House would become a monolith. There were rivalries between Nixon holdovers and assistants who had been associated with Ford on Capitol Hill and between Rumsfeld's aides and those of Rockefeller. There also was Ford himself. He was an incorrigibly informal human being. Although he was impatient with friction on his staff, it was not in his makeup to refuse access to old associates or administer draconian punishments to quell conflict. The solution arrived at was one in which nine aides nominally reported to Ford, but their access was coordinated by Rumsfeld, who became the president's right-hand man.

Ford's approach to organizing his presidency evolved with changing circumstances, showing that presidents need not be saddled with unproductive operating methods. It also varied from policy area to policy area, demonstrating that presidents can adapt their consulting procedures to their interests and the policy emphases of their administrations. His practices in the critical area of economic policy are of particular interest in that they exemplify the much praised but rarely practiced procedure of multiple advocacy in which policy disagreements are rigorously debated in the president's presence, with all important points of view accorded careful consideration.

These exchanges occurred in a body Ford established to combat the puzzling mixture of inflation and lack of economic growth the nation was experiencing: the Economic Policy Board. The EPB consisted of representatives of all of the administration's major economic bodies and was managed by a coordinator who was expected to be an honest broker of the policy process, not an advocate of particular policies. Ford met at least once a week with the EPB, welcoming debate and constructive disagreements.[11] Ford conducted these forums as if he were a judge in a courtroom:

> At the end of a discussion he would pause, ask if anyone had anything further to say, and go to the Oval Office. There he would make his decision, without delay, and in writing—he wanted no misunderstanding about his intention. Once he decided, he didn't worry or second-guess himself; he moved on to the next task at hand.[12]

Ford was not a natural administrator, but he was an experienced political professional. His practice, he remarked in his memoirs, was to steer clear of jurisdictional rivalries, avoid having confidants within his cabinet, have private sources of advice outside the cabinet, leave "management and program implementation to the department heads," and encourage dissent when he was making up his mind, but reserve the final decisions for himself.[13]

BATTLING ADVERSITY

Some presidents take office riding tailwinds. Harry Truman assumed his responsibilities shortly before V-E Day, and three months later he had the political good fortune of presiding over the end of the war in the Pacific. George H. W. Bush entered office with a booming economy, and before the end of his first presidential year the communist empire in Eastern Europe had collapsed.

Ford had to battle headwinds. He never recovered from having pardoned Nixon. The economy was in grievous shape. The Democrats controlled Congress, increasing their majority by six seats in the Senate and fifty-two in the House in the 1974 midterm elections. Ford barely had his own team in place before he had to think about reelection. By early 1976, the political season was underway. Ford was buffeted from within his party by California governor Ronald Reagan, who sought to deny him the Republican nomination, and from the Democratic side by Georgia governor Jimmy Carter, who railed against all Washington politicians, including Ford.

Ford also suffered from his own real and perceived limitations. His ponderous speaking style and even his body language were liabilities. Early in his presidency, he bumped his head while debarking from a helicopter and thereafter late-night television comedians portrayed him as a bumbling incompetent. Ford might have reversed such impressions by communicating a persuasive conception of where he proposed to take the nation, but his years as a legislative broker did not equip him to enunciate a rhetorical framework for his policies.

Ford never became bitter or defensive. In an October 1974 interview, Ford said of the presidency, "I love it. It's sort of got my adrenaline going again." Despite the firestorm of criticism occasioned by his pardon of Nixon the previous month, his comment was: "I feel great. Every day from the point of view of focusing and meeting the problems, I think we're doing better."[14] Ford's modus operandi helped him maintain his positive outlook. If he had stipulated his operational code, it might have boiled down to four maxims:

1. *Be open.* Ford was utterly "non-Nixonian." In October 1974, when a subcommittee of the House Judiciary Committee asked him to send an emissary to testify on the reasons behind the pardon of Nixon, he startled the Washington establishment by saying he would testify himself, the first such presidential testimony on Capitol Hill since Lincoln. He also made himself accessible to the press, reversing Nixon's practice of holding few press conferences, and gave scores of interviews to journalists. Despite two attempts on his life, he traveled extensively throughout the nation, making himself available in a variety of public forums.

2. *Be presidential.* To counter the imagery of a bumbler who had played too much football in an era of inadequately padded helmets, Ford's White House took every opportunity to publicize the calm, incisive manner in which he dispatched his presidential obligations. Beyond public relations, there was the reality of being president. Apart from the pardon of Nixon, Ford's most noteworthy action occurred in May of 1975, when Cambodian naval forces seized the American merchant ship *Mayaguez* and showed signs of taking its crew as hostages. Ford promptly ordered the military into action, recovering the ship and its crew. Although the number of American marines killed in the rescue exceeded the number of crew members, Ford was credited with an incisive and effective use of presidential power.

3. *Cooperate with Congress, but wield the veto.* Ford vied with the heavily Democratic Congress on principled grounds, never adopting the confrontational style of Nixon. He was consistently ready to negotiate with Congress, using his old contacts and friendships to

win support for his initiatives. He also made extensive use of his constitutional power to nullify legislation, vetoing sixty-six bills, with only twelve overrides. Only FDR, Truman, and Grover Cleveland wielded the veto more frequently, and they mainly rejected bills introduced by members of Congress to assist particular constituents, whereas all but five of Ford's vetoes were of substantive legislation.

4. *Be patient.* Ford cultivated the image of being another Harry Truman, but his motto might better have been "All things come to him who waits" than "The buck stops here." Rejecting Democratic efforts to end the recession by deficit spending, he persisted in orthodox economic practices. By 1976 the economy was on the upswing, but Ford then had to face the criticism of Reagan and Carter. Instead of immediately going on the stump, he employed a Rose Garden strategy, carrying out his responsibilities from the White House in a manner calculated to bring him favorable attention.

After a series of closely contested primary contests, Ford triumphed over Reagan. He began the general election campaign far behind Carter but closed much of the gap. A shift of less than ten thousand votes in Ohio and Hawaii would have enabled him to carry the electoral college and made him a two-term president, instead of a seemingly transitional figure whose experience would be deemed of little interest.

SIGNIFICANCE

Public Communication   Although the presidency of Gerald Ford is a surprisingly fertile source of insights into how presidents can advance their purposes, the lessons of his performance as a public communicator are largely negative. As a public speaker, Ford was reminiscent of the man from Missouri whose portrait he placed in the Cabinet Room: Harry Truman. He was a plodding speaker, whose rhetorical limitations made him less able than a Roosevelt, Kennedy, or Reagan to put a good face on political misfortune. Ford also resembled Truman in being verbally accident prone, most notoriously his assertion in his second debate with Jimmy Carter that Eastern Europe was not under communist control.

Organizational Capacity   Ford's organizational legacy includes his painfully won demonstration that it is no longer feasible to operate an effective presidency without an able and experienced White House chief of staff. There is in general much to be learned from the intelligently structured staff procedures of Ford's White House. Of particular interest is his Economic Policy Board, which employed the principles of multiple advocacy that served well in Eisenhower's foreign policy advisory arrangements. A policy mechanism like the EPB would have been useful to a number of Ford's successors, particularly Carter.

Political Skill   Ford's political skills were those of an experienced legislative pragmatist. His success in cultivating the support of lawmakers contrasts with the difficulty a number of other presidents had in dealing with their counterparts at the other end of Pennsylvania Avenue. Ford also adapted readily to the instruments of presidential power, demonstrating the value of the veto to a chief executive faced with a Congress dominated by the opposition party.

Vision   It might be assumed that the eminently practical Gerald Ford possessed little in the way of political vision. But in fact he had clear, internally consistent policy convictions, particularly in the domestic sphere. During his years on the House Appropriations Committee, Ford formed conservative, market-oriented political beliefs that became as much a part of his worldview as his sturdy work ethic and strong religious convictions. These made his actions predictable to his allies and opponents, but did not prevent him from maintaining amiable personal relations with his Democratic opponents.

Cognitive Style   Despite his portrayal on *Saturday Night Live* as a presidential dullard, Ford brought an open mind and thoughtful intelligence to his responsibilities. Alan Greenspan, who chaired Ford's Council of Economic Advisors (CEA), has provided an insightful account of Ford's cognitive and emotional qualities. His first impression, Greenspan remarked, was that Ford lacked the capacity to engage in abstract reasoning. The consistency of Ford's concrete economic decisions persuaded him otherwise.

It was Greenspan's further observation that Ford found it enjoyable to discuss economics with him, even when there was no pending decision that made doing so necessary. Similarly, Greenspan's CEA colleague Burton Malkiel commented that although it took Ford some time to grasp difficult economic concepts, "He always ended up with a very firm grasp of the issues and a complete mastery of the complexities that might be involved. He loved to hear things argued out in front of him and would often ask the most insightful questions of the participants in the debate."[15]

Emotional Intelligence   It is not necessary to depict Ford as a closet intellectual to appreciate the personal strengths he brought to the presidency. He was patently emotionally stable, and his self-esteem was not wrapped up in the fate of his policies. "You never got negative emotional vibrations from the man," Greenspan recollected, "except when he was mad for reasons that were absolutely objective." The practical significance of Ford's emotional soundness was underscored by Henry Kissinger, who stayed on to head Ford's foreign policy team. In contrast with Nixon, Kissinger found Ford to be straightforward and direct.

> Ford's associates never needed to fear that he might be leaving other colleagues with some different impression from their own. There was none of that almost surreal uncertainty about the President's ultimate intentions that had made service in the Nixon White House such an emotional roller coaster. Disagreements did not lead to competing conspiracies; Ford would have them out in front of him and there was no ambiguity about the outcome.[16]

Ford's own remark about himself upon assuming the vice presidency in December 1973 was that he was "a Ford, not a Lincoln." In the second half of the 1970s, it was more to the point for the nation that he was not an emotionally roiled Lyndon Johnson or Richard Nixon.

Jimmy Carter launched his presidency with an outburst of populist symbolism, walking down Pennsylvania Avenue from the Capitol to the White House with his wife. There was an initial payoff from this public relations blitz, but by the summer of his fourth year in the White House, Carter's approval ratings had descended to the lowest level in the history of presidential polling. During the Carter years, the economy was beset by a combination of high inflation and economic stagnation. Carter's presidency also suffered from his own reluctance to engage in normal political give and take, which antagonized the members of the political community whose support was needed to enact his program.

(Jimmy Carter Library)

Jimmy Carter
and the Politics of Rectitude

I'm Jimmy Carter and I'm running for president. I will never lie to you.

— REPEATED CARTER
CAMPAIGN STATEMENT

A nation's domestic and foreign policies should be derived from the same standards of ethics, honesty and morality which are characteristic of the individual citizens of the nation. The people of this nation are inherently unselfish, open, honest, decent, competent, and compassionate. Our government should be the same, in all of its actions and attitudes.

— JIMMY CARTER,
Why Not the Best?

Everybody has warned me not to take on too many problems so early in the administration, but it's almost impossible for me to delay something that I see needs to be done.

— PERSONAL DIARY ENTRY,
JANUARY 29, 1977,
IN JIMMY CARTER,
Keeping Faith

I had a different way of governing than my predecessors. I was a southerner, a born-again Christian, a Baptist, a newcomer. Very few of the members of Congress, or members of the major lobbying groups, or the distinguished former Democratic leaders had played much of a role in my election. As an engineer and as a governor, I was more inclined to move rapidly and without equivocation and without the interminable consultations and so forth that are inherent, I think, in someone who has a more legislative attitude, or psyche, or training, or experience.

—JIMMY CARTER,
INTERVIEW, 1982

Every president from Franklin Roosevelt to Gerald Ford had spent a decade or more in responsible public positions in and out of the nation's capital before entering the White House. Jimmy Carter's previous governmental service consisted of one term as governor of Georgia and two as a member of that state's legislature. That someone with modest political experience, none of which was national, could become president of the United States would have been highly unlikely until the 1970s. Carter made his way to the White House at a time when established leaders were in ill repute, and he won his party's nomination as a result of the post-1968 presidential nominating process, which drastically reduced the influence of traditional political party power brokers.

Carter stood out in another respect. Public figures regularly refer to God in American politics, and in most jurisdictions, a leader's assertion that he or she did not believe in a supreme being would be a ticket to oblivion. Religious doctrine, however, rarely finds its way into public affairs, except indirectly through such issues as school prayer, abortion, and gay rights. Carter stands alone among the modern presidents in the centrality of religious principles to his political leadership and, indeed, his very being.

In the Hollywood classic *Mr. Smith Goes to Washington,* an idealistic political outsider prevails over Washington officialdom. For a few short months, Jimmy Carter seemed to be another Mr. Smith, but his honeymoon ended well before the end of his first year in the White House. By the summer of 1980, Carter's approval ratings had reached abysmally low levels, and very little of his policy agenda had made its way into the statute books. In November, the voters returned him to private life, where he earned ironic acclaim for his Nobel Prize–winning performance as an ex-president.[1]

THE MAKING OF JIMMY CARTER

Jimmy Carter was born on October 1, 1924, in the rural hamlet of Plains, Georgia. He was the first child of James Earl Carter, Sr., a farmer and businessman with extensive land holdings, and Lillian Carter, a nurse who provided the bulk of the community's medical care.

Earl Carter was a self-assured disciplinarian who held the conservative racial attitudes typical of southern white males of his generation. He employed about two hundred African Americans as tenant farmers and employees, treating them benignly but never as equals. In his campaign autobiography, Jimmy Carter describes his father as his "best friend" and the main influence on his early development, but goes on to add that "from the time I was four years old until I was fifteen years old he whipped me six times and I never forgot any of those impressive experiences."[2]

Lillian Carter was a racial moderate and free spirit who joined the Peace Corps in her late sixties, serving as a public health nurse in rural India. She was a Methodist and her husband was a Baptist. Neither she nor her husband was responsible for the depth of their eldest child's religious commitment, but they were the source of his strong sense of responsibility and work ethic.

Carter was a star student in Plains High School, graduating at age sixteen. He was admitted to the U.S. Naval Academy in 1943, where he thrived on the school's engineering curriculum, ranking in the upper tenth of his class. He spent seven years as a naval officer, the last of them in the nuclear submarine program headed by the notoriously demanding Admiral Hyman J. Rickover. When Carter acknowledged to Rickover that he had not always done his best in his studies at Annapolis, Rickover asked, "Why not?" The question became the title of Carter's autobiography.

In 1953, Carter returned to Plains to be at the bedside of his dying father. As local citizens joined him in paying their respects to "Mr. Earl," Carter realized that his father was "an integral part of the community" with "a wide range of varied but interrelated interests and responsibilities," including service as a state legislator. Concluding that he wanted to emulate his father and spend the remainder of his life as a civilian with an "opportunity for varied public service," Carter resigned his commission. He took over the family business, which he made into a prosperous concern, and became active in civic and church affairs.[3]

POLITICAL EMERGENCE

In 1962, Carter won election to the state legislature, where he earned a reputation as a reformer and political gadfly. In an early display of his trademark preoccupation with detail, he undertook to read each of the hundreds of bills that came to a vote every year, taking a speed reading course to do so. One result, Carter wryly noted, was that he became "an expert on many unimportant subjects."[4] Another was that he became deeply informed about Georgia's government. He became an advocate of such good-government reforms as laws that open official meetings to the public, state-of-the-art budgeting procedures, and a variety of other measures designed to reduce waste and inefficiency.

In 1966, Carter embarked on the pursuit of higher office that culminated a decade later with his election to the presidency. He entered the crowded Georgia Democratic gubernatorial primary, honing his skills as a campaigner and building a statewide network of supporters. Carter called for fiscal prudence, government reorganization, and greater governmental responsiveness to the people, but his appeal was not just to policy. He drew attention to his personal character, making such avowals as, "I'll never tell a lie," "I'll never betray your trust," and "I'll never make a misleading statement or avoid a controversial issue."[5]

Carter was the close runner-up to a pair of far more established candidates, the prominent segregationist Lester Maddox and former governor Ellis Arnall, a nationally known southern moderate. Rather than rejoicing at his strong first-time showing, Carter sank into depression. Seeking solace in his faith, he underwent a classic born-again experience—not an instant epiphany but an intensely felt expansion of spirituality. From then on, religion became his driving force. He participated in retreats, went on evangelical missions, and prayed daily.

Carter resumed his political climb, spending the next four years preparing for another run for governor. In 1966, Maddox had monopolized the white supremacist vote, and Carter was in competition with Arnall for moderates' support. In 1970, Carter's principal opponent was a moderate. In a tactic later held up as evidence of his opportunism, Carter courted the white supremacists who had backed Maddox four years earlier.* He won the Democratic primary and general elections and was inaugurated governor in January 1971.

GUBERNATORIAL STAGING POINT

Upon taking office, Carter incensed his segregationist supporters by declaring in his inaugural address that "the time for racial discrimination is over" and that "no poor, rural, weak, or black person should

---

*Carter never employed racist language in the campaign, but his forces circulated a photograph of his opponent being doused with champagne by a black basketball player at a victory celebration of a team he owned. At the same time, he forged personal ties to individual African Americans, often alluding to their common links to evangelical Christianity.

ever have to bear the additional burden of being deprived of the opportunity of an education, a job, or simple justice."[6] Carter's call for racial justice earned him national attention and praise. In May 1971, his picture appeared on the cover of *Time,* accompanied by a story referring to him as a promising leader of the emerging progressive forces of the "New South."

By then Carter was in the process of seeking support for a sweeping governmental reorganization plan that became the centerpiece of his legislative program. He surrounded himself with a dedicated staff of former campaign workers, many of whom were to serve him in the White House. The most important of them were his chief political operative, Hamilton Jordan, and his press secretary, Jody Powell.

Carter quickly evinced the leadership style he was to bring to the White House. His outward manner was more that of a moralist and social engineer than a conventional politician. He advanced a blend of domestic liberalism and economic conservatism that cut across traditional ideological divisions. He was deeply committed to addressing public problems comprehensively rather than incrementally.[7]

Carter was a loner who spent long hours digesting option papers, often communicating with his aides in writing rather than face-to-face. He preferred appealing directly to the public for support of his program to negotiating its terms with other policymakers, although he seemed almost defiantly bland when he addressed large audiences. However, he was far more effective in face-to-face persuasion, where he was advantaged by his clarity of mind and serene self-confidence.

By the end of his term, Carter was able to point to such accomplishments as judicial reform, improved mental health facilities, and government reorganization. He also drew attention for his actions in the area of race relations, many of which were in the realm of symbolism. He increased the number and visibility of African Americans in state government, employed a black state trooper as his escort, and placed portraits of prominent Georgia blacks in the state house rotunda, among them one of Martin Luther King, Jr., whose widow and father became important supporters of Carter's presidential candidacy.

SCALING THE HEIGHTS

In seeking the presidency, Carter showed none of the reluctance to adapt to existing political arrangements that he later displayed in the White House. Studying Democratic party rules with Talmudic closeness, Carter's strategists noted that the number of primaries would increase in 1976 and that even losers would reap a portion of a state's representation at the Democratic Convention. They concluded that Carter should run in all primaries. This placed him on the ballot everywhere and meant that even if his campaign lost its initial momentum, he would continue to amass delegates. They also decided that rather than waiting for the New Hampshire primary in late February, Carter should contest the little-noticed Iowa precinct caucuses in mid-January.

Carter visited Iowa early and often, and his staff built the state's strongest Democratic candidate organization. The investment paid off. Running as the principal moderate in a field of liberals, Carter received 28 percent of the vote. Although 38 percent of the delegates voted for uncommitted slates, the national media declared Carter the winner. Suddenly, "Jimmy Who?" had no difficulty reaching the public. The morning after the Iowa caucuses, Carter appeared on all three network talk shows. In the coming weeks, he was the subject of cover stories in *Time* and *Newsweek*.

Five weeks later in New Hampshire, Carter again ran as a moderate in a field composed entirely of liberals, coming out first. Vindicating his strategy, Carter steadily accumulated delegates. By June his nomination was certain, the other candidates dropped out, and Democratic regulars such as Chicago Mayor Richard Daley endorsed him.

Carter began the general election campaign with a lead over President Ford, who had barely survived Ronald Reagan's effort to deny him the nomination, but steadily lost ground. Ford's strategy was to play up his status as chief executive, carrying out his official responsibilities in a high-profile manner. Carter damaged his own cause by his awkward attempts to clarify his policy stands. He also hurt himself by granting an interview to *Playboy* in which he made the strange confession that he had "committed adultery" in his heart "many times" and therefore would not condemn a man "who screws a whole bunch of women."[8]

By Election Day, the candidates were in a dead heat. It took until early in the morning of November 5 for Carter to be declared the victor with 50.1 percent of the popular vote. His electoral vote margin was 57, the smallest plurality since 1916.

MANUFACTURING A MANDATE

Having won so narrowly, Carter set out to build the public support he would require to advance his agenda. Setting up his transition headquarters in his home town, he promulgated strict conflict-of-interest rules, announced his intention to reduce the perquisites of government officials, and let it be known that his nine-year-old daughter would be attending a predominantly black public elementary school in the District of Columbia.

He took the presidential oath as "Jimmy Carter" rather than "James Earl Carter," wearing a business suit rather than the traditional top hat and morning coat, and walking from the Capitol to the White House hand-in-hand with his wife. Continuing in a populist mode, he delivered what his White House billed as a fireside chat on February 2. Seated before a crackling fire and wearing a cardigan sweater to symbolize energy conservation, Carter announced that in ninety days he would send Congress a comprehensive bill addressing the nation's energy shortage. The following month, he appeared on a call-in radio program and participated in a Massachusetts town meeting, spending the night in the spare bedroom of a local family.

Such efforts played well. In February, when Gallup reported its first assessment of Carter's support, his approval level was already 66 percent. By mid-March it was 75 percent, but he was off to a less auspicious start with the public officials at home and abroad whose support he would need to achieve his aims.

COLLIDING WITH OFFICIALDOM

Carter's initial international difficulties resulted from the high priority he placed on human rights. Upon taking office, he and his foreign policy team criticized a number of nations they deemed deficient in this regard, including the Soviet Union. Carter received a stinging rebuke from Soviet general secretary Leonid Brezhnev for injecting himself in the internal affairs of the Soviet Union. The first meeting of Secretary of State Cyrus Vance with the Soviets on disarmament ended in an impasse.

Carter's domestic collisions began before he took office. During the transition, he paid a courtesy call to Speaker of the House Thomas P. O'Neill. When the Massachusetts Democrat stated his willingness to advise him on congressional relations, Carter spurned the offer. He had faced opposition from lawmakers in Georgia, he explained, and had overcome it by taking his case to the people. Hamilton Jordan had a similarly unpromising encounter with O'Neill, seating the Speaker's guests in the second balcony at a major inaugural event and failing to make amends when O'Neill complained about the affront. (O'Neill reported that Jordan, whom he came to call "Hannibal Jerkin," met with him only three times in the four years of the Carter presidency.[9])

Frictions proliferated after the new administration was in office. Carter lined up key Democratic lawmakers behind a controversial tax rebate and then dropped the proposal without warning. He canceled nineteen water projects, many of them in the districts of the members of Congress whose support was essential to his program. His chief congressional lobbyist became notorious for failing to return the calls of legislators. Meanwhile, he flooded Congress with legislative proposals, not taking account of its capacity to process them.[10]

Before the year was out, Carter's legislative program was faltering. Most serious was Congress's inaction on his flagship energy bill. True to his word, Carter had dispatched an energy measure to Congress three months after his fireside presentation. However, it had been hatched in secret by a task force headed by Carter's politically insensitive energy secretary, James R. Schlesinger. Because there was no consultation with Congress or the affected interests, the bill lacked a base of political support. It also was staggeringly complex in its provisions, which came under the purview of over a dozen congressional panels.

In the House of Representatives, Speaker O'Neill came to Carter's assistance by constituting a special energy committee, but in the Senate the Democratic leadership insisted that it be divided up among the committees concerned with its provisions. In November, Carter postponed a major overseas trip to push the measure, but to no avail. It was not until late the following year that Congress acted, passing a measure that was much watered down from the one on which Carter had expended so much political capital.

PLUNGING PUBLIC SUPPORT

Public approval of Carter's performance tracked the principal events of his presidency, rising and falling in a sequence of increasingly steep declines. An early source of Carter's difficulties was a controversy in the summer of 1977 over whether Carter's friend and budget director, Bert Lance, had engaged in shady banking practices in Georgia before joining the administration. Carter initially stood behind Lance, opening himself to the charge that he was prepared to bend the high standards he had set for his administration where his associates were concerned.

In 1978, Carter won Senate approval of a treaty transferring control of the Panama Canal to Panama, applying himself with fierce intensity to overcome conservative opposition to "giving away" the canal. The Senate ratified the treaty after thirty-eight days of debate. During the ratification struggle, the rest of his program languished, including the long-delayed energy bill. Carter acknowledged in his diary that he found it difficult "to concentrate on anything but Panama" during the ratification fight.[11]

Despite Carter's success on Panama, his public support continued to decline. More damaging than specific events was the increasingly problematic economy, which alternated between bursts of inflation and slowdowns in production throughout Carter's term. Most disturbing to the public was soaring rates of inflation, peaking at 18 percent in 1980. Moreover, the Carter administration never settled on a consistent strategy for curbing prices and encouraging growth, wavering between efforts to stimulate the economy and rein in prices. The nation's economic woes could not be attributed exclusively to Carter, but a president rarely goes unpunished for economic distress that occurs on his watch.

CARTER THE PEACEMAKER

In 1978, Carter registered a triumph that temporarily improved his standing—his feat of personally negotiating a peace agreement between Israel and Egypt. The possibility of an accord between those historic enemies arose in November 1977, when Egyptian prime minister Anwar el-Sadat flew to Jerusalem to address the Israeli parliament, calling for peace between his nation and the Jewish state. The two nations began discussions, but they quickly broke down. Ignoring the near-unanimous advice of his aides not to put his prestige on the line for such a high-risk cause, Carter invited Sadat and Israeli prime minister Menachem Begin to meet with him at Camp David in a last-ditch effort at reconciliation.

Carter proved to be an ideal negotiator. Spurred by the knowledge that it was the Holy Land in which he was seeking to make peace, he displayed none of his usual reluctance to compromise. He placed himself totally in charge of the deliberations, persuading Sadat and Begin to remain at the presidential retreat for an astounding thirteen days. He was served well by his single-mindedness, his capacity to master details, and his facility for one-to-one persuasion.

Carter finally secured an agreement, after personally intervening when each of his foreign counterparts threatened to walk out. On September 17, Sadat and Begin joined Carter in the White House East Room, where they signed the accords in the presence of a large audience of political luminaries. The Egyptian and Israeli leaders were lavish in their praise of the American president. For a brief period, the qualities for which Carter had often been faulted became virtues. It was widely asserted that few other high officials would have had the will and skill to bring about such an impressive accomplishment.

In the summer leading up to Camp David, Carter's approval level had declined to 39 percent, the lowest level of his presidency. In the three months after Carter's success, it averaged 50 percent, but by June 1979 it had gone down to 29 percent. The overriding problem continued to be the economy. The political costs of the nation's economic woes were exacerbated in 1979 when Muslim fundamentalists seized power in Iran, cutting off its oil supply to the United States. Before long there were long lines at gas stations, and Carter was being blamed for a worsening situation in the very domain he had given his highest priority.

On July 4, 1979, Carter canceled a planned vacation in order to prepare what would have been his fifth speech on the nation's energy problems. Then he abruptly called off the address, retreated to Camp David, and consulted on the nation's problems with over one hundred prominent individuals, including political and business leaders, members of the clergy, and a handful of academics.

In mid-July, Carter finally addressed the nation. Focusing more on the nation's morale than its energy resources, Carter declared that the United States faced a "crisis of confidence that strikes at the very heart and soul of our national will." Its elements, he averred, were pessimism about the future, excessive materialism, and loss of respect for institutions such as the government, churches, and news media. Late in his remarks Carter proposed a long-range program designed to free the nation from its dependence on foreign energy sources, asserting that a solution of the energy crisis would "rekindle our national sense of unity, our confidence in the future."[12]

FINAL TRAVAILS

Despite assertions by his critics that it was his presidency rather than the nation that was in crisis, Carter's address was well received by the press and opinion leaders. Two days after his speech, however, he negated its positive effect by unexpectedly demanding letters of resignation from his entire cabinet. He accepted those of Transportation

Secretary Brock Adams, Treasury Secretary W. Michael Blumenthal, Health, Education, and Welfare Secretary Joseph A. Califano, Jr., and Energy Secretary James Schlesinger. He also named Hamilton Jordan his chief of staff, abandoning his practice of managing his own White House.

This draconian action led to expressions of concern about Carter's sense of proportion and even his emotional stability. Against the backdrop of such concerns, two overseas crises transformed the domestic political climate. On November 5, a mob of Iranian students stormed the American embassy in Tehran, taking ninety hostages. On December 27, the Soviet Union invaded Afghanistan. The short-run effect of the overseas turmoil was typical of the initial stage of many international crises—the public rallied around Carter. His approval rating surged from 32 percent in early November to 56 percent in January, but by April it was down to 39 percent.

Carter was challenged for the 1980 Democratic nomination by Senator Edward Kennedy. Surveys had repeatedly shown Kennedy to be more popular than Carter among Democrats, but the Massachusetts Democrat proved ineffective in stating his case, and Carter became the party's nominee again. Meanwhile, the economic deterioration continued, the hostage crisis dragged on, and Carter's ratings began their final plunge. By July 1980, they were down to an all-time presidential low of 21 percent.

The Republicans added to Carter's woes by nominating a candidate whose capacity for communicating to the public was as great as Carter's was slight: Ronald Reagan. Early in the campaign, the polls showed a substantial lead for Reagan, but the gap narrowed when the former California governor made a number of gaffes, calling the Vietnam War a "noble cause" and expressing doubt about the validity of the theory of evolution.

On October 28, Carter and Reagan confronted each other in an hour-and-a-half nationally televised debate. Carter contended that his experience made him the better candidate. Reagan's response was to urge the viewers to ask themselves: "Are you better off now than you were four years ago?" Although it is difficult to establish a causal link between campaign rhetoric and election outcomes, the voters appear to have answered in the negative. On Election Day, they accorded Carter a mere 41 percent to Reagan's 51 percent. (The remaining 8 percent went to independent candidate John Anderson.) In January 1981, Carter returned to Georgia to commence his much praised post-presidential career.

SIGNIFICANCE

Public Communication   As a public communicator Carter began well but faded rapidly. The Inauguration Day procession of the Carter family down Pennsylvania Avenue was arresting political drama, as was the populist symbolism of Carter's early media appearances. The cardigan sweater phase of the Carter presidency was a communications success. *Time* declared that he was "winning converts by the millions with his revivalist, meet-the-masses approach to the presidency." *Newsweek* wrote of his "genius for intimacy with his public." His support level averaged 71 percent in his first two months in office, and it remained above 60 percent through the summer.[13]

As the year continued, Carter's limitations as a public communicator began to manifest themselves. His speeches suffered because they reflected the absence of organizing principles in his program. He read their lines in an uninflected voice, barely moving his lips, and pausing at inappropriate points. It was evident that his presentations would profit from coaching and rehearsals, but he spurned suggestions that he invest effort in improving his speaking style. The overall tone of Carter's communications is well captured by the title of a widely read article by his former speechwriter James Fallows: they were "passionless."[14]

Organizational Capacity   In the realm of organization, Carter was also wanting. In the spirit that led him to carry his own garment bag, Carter announced his intention to reduce the size of the White House staff and do without a chief of staff. The implication was that he was no imperial president, hiding behind a phalanx of White House gatekeepers. Gerald Ford had attempted the same experiment and concluded that he needed a Washington-wise aide to coordinate his operations. That lesson was lost on Carter, whose difficulty of coordinating his White House was exacerbated by his solitary work habits.

The organization of the Carter presidency was at its worst in foreign affairs. Carter received conflicting advice from his secretary of state, Cyrus Vance, who favored measured diplomacy with the communist world, and national security adviser, Zbigniew Brzezinski, who advocated a more confrontational stance. Because he lacked a mechanism for reaching his own conclusions, Carter fell under the sway of Brzezinski, who had proximity to the Oval Office, rather than closely considering alternative policy options.

Political Skill   It might be assumed that Carter offers only warnings in the realm of political skill, but that would ignore his brilliant campaign for the 1976 Democratic nomination and his stunning achievement at Camp David. As in the case of his difficulties as a communicator, Carter's deficiencies as a political operator appear to have been a function of his fixed conceptions rather than innate incapacity. The precise content of those preconceptions is unclear, but they plainly were bound up in his identities as a Christian and an engineer. Rather than viewing compromise as the essence of politics, he seems to have perceived it as a readiness to do what one knows is wrong.

Whatever the cause of Carter's political failures, his actions provide future presidents with a multitude of cautions. A president who studied the Carter experience would be alert to the dangers of raising unrealistic expectations, failing to build bridges to Capitol Hill, and overloading the national policy agenda. One who ignored Carter's failures would risk repeating them, which is precisely what President Bill Clinton did in his 1993 effort to reform the national health care system. Clinton too commissioned a task force that had a controversial head (his wife), met in secret, and did not consult with Congress. His task force also reported a massively complex bill, which in his case went down to defeat rather than being passed in a much modified form.

Vision Carter did not lack vision in the spiritual sense of the term. His human rights policy reflected his own lofty ideals. Because it was fundamentally an ideal, however, it failed to account for such political realities as the need of the United States to retain the support of a number of nations that had less than stellar human rights records, for example China. It therefore did not provide the Carter administration with a clear road map for its relations with the world.

Carter's domestic policies were devoid even of broad inspirational principles. As Fallows observed:

> No one could carry out the Carter program, because Carter had resisted providing the overall guidelines that might explain what his program is. . . . I came to think that Carter believes fifty things, but no one thing. He holds explicit, thorough positions on every issue under the sun, but he has no large view of the relations between them.[15]

Cognitive Style Carter took pride in his intellectual strengths, which were impressive but highly circumscribed. He could and did master complex policy provisions, often revealing a fuller grasp of the details of a program than the member of his administration who was responsible for it. He was better at the specific than the general, however. He lacked the capacity of an Eisenhower to get at the heart of a problem or the ability of a Nixon to set long-run goals. As Fallows put it, Carter thought in terms of lists of proposals rather than larger programs. The order of the items on the lists did not matter, nor did "the hierarchy among them."[16]

Emotional Intelligence For all of his self-composure, Jimmy Carter falls in the category of chief executives whose emotional susceptibilities complicate their public actions. His weaknesses paralleled his predilection for such authoritarian role models as the father who sometimes whipped him and the taskmaster under whom he served in the navy, Admiral Rickover. He was fixed in his ideas and unwilling to brook disagreement.

Carter's policies toward Korea illustrate these traits. Shortly after declaring his presidential candidacy, he proposed to withdraw American troops from South Korea. Thereafter his mind was made up. As president-elect, he refused a CIA briefing on Korea. As president, he was undeterred by the expressed concern of South Korea that removing the American military would trigger an invasion of South Korea by the heavily armed and erratic leadership of North Korea. Nor did it matter to him that his own national security team was opposed to such a move.

Carter's "iron-willed resolve" to withdraw American forces from Korea "posed an ethical and professional dilemma for many officials of his government," according to a close observer of U.S. policy toward Korea. Unlike the usual struggle of contending forces within an administration "for the president's mind," there was a struggle "against the president's mind."[17]

Carter was not marked by the imperiousness of Lyndon Johnson or the deep suspiciousness of Richard Nixon. What Carter did have in common with Johnson and Nixon was an emotionally driven limitation in his ability to get the most out of what otherwise were highly impressive abilities.

Ronald Reagan is shown here with Mikhail Gorbachev in the first of their four summit conferences. In 1983, Reagan had excoriated the Soviet Union, calling it an Evil Empire. In March 1985, Gorbachev was installed as General Secretary of the Soviet Communist party. Recognizing the new Soviet leader as a man with whom the United States could do business, Reagan met with Gorbachev every year of his second term. Together they presided over the termination of a four-and-a-half-decade, potentially lethal, superpower confrontation.

(Ronald Reagan Library)

CHAPTER 10

Ronald Reagan:
The Innocent as Agent of Change

Government is not the solution to our problems; government is the problem.

—RONALD REAGAN,
INAUGURAL ADDRESS,
JANUARY 20, 1981

I urge you to beware the temptation [to declare] both sides equally at fault, to ignore the facts of history and the aggressive impulses of an Evil Empire.

—RONALD REAGAN, ADDRESS TO
PROTESTANT EVANGELICALS IN
ORLANDO, FLORIDA,
MARCH 9, 1983

I was talking about another time, another era.

—REAGAN'S RESPONSE TO A QUESTION
ABOUT WHETHER HE STILL CONSIDERED
THE SOVIET UNION TO BE AN EVIL EMPIRE,
MOSCOW SUMMIT,
MAY 30, 1988

DAVID BRINKLEY: Did you learn anything as an actor that
has been useful to you as president?
REAGAN: There have been times in this office when I have wondered how you could do this job if you hadn't been an actor.

                 —TELEVISED INTERVIEW WITH
        DAVID BRINKLEY, DECEMBER 22, 1988

Ronald Wilson Reagan was at once innocent of much that went
on in his own presidency and an overshadowing political presence in his times. Before his first year in the White House was over,
Reagan presided over a fundamental reorientation of public policy in
the realms of taxes and spending. In his second term, he played a significant part in the peaceful termination of a global conflict that
threatened the survival of humankind.

If one asks whether Reagan was a leader whose actions were determined by circumstances or one who shaped historical outcomes, he
has to be placed in the second category. But much of his impact was
inadvertent, and he was more dependent than any other modern president on others to accomplish his aims. As a result, the policies of Reagan's presidency were to a large extent a function of the shifting cast of
aides who served him.

THE RISE OF A CAREER COMMUNICATOR

Ronald Reagan was born on February 6, 1911, in Tampico, Illinois, a
small town sixty miles west of Chicago, and raised in the somewhat
larger nearby town of Dixon. His father was an ebullient Irish
Catholic salesman with the gift of gab and a drinking problem. His
mother, who was Protestant, taught her children to love their father
and think of his alcoholism as an illness. His father's drinking did not
prevent Reagan from growing up with a sunny disposition. As an

adult he had a number of traits that are common in children of alcoholics, including discomfort with conflict, remoteness in personal relationships, and a tendency to put a rosy gloss on harsh realities.[1]

In high school, Reagan was captain of the football team, president of the student body, and an active participant in dramatics. The motto he chose to appear with his yearbook picture was: "Life is one grand, sweet song, so start the music." In the small Illinois denominational college he attended, he again took part in sports, dramatics, and student governance, graduating in 1931. Reagan's ambition was to become an actor, but he settled for a job as sportscaster for an Iowa radio station. His forte was embellishing the wire service's bare-bones running accounts of games with imagined descriptions of ballpark atmospherics.

In 1937, Reagan was signed to a contract by Warner Brothers. By 1964, he had appeared in fifty-three films, earning a reputation as a solid performer who put serious effort into his parts. As a New Deal Democrat and four-time Roosevelt voter, Reagan became a regular speaker for his party's candidates. He was also active in the Screen Actor's Guild, leading it in collective bargaining negotiations and serving as its president during the postwar controversies over alleged communist infiltration of the film industry.

Reagan's political style was molded by his enthusiasm for FDR, his union experience, and his background as an actor. He took Roosevelt's use of the presidential pulpit as the prototype for his own political leadership. His experience as a labor leader helped shape the bargaining skills that he employed to good effect in Sacramento and Washington. Hollywood prepared him to take part in the staged public events that were a central feature of his governorship and presidency, and his screen persona as an unassuming, personable middle American was the model for his political personality as a congenial citizen-politician bent on restoring the nation to its traditional values.

EMERGENCE AS A CONSERVATIVE

Reagan campaigned against Richard Nixon in his 1950 race for senator from California. He campaigned *for* Nixon in his 1960 presidential campaign. By that time Reagan had become a dedicated conservative. His conversion reflected his rise to affluence in Hollywood and his extended immersion in corporate America in the 1950s, when he served as a corporate spokesman for the General Electric Company. In that capacity he hosted a weekly television drama and visited GE plants throughout the nation, meeting with executives, addressing employees, and speaking to civic groups. He spent much of his time on the road, giving several talks a day for weeks on end. Gradually he took on the worldview of his business audiences.

By the end of the 1950s, Reagan had become much in demand on the conservative speaking circuit. In 1962, he completed his metamorphosis to conservatism by registering as a Republican. In just two more years, he became one of his party's most prominent figures. The context was the ill-fated 1964 presidential campaign of Arizona senator Barry Goldwater.

Two weeks before Election Day the party broadcast a prerecorded fund-raising appeal by Reagan. Speaking with an ease and fluency that derived from his years as a public speaker, Reagan warned his audience that individual freedom was in decline and world communism and big government ascendant. He closed by declaring that America faced a choice between preserving its status as "the last best hope of man on earth" or falling into "a thousand years of darkness."[2]

Reagan's broadcast brought in a cascade of contributions. The day after it was aired, a group of Republicans formed an organization dedicated to advancing his political future. Shortly thereafter, he was approached by several wealthy California businessmen who urged him to run against the state's two-term Democratic governor, Edmund Brown, in 1966. Reagan agreed, and his sponsors commissioned a team of top-flight political consultants to manage his campaign.

FROM SACRAMENTO TO WASHINGTON

Reagan conducted a vigorous race, calling for lower taxes and less government. He castigated Brown for mismanaging the state and tolerating student protests on the state's college and university campuses.

The Brown forces derided him as a mere movie actor, but Reagan turned the tables, asserting that what was needed in government was not career politicians but ordinary citizens who would bring common sense to bear on the problems of the day.

Reagan carried all but a handful of the state's counties, overwhelming Brown by nearly a million votes. In his inaugural address, he declared that "for many years now, you and I have been shushed like children and told there are no simple answers to the complex problems which are beyond our comprehension." The truth, he asserted, is that "there *are* simple answers—there just are not easy ones. The time has come for us to decide whether collectively we can afford everything and anything we think of simply because we think of it."[3]

The time had also come to begin governing, and that proved less than simple and easy for an inexperienced citizen-politician. The fifty-five-year-old Reagan had little understanding of such basics as what positions he needed to take on pending legislation to fulfill his campaign promises, the status of the state's finances, or even how the state budget was prepared. Reagan adapted to his new role by relying on aides to furnish the details of his programs, concentrating his own efforts on negotiation and public communication.

A variety of conservative policies were instituted during Reagan's eight years in Sacramento, including tightened welfare requirements, the assessment of fees in the state's colleges and universities, and measures designed to reduce the costs of government. Reagan's conservatism did not keep him from bending to political realities, and he went along with a tax increase when it became clear that the state was in danger of running in the red.

Even before he had completed his first term as governor, Reagan's supporters embarked on the campaign that was to bring him to the White House. In 1976, he made his first serious effort to win the GOP nomination, coming close to depriving President Ford of the opportunity to seek an elected term. Then, in 1980, Reagan swept the primaries, winning the nomination and choosing the moderate George H. W. Bush as his running mate. At the start of the campaign Reagan was well ahead of the highly unpopular Jimmy Carter in the polls, but the gap narrowed.

Reagan triumphed on Election Day, winning 90 percent of the electoral vote and 51 percent of the popular vote to Carter's 41 percent. (The remaining 8 percent went to independent candidate John Anderson.)

REAGAN IN OFFICE

Reagan's performance in what his biographer Lou Cannon calls the "role of a lifetime"[4] reveals the poverty of the distinction between presidents who are activists and those who are fundamentally passive. As the spokesman-in-chief and principal negotiator of his presidency, Reagan was unsparing in his efforts. He was more than its star performer, however. He was its producer, setting the tone and direction for his administration's policies.

When it came to the administration's internal workings, however, Reagan had a distinctly hands-off manner. Examples of his lack of information and initiative abound. His first-term treasury secretary, Donald Regan, relates that during his four years as Reagan's chief financial officer, Reagan never sought him out for a one-to-one discussion. His White House aide Michael Deaver reports that at a reception for city executives, Reagan mistook his secretary of housing and urban development for a mayor. Budget director David Stockman describes a larger pattern of political remoteness in his account of the enactment of the 1981 tax and budget cuts, reporting that Reagan remained above the fray of his cabinet, allowed himself to be misled by his advisers, and was uninformed on the details of the tax and spending reductions.[5]

The most rounded account of Reagan's leadership style is by his former domestic policy adviser, Martin Anderson. It shows that Reagan's leadership had a distinct pattern that helps explain how he could have had such a great historical impact despite his remoteness from the specifics of politics and policy. First, because he had strong general convictions, Reagan was able to set his administration's overall priorities. Everyone knew that he placed the defense buildup and his economic program ahead of everything else. Second, he was tactically flexible, showing no regret when he had to adjust to political opposition or to changed circumstances. Third, he was a good negotiator, setting his demands higher than the minimum he would accept, and accepting what he could get. Fourth, he made decisions easily and promptly.

Reagan also delegated authority readily, Anderson adds, but delegation was his Achilles' heel. Reagan's practice was to make decisions on the basis of the options his aides presented to him. He neither questioned the choices he was given nor sought to shape them. When he had competent aides, his presidency went well. When they were deficient, the results could be disastrous.[6]

A DRAMATIC FIRST-YEAR SUCCESS

The Reagan administration burst into office with a display of political effectiveness that will be studied for years to come. By the summer of 1981, Reagan and his associates had persuaded Congress to institute the greatest change in government priorities since the New Deal. One source of Reagan's success was the caliber of his staff, especially the triumvirate of aides who managed his White House. His chief of staff, James Baker III, was one of the most skilled Washington operators of his time. Michael Deaver was the choreographer of the news-making events that kept Reagan at the forefront of national attention. His former California aide, Edwin Meese III, was the White House emissary to the Republican right.

Other reasons for Reagan's accomplishments include his single-minded focus and early start. From the beginning of the transition, he made it clear that his economic program would be his "first, second, and third priority."[7] Those of his supporters primarily concerned with social issues such as abortion and school prayer had to settle for symbolism. To create momentum, Reagan set up his transition operation before he even secured the nomination. He located it in Washington, placed it under the direction of a respected lobbyist, and visited the capital himself soon after the election, cultivating legislators, ingratiating himself with the city's power brokers, and making it evident that he would be a determined, forceful player in national policymaking.

Finally, there was Reagan himself. He was his program's principal spokesman and salesman. His timing was unerring. He urged voters to contact their legislators just before key roll calls, winning over members of Congress whose votes were in doubt. He even turned an attempt on his life to his program's advantage, marking the end of his convalescence with a masterful address to a joint session of Congress.

The upshot was the passage of two measures that reduced the next year's domestic spending by $35.2 billion, while cutting personal income tax rates by 25 percent over the next three years. Despite Reagan's faith in the notion that such a tax reduction would pay for itself by strengthening the economy, the result was a budgetary deficit of record proportions and the likelihood of more red ink for the foreseeable future. An unintended additional consequence was that the deficit advanced Reagan's larger purposes, constraining future demands for costly domestic programs.*

A MID-PRESIDENCY DEBACLE

The 1981 enactments had barely been signed when it became evident that a steep recession was underway. Reagan's political stock nosedived, but by 1984 both the economy and Reagan's public support were on the rise. On election day, Reagan polled 59 percent of the popular vote and 98 percent of the electoral vote, losing only the District of Columbia and the home state of his Democratic opponent, Minnesota senator Walter Mondale.

Reagan's second term began with a seemingly minor set of personnel changes. Michael Deaver left government. Edwin Meese became attorney general. White House chief of staff Baker and Treasury Secretary Donald Regan decided to swap positions. Reagan gave the go-ahead, raising no questions about the pros and cons of the change.

In contrast to the politically astute Baker, Regan was politically tone deaf. Regan, a former chairman of Merrill Lynch and a devotee of top-down management, restructured the White House along hierarchical lines, putting himself in control of access to the president. In

---

*It sometimes is claimed that this was Reagan's intention, but Reagan was no Machiavelli. He was a congenital optimist who had no difficulty believing that a tax cut would increase revenues by fostering prosperity.

focusing on the top of the White House pyramid, Regan was inattentive to its base. In the second year of his tenure, a major political scandal erupted at the lower levels of the White House. Its key perpetrators were the fourth of Reagan's six national security advisers, Admiral John Poindexter, and marine Colonel Oliver North, an obscure functionary on the NSC staff. In November 1986, it came out that Poindexter and North had engaged in the covert sale of arms to the revolutionary regime of Iran. Their hope was to persuade Iran to intervene with a group of Islamic militants who were holding a number of Americans hostage in Lebanon. Before the month was over, there was a bizarre further disclosure. North and Poindexter had secretly used the profits from the arms sales to aid the rebel contra guerrillas seeking to overthrow the left-leaning government of Nicaragua.

Reaction on Capitol Hill was explosive. The White House had failed to inform relevant legislators of these actions and had ignored legislation explicitly barring the nation's intelligence agencies from providing assistance to the Central American rebels. Reagan lost his customary aplomb. After a stumbling effort to minimize the disclosures, he admitted that he had not been "fully informed" of the actions of his aides.[8]

When the Iran-contra revelations broke, Reagan was riding high: his approval had exceeded 60 percent in fifteen successive Gallup soundings. In the course of the next month, it plunged to 47 percent, remaining in that range throughout 1987. Investigating committees were constituted on both sides of Capitol Hill, and for much of the year the nation was focused on the televised spectacle of North and Poindexter insisting that they had acted to advance Reagan's policies but kept him uninformed so he could preserve "deniability." It was not until March 1988 that more than half of the public expressed favorable views of Reagan's job performance, and his ratings never reached their pre-Iran-contra heights.[9]

WINDING DOWN THE COLD WAR

One aspect of his administration's policies in which Reagan was emphatically not out of the loop was relations with the Soviet Union. In the initial news conference of his first term, Reagan described détente as "a one-way street that the Soviet Union has used to pursue its own aims." In March 1983, he went so far as to denounce the Soviet Union as an "evil empire."[10]

Shortly after his evil empire speech, Reagan took a step that Kremlin leaders found more threatening than his rhetoric: he announced his administration's plan to develop a space-based Strategic Defense Initiative (SDI) designed to intercept incoming enemy missiles. Reagan viewed SDI as a defensive shield that would contribute to world peace by eliminating the danger of nuclear war. The Soviet leaders saw it as an effort to extend the arms race into space, forcing huge new military expenditures on their already faltering economy.*

It would have been difficult for any American president to reach an accommodation with the leaders of the Soviet Union during Reagan's first term. Leonid Brezhnev was in his final years when Reagan took office and was increasingly incapacitated. Brezhnev was followed by two additional geriatric Politburo members, each of whom died slightly over a year after taking office. Then, on March 11, 1985, the Soviet Communist party installed the vigorous fifty-five-year-old Mikhail Gorbachev as general secretary.

Trusting his instincts and ignoring those of his aides who were skeptical of Gorbachev, Reagan set about to establish a working relationship with the new Soviet leader. He was encouraged to do so by his wife, Nancy, who did not want her husband's legacy to be that of intensifying the cold war. He was able to manage the negotiations needed to wind down the cold war because he had at his disposal the services of one the nation's most able and bureaucratically experienced public servants, Secretary of State George Shultz.

The story of how Reagan reached out to the new Soviet leadership can be summarized by reviewing his summit conferences with Gorbachev. The 1985 Geneva summit was an occasion for breaking the ice and conveying the symbolism of a new beginning. The 1986 summit in Reykjavik, Iceland, witnessed a veritable frenzy of bargaining as the

---

*Ironically, SDI did contribute to the reduction of cold war tensions, but not because of the reasons for which Reagan favored it. It made the Soviet leaders more pliable by threatening to impose unacceptable costs on the already strained Soviet economy.

two sides debated—but finally rejected—the revolutionary possibility of scrapping their nuclear arsenals. The 1987 Washington summit saw the signing of the first cold war pact providing for arms reductions. The 1988 Moscow summit was the occasion for the exchange of documents that made the arms reduction treaty official. It also was marked by the two leaders ambling through Red Square and Reagan's assertion that he no longer viewed the Soviet Union as an evil empire.[11]

Reagan was far from the sole cause of the dramatic improvement in Soviet-American relations of the second half of the 1980s. That transformation would have been out of the question without the rise of Gorbachev, the elimination of state repression in the Soviet Union, and the collapse of the Soviet empire in Eastern Europe. Still, if Reagan had responded to Gorbachev in a spirit of confrontation, it would have been impossible for the Soviet leader to resist his hard-liners.

Instead, Reagan formed a personal bond with Gorbachev and supported those of his own aides who were prepared to find an accommodation with the Soviet Union, contributing to the end of the cold war simply by being who he was. Like Richard Nixon, he was too well known as an anticommunist to be vulnerable to attack from the right. In short, he was capable of a paradoxical moderation that would have been less feasible if he had been a moderate.

SIGNIFICANCE

Public Communication   Given the centrality of appeals to the public in the modern presidency, it is remarkable that Reagan was the first White House occupant who had been a career public communicator before entering politics. Reagan turned his professionalism to good advantage, carrying off his rhetorical responsibilities with a virtuosity exceeded only by FDR. He and his aides made effective use of the "line-of-the-day" approach to presidential public messages, taking pains not to diffuse Reagan's communications by confining him to the single daily public appearance that best advanced his administration's purposes. They also were masters at the atmospherics of presidential communication, consistently providing television with irresistible images that dominated the evening news.

Organizational Capacity As a communicator Reagan offers lessons that any chief executive can take to heart. The organizational side of his presidency is mainly a source of warnings. Reagan appears to have had no general views about presidential organization, but his presidency was a laboratory for examining the impact of a president's advisers on his performance. When Reagan's assistants took advantage of his strengths and protected him from his weaknesses, the results often were impressive, as in the enactment of his 1981 economic program. When the reverse was the case, there was a danger of such misadventures as the Iran-contra affair.

Political Skill For all of his limitations, Reagan possessed exceptional political skills. He was as active in selling his policies within the political community as in promulgating them to the public. He excelled in the acts of bonhomie that were alien to Jimmy Carter, easily ingratiating himself with lawmakers. Yet he was far more than a front man: He was decisive in setting the direction of his administration's program.

Reagan also had impressive negotiating skills. These are illustrated in an account by the former Kennedy and Johnson administration treasury secretary Douglas Dillon, who served with Reagan on a task force charged with reevaluating the CIA's mission in the wake of its use for domestic political espionage by the Nixon administration. Some members of the group favored a largely uncurbed CIA; others wanted to rein it in. When Reagan, who had missed the early meetings, finally made it to a session, he spent part of his first morning listening to the debate. Then he picked up a pen and began writing, finally reading a compromise wording. He asked the proponents of the polar positions if they could accept it, and they acknowledged that they could. He later explained to Dillon that he was doing no more than he had as a labor leader in Hollywood.[12]

Vision No matter what their views of Reagan, no one would accuse him of lacking vision. It was evident to all that he was committed to a handful of verities—a strong military, low taxes, and less government involvement in the economy. It also was clear that he was adamantly opposed to the Soviet Union—until Mikhail Gorbachev transformed the Soviet reality. Reagan's convictions provided a steady beacon for his political counterparts. As George Shultz put it, "Maybe you didn't agree with him and maybe you did. But there it was. What you saw was what you got."[13]

Cognitive Style   Reagan's cognitive limitations were worrisome. This was a president who never grasped the logic of nuclear deterrence and genuinely believed that it would be possible to produce an invulnerable space shield. Still, there was more to Reagan's intellect than met the eye. That was the conclusion of the *Washington Post*'s Lou Cannon, who covered Reagan for twenty years. Drawing on the Harvard psychologist Howard Gardner's notion of multiple intelligences, Cannon concludes that while Reagan was not well endowed with logical abilities, he was gifted at interpersonal relations and strategic use of verbal and body language. These are traits that are more common with actors than politicians. Reagan succeeded in turning them to good political effect.[14]

Emotional Intelligence   Reagan was like FDR in that his leadership was better served by his temperament than his intelligence. Despite having had to cope with an alcoholic father, he projected a sense of self-assurance and equanimity. As George Shultz put it, Reagan "was and is comfortable with himself."[15] He was confident in his own perceptions, feeling free to ignore his conservative base, when he sensed that the United States could do business with Mikhail Gorbachev.

Reagan was also like FDR in not revealing his inner self. His aides held him in great respect, but they felt that he never fully bonded with them. He was marked by a discomfort with face-to-face disagreement that limited his ability to get the most from his advisers. Still, he showed no sign of the insecurity, anger, and other disruptive emotions that intruded into the leadership of a number of other chief executives. Reagan may not have been the epitome of mental health, but his emotional qualities were well suited to the role in which he was cast by the American people.

George H. W. Bush is shown here with his principal ally in the 1991 Gulf War, British prime minister Margaret Thatcher. Bush displayed great skill in orchestrating the campaign that drove the forces of Saddam Hussein's Iraq from Kuwait. He was less adept in the manner in which he brought the war to a close, leaving Saddam Hussein in power. In 1990, Bush signed off on a tax increase he had promised he would never countenance. He also gave the impression of floundering in the final year and a half of his presidency, when the economy experienced a sharp downturn.

(George Bush Presidential Library)

CHAPTER 11

The Highly Tactical Leadership of George H. W. Bush

The Congress will push me to raise taxes, and I'll say no. And they'll push, and I'll say no. And they'll push again, and I'll say to them, "Read my lips. No new taxes."

—GEORGE H. W. BUSH, SPEECH ACCEPTING THE
REPUBLICAN PRESIDENTIAL NOMINATION,
AUGUST 19, 1988

This one compromise that—where we begrudgingly had to accept revenue increases—is the exception that proves the rule.

—GEORGE H. W. BUSH,
PRESS CONFERENCE,
OCTOBER 27, 1990

As Commander in Chief, I can report to you our armed forces fought with honor and valor. And as President, I can report to the Nation aggression is defeated. The war is over.

—GEORGE H. W. BUSH, ADDRESS BEFORE
A JOINT SESSION OF CONGRESS ON THE
CESSATION OF THE PERSIAN GULF CONFLICT,
MARCH 6, 1991

Way back in 1945, Winston Churchill was defeated at the polls. He said, "I have been given the order of the boot." That is the exact same position in which I find myself today.

—George H. W. Bush, radio address
to the nation on the results
of the presidential election,
November 7, 1992

The first three years of George H. W. Bush's presidency witnessed the collapse of communism in Eastern Europe, the demise of the Soviet Union, and the dramatic military triumph of a U.S.-led military coalition over the forces of Saddam Hussein's Iraq. In March 1991, 89 percent of the public expressed approval of Bush's job performance—then the highest rating in the history of presidential approval polling. By July 1992, however, the economy was in a sharp downturn, and his approval level tumbled to 29 percent. In November, he was defeated for reelection in a three-way race with Arkansas governor Bill Clinton and the billionaire businessman H. Ross Perot, polling a mere 38 percent of the popular vote.[1]

It is necessary to go back to Franklin Roosevelt to find a chief executive with the rich governmental experience of George H. W. Bush. Like Roosevelt, he was the product of a privileged upbringing that instilled in him the ideal of public service. In sharp contrast to FDR, Bush resisted using the White House as a platform from which to educate the public and failed to associate himself with a clearly identifiable political program. These deficiencies were not problematic between 1989 and 1991, when his public support was buoyed by prosperity and military success, but they were his undoing in 1992, when circumstances changed and his presidency was at stake.

ACQUIRING AN ETHOS OF SERVICE

George Herbert Walker Bush was born on June 12, 1924, to Prescott Sheldon Bush and Dorothy Walker Bush and raised in the affluent exurban community of Greenwich, Connecticut. His father, a Wall Street investment banker and managing partner of Brown Brothers, Harriman, served as U.S. senator from Connecticut between 1952 and 1962 and was a strong supporter of President Eisenhower. His mother came from a prominent St. Louis family. Her father had founded the Walker Cup competition between American and British amateur golfers, and her family spent its summers at the gracious ocean-front compound at Walker Point in Kennebunkport, Maine, which Bush was to use as a presidential retreat.[2]

Bush's sense of civic responsibility was incubated at Greenwich Country Day School and Phillips Academy, in Andover, Massachusetts, which he attended from 1937 to 1941. Although he grew up during the Depression, he appears to have had little awareness of the political turmoil and economic distress of the 1930s. At prep school, Bush was an enthusiastic athlete and a much-liked participant in extracurricular activities. He graduated six months after Pearl Harbor and enlisted in the navy, becoming its youngest combat pilot. He flew fifty-eight missions in the Pacific, earning the Distinguished Flying Cross for completing a mission in a burning torpedo bomber before bailing out.

After the war, Bush attended Yale, where he earned a B.A. in economics, played varsity baseball, and belonged to the prestigious secret society, Skull and Bones. He graduated in 1948, spurned the opportunity to take a secure position on Wall Street, and moved his family to Texas, where he became a prosperous oilman. Once he was financially comfortable, Bush sought a career in public life, building what came to be regarded as a perfect resumé for a would-be president.

A GOVERNMENTAL POLYMATH

In 1964, Bush ran unsuccessfully as the Republican candidate for the Senate in his adopted state against the liberal Democratic incumbent,

Ralph Yarborough. Aligning himself with the fervent conservatism of his party's presidential candidate, Arizona senator Barry Goldwater, Bush condemned the Civil Rights Act of 1964 as an abrogation of states' rights, a stand he later said he regretted.

Between 1966 and 1970, Bush represented a prosperous Houston congressional district in the House of Representatives. He took more moderate stances in the House than he had in his campaign for the Senate, supporting the right of eighteen year olds to vote, abolition of the draft, and open housing. In 1970, Bush made a second unsuccessful run for the Senate and was then appointed ambassador to the United Nations by President Nixon. He took on the assignment with energy and enthusiasm, building a network of international contacts that would serve him well in the White House, particularly in the Persian Gulf War.

Following the 1972 election, Nixon asked Bush to become chairman of the Republican National Committee. Bush was reluctant to leave the United Nations but dutifully did so. As Watergate unfolded, Bush was one of Nixon's most loyal defenders, maintaining that it was inconsistent with Nixon's character to be involved in the sordid goings-on for which he was under investigation. In August 1974 the release of the smoking-gun tape proved Bush wrong, and he urged Nixon to resign.

During the Ford presidency, Bush added two more high-level positions to his curriculum vitae. In September 1974, he was appointed chief of the U.S. Liaison Office in the People's Republic of China, a responsibility he discharged with zest. Thirteen months later, Ford appointed him director of the CIA. The agency was under fire for employing such practices as assassination in the 1950s and 1960s and for engaging in domestic political activities during the Nixon presidency.

Bush instituted reforms designed to eliminate such abuses. He also authorized a controversial intelligence exercise in which a team of hawkish nongovernmental national security specialists was charged with producing an estimate of the Soviet threat for comparison with the agency's official estimate. That team's alarming assessment of

Soviet intentions and capabilities became an article of faith for such conservatives as Ronald Reagan, who held that the Soviet Union had taken advantage of détente to create a window of American military vulnerability.

Rise to the Presidency

After Ford's defeat, Bush returned to Texas, where he readied himself to seek the 1980 Republican presidential nomination. He announced his candidacy in May 1979, declaring that his extensive public service had prepared him to provide "the principled, stable leadership we must have in the decade of the eighties." He ran a spirited primary campaign, but was defeated by the highly popular Ronald Reagan. Searching for a running mate who would appeal to moderates, Reagan chose Bush for the second spot on the ticket.[3]

Although he was selected by Reagan for his centrist appeal, Bush rapidly moved to the right, disavowing his campaign assertion that Reagan's domestic program was based on "voodoo economics." During his eight vice-presidential years, Bush displayed his customary dynamism, traveling widely and expanding his already impressively wide acquaintance with foreign leaders. Like other vice presidents, Bush cultivated the impression that he was a force in the administration in which he served, but when questions were raised about whether he had played a part in the Iran-contra affair, he insisted that he had been "out of the loop."

Early in 1987, Bush announced his intention to seek the 1988 Republican presidential nomination. After a poor showing in the Iowa caucuses, he ran well in the primaries, in effect securing the nomination by the end of March. In his acceptance speech at the Republican convention, Bush made his highly publicized "no new taxes" pledge, called for an outpouring of voluntary activities to address the nation's social problems ("a thousand points of light"), and declared that if elected, he would work to bring about a "kinder, gentler America," implying that he would smooth out the rough edges of Reagan's domestic policies.[4]

Bush then embarked on an anything-but-gentle campaign, calling his Democratic opponent, Massachusetts governor Michael Dukakis, a "card-carrying member of the American Civil Liberties Union." He criticized Dukakis for vetoing a bill requiring public schoolteachers to lead their pupils in the Pledge of Allegiance and approving a prisoner furlough program under which an African American felon named Willie Horton was released from prison and went on to rape a white woman. Bush was elected with 54 percent of the popular vote. He then promptly returned to his gentlemanly mode, vowing to be "president of all the people," but saying little about what he hoped to accomplish.

In the 1988 campaign Bush left the impression that his presidency would be tantamount to a Reagan third term. But it quickly became evident that, at least in his leadership style, he was the near antithesis of his predecessor. Reagan was a quintessential message politician, whereas Bush was famously deficient in "the vision thing." Reagan had been disengaged from the inner workings of his administration; Bush had a hands-on approach to leadership. Most striking, once the electioneering was over, Bush seemed to go out of his way to avoid the rhetorical emphasis that led Reagan to be dubbed the "Great Communicator." He rarely addressed the nation from the Oval Office, rejected speech drafts containing soaring phrases, and was notorious for his garbled extemporaneous statements. As he once put it, "Fluency in the English language is something I'm often not accused of."[5]

COLD WAR ENDGAME

Bush also was the opposite of Reagan in his response to the sea change in the Soviet Union under Mikhail Gorbachev. As vice president, Bush had been uneasy about the stridency of Reagan's early anti-Soviet pronouncements. During Reagan's second term, he was equally unsettled by Reagan's readiness to reach out to Mikhail Gorbachev. So great was Bush's skepticism about whether the Soviet Union had been fundamentally altered under Gorbachev that in June 1988, he publicly distanced himself from Reagan, declaring that he still considered the Soviet Union a threat.[6]

On taking office, Bush acted on his skepticism toward the Soviet Union, placing East-West diplomacy on hold while his administration conducted an extensive foreign policy review. Meanwhile, he assembled a highly professional foreign affairs team. Drawing on his former colleagues in the Ford administration, he appointed Brent Scowcroft, who had been Ford's national security adviser, to the same position in his own administration. He also named Ford's former White House chief of staff, Dick Cheney, as secretary of defense, and he chose his close friend and Texas political ally, James Baker III, as secretary of state.

In May, Bush resumed negotiations with the Soviets, proposing sweeping cuts in NATO and Warsaw Pact forces in Europe. By summer, the cold war had assumed a dramatically new character. In a dizzying sequence of events, the nations of Eastern Europe rapidly cast out their communist governments. By the end of 1989, the communist regimes in Poland, Hungary, Bulgaria, Czechoslovakia, East Germany, and Romania had been replaced by governments free of Soviet control.

The political changes in Eastern Europe and the Soviet Union brought out the professionalism with which Bush approached global politics. When he held his first summit conference with the Soviet leader, Bush took pains to convene it in a neutral setting, holding the meeting on U.S. and Soviet naval warships off Malta. He gradually established a close working relationship with Gorbachev, going out of his way not to gloat over such events as the breaching of the Berlin Wall or engage in actions that would damage or embarrass Gorbachev domestically. He proceeded with particular caution during the intricate negotiations that led to the unification of East and West Germany in 1990.

Just as Bush was cautious in establishing political bonds with Gorbachev, he was wary about forging links with the leading Soviet opposition figure, the bumptious Boris Yeltsin. As late as July 1991, Bush visited Moscow, but did not schedule a meeting with Yeltsin, who by then was president of the Russian Republic. A month later, when a group of Soviet hard-liners staged an attempted coup against Gorbachev, Bush's caution again manifested itself. Instead of condemning the attempt, he issued the mild statement that the actions of the plotters were "extra-constitutional."

Bush's response to the failed coup epitomizes the reactive nature of his responses to the epochal events that ended the cold war. As his ambassador to the Soviet Union, Jack Matlock, put it, Bush tended to be suspicious of political change—"even when it was for the better." His strength was in "managing the present and avoiding the mistakes of the past." It was not in his nature to seek to mold the future.[7]

VICTORY IN THE GULF

To the extent that Matlock's judgment implies that Bush was a fundamentally passive leader, it does not apply to his response when Saddam Hussein's Iraq seized the Persian Gulf sheikdom of Kuwait on Thursday, August 1, 1990. Suddenly the Iraqi dictator was in control of one-fifth of the world's oil resources, and his forces were poised to seize the rich oil fields of neighboring Saudi Arabia.

On the morning of August 2, Bush made a rambling comment to reporters before a meeting with his national security team. His remarks left the impression that he considered the Iraqi takeover of Kuwait a fait accompli. After the meeting, Bush flew to Colorado to take part in a public event with British prime minister Margaret Thatcher. During the flight he conferred with Scowcroft. They concluded that the United States should do what was necessary to reverse the Iraqi takeover, a view that Thatcher strongly reinforced.

Bush spent the weekend at Camp David, where he deliberated and telephoned the foreign leaders he had come to know so well over the years. When he returned to the White House on Monday, the hesitancy evident on August 2 had evaporated. Striding from his helicopter, he paused and declared: "This will not stand, this aggression against Kuwait."[8] This was the first indication to the chairman of the Joint Chiefs of Staff, General Colin Powell, that Bush intended to evict Saddam from Kuwait and not just hold the line against a further Iraqi advance.

George H. W. Bush and Margaret Thatcher were representatives of the World War II generation for which it was an article of faith that one must never appease aggressors. Powell was a twice-wounded Vietnam veteran who took two lessons from that conflict: the United States should never embark on a major military action without domestic and international support and, if it did take action, it should do so decisively and have a strategy for extricating itself when its goal was accomplished.

In the months ahead, Bush, Baker, Scowcroft, and Cheney set out to meet Powell's criteria. By early 1991, they had dispatched an American military force of over a half-million to the Persian Gulf, equipped with a huge arsenal of technologically advanced weapons. Meanwhile, Bush and his associates set about forging an international coalition in support of the liberation of Kuwait. The culmination of their efforts was the passage on November 27 of Security Council Resolution 678 authorizing the use of force if Iraq did not withdraw from Kuwait. Early in January, Bush asked for and received a congressional resolution of support for military action if Iraq did not meet the U.N. deadline for withdrawing from Kuwait: January 15, 1991.

The war itself was an anticlimax. It began on January 16 with a massive campaign of precision bombing. By February 24, when the ground phase of the allied action commenced, Iraq's front-line troops had been devastated. The American-led forces launched a massive attack on the undefended west flank of the Iraqi forces, and resistance crumbled.

On February 27, Bush ordered a cease-fire. Saddam Hussein remained in power, but the U.N. mandate had been fulfilled with a minimum of U.S. casualties. In the next Gallup presidential approval poll, Bush's level of support soared to 89 percent. There followed a wave of announcements by prominent Democrats that they did not plan to seek their party's presidential nomination in 1992.

THINGS FALL APART

In contrast to his energetic involvement in international affairs, Bush seemed almost without interest in domestic policy. That impression is misleading. He presided over two major domestic policy reforms: an extensive revision of the Clean Air Act and the passage of the Americans with Disabilities Act, a civil rights policy departure that guarantees the handicapped access to services and facilities. Still, he was too much an incrementalist to enunciate a broad set of goals in domestic affairs. As he put it in his inaugural address:

> Some see leadership as high drama and the sound of trumpets calling. And sometimes it is that. But I see history as a book with many pages—and each day we fill a page with acts of hopefulness and meaning.[9]

There was one politically costly domestic theme that did run through the Bush presidency. It followed from his categorical no-new-taxes pledge in the 1988 campaign. Bush made that declaration to combat the impression he was a closet moderate rather than a true Reaganite. In doing so, he set himself up for a fall, since it was predictable that the mounting deficits resulting from Reagan's tax cuts would make it necessary for him to seek new revenues.

In 1990, he did exactly that. After extensive negotiations with the leaders of the two congressional parties, he agreed to support a tax increase. Bush could have derived political capital from the compromise by stressing its constructive features, but he made no serious attempt to justify the increase, and he worsened matters with a dismissive comment when reporters asked him about his change of position during one of his morning jogs. Pointing to his buttocks, he tossed off the throwaway line, "Read my hips."[10]

Having failed to establish an identifiable domestic record, Bush experienced a hemorrhage of political support when the nation's focus shifted to matters closer to home, as it did later in 1991. By then the United States had slipped into a sharp economic recession, and the glow of military success in the Gulf War had worn off. By 1992, when the election season was underway, Bush's approval level had plunged to the 30 to 40 percent range.[11]

Bush was challenged in the Republican primaries by the fiery

Republican conservative Patrick Buchanan. Meanwhile, he was also being attacked by contenders for the Democratic nomination and the crankily charismatic independent candidate, H. Ross Perot. After emerging victorious from the primaries, Bush went on to conduct a campaign devoted more to deriding his Democratic opponents than defending his own achievements.

Bush received a mere 38 percent of the popular vote, the smallest vote for an incumbent president since 1912. His Democratic opponent, Arkansas governor Bill Clinton, received 43 percent of the vote, and Perot the remaining 19 percent. Bush then retired to what gave every sign of being a highly contented private life, removing himself to the political sidelines. Departing from precedent, he refused to write his memoirs, although he and Scowcroft coauthored a volume on his administration's major foreign-policy decisions.[12]

SIGNIFICANCE

Public Communication   In the realm of public communication, Bush made the most of his detailed command of policy. He appeared before the press regularly in the White House situation room, conducting the kinds of factual briefings that are usually the responsibility of lesser officials. He addressed reporters by name, took an interest in them as individuals, and often sent them handwritten notes. All of this was to his advantage, but in leaning over backward to avoid Reaganesque oratory, he deprived his presidency of the teaching function that enabled presidents such as Roosevelt, Kennedy, and Reagan to frame public perceptions, place their administrations in a favorable light, and buffer themselves from negative developments.

Organizational Capacity   Bush's organizational legacy is mixed. He had an impressive capacity to select and motivate able advisers. In 1997, Hofstra University convened a conference on Bush's presidency. The alumni of his administration were effusive in expressing respect and affection for their former boss, much more so than veterans of many earlier presidencies.

There may, however, have been a less positive side to the bonding of Bush with his aides. Students of decision making argue that highly cohesive leadership groups tend to find it difficult to ask hard questions about political realities.[13] The available record on the Bush administration's decision making on Iraq suggests that Bush did not rigorously debate the widely discussed option of freeing Kuwait by applying sanctions to Iraq rather than force. It also suggests that in calling a halt to the hundred-hour intervention, they did not give careful attention to the possible costs of leaving Saddam Hussein in power.

Political Skill Bush provides many illustrations of political skill. Examples include his subtle maneuvering in connection with the unification of Germany and expert use of "Rolodex diplomacy" to mold an international coalition to support the liberation of Kuwait. He also was consistently attentive to Congress, visiting Capitol Hill regularly and even working out in the congressional gym. However, his skills were more tactical than strategic. His most impressive feat was his success in mustering support for the Gulf War, but he and his associates made their hasty decision to bring the war to a halt with insufficient deliberation.

Vision That George H. W. Bush lacked "the vision thing" is no less accurate for being a cliché. In the absence of a larger direction, there was a situation-determined quality to the Bush presidency. Internationally, this manifested itself in his cautious relations with the Soviet Union and lack of deliberation over ending the Gulf War. Domestically, it accounts for the failure to communicate a sense of how he would address the nation's economic problems that contributed to his electoral defeat.

Cognitive Style Lack of vision need not imply cognitive limitations. Bush was far from intellectually handicapped. One need only read the richly informative transcripts of his briefings of the press to recognize that he was fully on top of his administration's policies. However, he was insensitive to abstractions, a cognitive deficiency that contributed to his highly tactical presidential leadership.

Emotional Intelligence Whatever his cognitive capacities, Bush was well supplied with emotional intelligence. His immersion in a near-frenetic athletic regimen seems to have kept him on an even keel. He also was generous, polite, and forbearing. The only circumstances in which his feelings seemed to get the better of him were those that engaged his patriotism—hence, his highly personalized responses to such authoritarian figures as Saddam Hussein and the Panamanian strongman Manuel Noriega. But compared with such presidents as Johnson and Nixon, Bush was a model of emotional balance. His presidency may have lacked monumental achievements, but it was free of character-based calamity.

Hillary Rodham Clinton looks on as her husband addresses congressional Democrats following the December 1998 vote of the House of Representatives to impeach him. Three months earlier, Clinton had confessed to his sexual involvement with White House intern Monica Lewinsky. The Clinton presidency has been fraught with difficulties, and Clinton has achieved far less than might have been expected of a chief executive with towering political skills and policy aspirations.

CHAPTER 12

The Undisciplined Bill Clinton

There is nothing wrong with America that cannot be cured by what is right about America. And so today we pledge an end to deadlock and drift, and a new season of American renewal has begun.

—BILL CLINTON,
INAUGURAL ADDRESS,
JANUARY 20, 1993

Keep in mind the ultimate purpose of deficit reduction is to improve the economy by getting interest rates down, freeing up tax funds that we would otherwise have to spend on servicing the debt, and improving the climate for new jobs. It's also clear that we have to have some investment incentives. People have to take this money we're going to save through reducing the deficit, turn around and invest it in the economy. And if you raise tax rates on upper income people and then you provide only in a very targeted way to in effect lower their tax burden by having them create jobs, then you win either way, because either way you reduce the deficit and you improve the economy. That's what we are trying to do.

—BILL CLINTON, REMARKS AND AN EXCHANGE
WITH REPORTERS AFTER A MEETING WITH
CONGRESSIONAL LEADERS, JULY 15, 1993

I was always worried that I never would quite fit in modern politics, which is so much television and the thirty-second sound bite and look macho, whether you are or not, and all that sort of stuff.

—BILL CLINTON,
REMARKS AT A FUND RAISER FOR
MAYOR DAVID DINKINS IN NEW YORK CITY,
SEPTEMBER 26, 1993

I want to say again to the American people how profoundly sorry I am for what I said and did to trigger these events and the great burden they have imposed on the Congress and the American people.

—BILL CLINTON,
STATEMENT AFTER ACQUITTAL IN
SENATE IMPEACHMENT TRIAL,
FEBRUARY 12, 1999

No one who is indifferent to politics becomes president of the United States, but some chief executives stand out as political in every fiber of their being. Guile, maneuver, and wheedling are second nature to them, and they are political in their private as well as their public lives. As of 1992, the modern presidents who best fit this description were Roosevelt, Johnson, and Nixon. In 1993, the first chief executive to be born after World War II joined their ranks: William Jefferson Clinton.

Besides being political to the core, Clinton was notable for his intelligence, energy, and exceptional articulateness. He also was marked by a severe lack of self-discipline that led him into difficulties, and a resiliency and coolness under pressure that enabled him to extricate himself from many of this predicaments.

A Young Man from Hope

Bill Clinton was born on August 19, 1946, in a southwest Arkansas hamlet with the politically valuable name of Hope. His father, William Jefferson Blythe, was a traveling salesman who died in an automobile accident three months before Bill's birth. His mother, Virginia, was a nurse whose optimistic outlook and ability to rebound from the deaths of three husbands was a prototype for her son's capacity for political regeneration. When Bill was four, she married Roger Clinton, a car salesman, who proved to be an alcoholic and a wife abuser.

In an event that was to be featured in the Clinton campaign video, "The Man from Hope," the fourteen-year-old Bill stood up to his drunken stepfather, forbidding him ever again to strike his mother. Bill later testified against Roger Clinton in his mother's divorce proceedings, but the divorce was barely final before she remarried her former husband. Sometime later, Bill took his stepfather's last name to signal his solidarity with his family.[1]

Bill gave no outward sign of the turmoil at home. He sailed through school thanks to his quick mind and near-photographic memory. From his earliest years, Clinton exhibited what an Arkansas observer refers to as "a compulsive need to meet people, to know them, to like them, to have them like him," which enabled him to win over most people he encountered, but alienated some who viewed him as an opportunist and gladhander.[2]

Like Ronald Reagan, Bill Clinton had a number of traits associated with children of alcoholics. His own assessment of the matter is very much that of others:

> In an alcoholic family, I grew up with much greater empathy for other people's problems than the average person. . . . I learned some good skills about how to keep people together and try to work things out. On the negative side, if you grow up in an environment that causes you to want to avoid trouble, you tend to try to keep the peace at all costs. . . . All my life, I've had to work to draw the line in the dirt, to make conflict my friend, not my enemy.[3]

Clinton was president of his high school freshman and sophomore classes, a National Merit scholar, and an avid participant in extracurricular activities. At age sixteen, while visiting Washington with a youth group, he shook hands with President Kennedy, an event that reinforced his captivation with politics. That interest led him to attend Georgetown University, in the nation's capital, where he stood out academically, was active in campus politics, and found employment with Arkansas senator J. William Fulbright, chairman of the Foreign Relations Committee.

Fulbright became Clinton's exemplar in two respects. He was a Rhodes scholar and the most prominent congressional opponent of President Johnson's Vietnam policy. Clinton became an antiwar activist, and he also won admission to the Rhodes program, attending Oxford between 1968 and 1970.

FROM OXFORD TO LITTLE ROCK

While at Oxford, Clinton read omnivorously, traveled widely in Europe, and participated in protests against the Vietnam War. He also engaged in a sequence of actions that enabled him to avoid military service but later plagued him politically. After receiving a draft notice, he arranged for it to be quashed by joining a Reserve Officer Training Corps unit at the University of Arkansas Law School. When the Selective Service system began cutting back on draft calls and instituted a draft lottery in which the odds of being inducted were low, he resigned from the ROTC, explaining in a letter to his former commander that he had joined in order to avoid service in a war to which he was opposed, while preserving his "political viability."[4]

After Oxford, Clinton entered Yale Law School, where he met his wife-to-be, the equally high-achieving Hillary Rodham. Upon graduation, he joined the faculty of the University of Arkansas Law School. In 1976, he was elected state attorney general. Two years later, at age thirty-two, Clinton won the Arkansas governorship, receiving national attention as the nation's youngest state chief executive in four decades. Two years after that he became the nation's youngest *ex*-governor, after being defeated for reelection by a little-known Republican banker.

The consensus in Arkansas political circles was that Clinton had brought this reversal on himself by advancing large numbers of policy initiatives with little regard for their political feasibility and steeply increasing automobile license fees. He and Hillary had compounded his difficulties by defying the conservative mores of Arkansas. He staffed his office with left-leaning, out-of-state political activists; she kept her maiden name, dressed unfashionably, and otherwise made it evident that she was not a conventional political helpmate.

Clinton was stunned, but he mounted a drive to regain the governorship. He taped a television commercial apologizing for the shortcomings of his governorship, and he and Hillary transformed their political personae. He recast himself as a pragmatic moderate, focusing on issues with mainstream appeal. She adopted her husband's last name, acquired a fashionable wardrobe, and became her husband's partner in public affairs. In 1982, Clinton regained the governorship, retaining it until he became president. Meanwhile, he became active in national politics, chairing the National Governors Association and helping found an organization of moderate Democrats who sought to move their party to the center of the national political spectrum.

FROM LITTLE ROCK TO WASHINGTON

In October 1991, Clinton announced his presidential candidacy, billing himself as a new-style Democrat who combined sympathy for the underprivileged with a hardheaded emphasis on individual responsibility. His pursuit of the nomination had barely begun when his campaign was dealt two blows that might well have been fatal to a less resolute candidate. One was a detailed report in the *Wall Street Journal* of his tangled efforts to avoid military service during the Vietnam War. The other was the assertion of an Arkansas nightclub singer that she and Clinton had been lovers for the past decade.[5]

Clinton explained his efforts to avoid the draft by saying that he, like other loyal young men, had been torn between his love of country and his abhorrence of what he regarded as an immoral conflict. He and Hillary dealt with the sexual accusation by appearing together on national television and acknowledging that he had "caused pain" in their marriage, but they had resolved their problems. Despite the two revelations, Clinton received a larger-than-predicted vote in the New Hampshire primary. Dubbing himself the "Comeback Kid," he went on to sweep the southern primaries and clinched the nomination in June.[6]

Clinton broke precedent by naming a demographically similar running mate: his fellow southern moderate and baby boomer, Tennessee senator Albert Gore, Jr. The two men and their wives conducted a highly telegenic campaign, barnstorming through small town America in a campaign bus and defeating Bush in a three-way contest with independent candidate and Texas billionaire H. Ross Perot. The Democrats maintained control of Congress but lost ten seats in the House of Representatives.

In the weeks just after his election, Clinton won praise for his assertion that he intended to focus on the nation's depressed economy "like a laser beam," as well as the mastery of economic issues he displayed at a postelection conference on the nation's finances. In mid-December, an ABC–*Washington Post* survey found that 72 percent of the public approved of Clinton's conduct of the transition, but the glow was gone by inauguration day.[7]

HITTING THE GROUND STUMBLING

Clinton's assumption of office was marred by a pair of contretemps that set the tone for the initial phase of his presidency. During the transition, he let it be known that he planned to appoint a woman to the key cabinet position of attorney general. However, his first nominee had to withdraw when it came out that she had employed two illegal aliens as household help and failed to pay their social security taxes. He finally nominated his eventual appointee in the second week of February. Clinton also announced that he would fulfill one of his less publicized campaign promises by instructing the armed forces to end the policy of barring homosexuals from its ranks. There was a barrage of protest, which continued until Clinton beat a retreat, permitting the military to discharge open homosexuals but instructing it not to ask recruits their sexual orientations.

Much of what could go wrong for Clinton did go wrong in the initial hundred-day period that has come to be taken as a yardstick of how well a new president has adapted to his responsibilities. Congress failed to enact an economic stimulus bill that was central to his legislative program, and reports of real or purported gaffes by the new administration filled the media. One story alleged that flights had been held up at Los Angeles International Airport while a Hollywood hairdresser cut Clinton's hair aboard *Air Force One*. By June, Clinton's approval rating was down by twenty points from its initial 58 percent.

Just as the political world began to write Clinton off, he displayed the capacity for self-correction that has been his hallmark. He added a number of Washington-wise professionals to his White House staff, which he had initially populated with Arkansans and former campaign aides. He also began to turn his political and rhetorical skills to his advantage. By year's end, Clinton had triumphed in a hard-fought budget agreement, given a dazzling presentation of his proposed reform of the health care system to a joint session of Congress, brokered passage of the landmark North American Free Trade Agreement (NAFTA), and presided over a ceremony on the White House lawn in which Israeli premier Yitzhak Rabin and Palestinian Liberation Organization chairman Yasir Arafat signed a peace accord.

In January 1994, Clinton's approval level was back to 58 percent, but the new year proved trouble laden. In January, in a move he would later have cause to regret, Clinton requested the attorney general to appoint an independent counsel to investigate charges that he and Hillary had engaged in fraud in connection with a 1980s Arkansas real estate venture called the Whitewater Development Corporation. Several months later, the judicial panel supervising the inquiry replaced the original appointee with the zealous Kenneth W. Starr, who made it his mission to search for wrongdoing on Clinton's part. Meanwhile, there was another development that was to converge with Starr's probe in Clinton's second term: a former Arkansas state employee named Paula Jones filed a lawsuit against him, accusing him of crude sexual advances toward her while he was governor.

The most damaging blow of the year for Clinton was the failure of his most ambitious policy initiative, a bill guaranteeing health care to all Americans. Clinton had entrusted its drafting to an administration task force under the direction of the first lady. The task force came under attack because it met in secret, thrust a presidential spouse into an unprecedented policymaking role, and excluded Congress and the affected interests from its deliberations. What emerged from the task force was a highly complex 1,300-page bill, which was reported late, enabling its opponents to mobilize against it. The bill died in committee not long before the 1994 congressional election.

Clinton's first two years in the White House were marked by such legislative successes as NAFTA, the creation of a youth volunteer corps, a major deficit-reduction measure, and a law permitting family members to take unpaid leave to attend to children and sick relatives. But what was most apparent to the public was the administration's miscues and failures. In the months leading up to the mid-term congressional election, Clinton was again in public disfavor, with more respondents expressing disapproval than approval of his job performance in every Gallup poll from July 1 to election day.

THE COMEBACK KID

The 1994 GOP congressional election campaign was unprecedented in its effectiveness. Its mastermind was the abrasively entrepreneurial Georgia congressman Newt Gingrich, who persuaded Republican House candidates to commit themselves to a ten-point conservative legislative program called the Contract with America. Gingrich's strategy produced stunning results. The Republicans won control of Congress for the first time in forty years, gaining fifty-two seats in the House and eight in the Senate. No other first-term president since Truman in 1946 had been so crushingly repudiated.

Clinton responded by seeking advice from Dick Morris, a New

York political consultant who had counseled him following his 1980 gubernatorial defeat. Because Morris had become an adviser to such conservative Republicans as North Carolina's Jesse Helms and Mississippi's Trent Lott, Clinton conferred with him in secret. Morris urged Clinton to return to the centrist themes on which he ran in 1992 and position himself as the moderate alternative to the liberal Democrats and conservative Republicans on Capitol Hill.

On January 5, Gingrich convened the newly elected House of Representatives with all of the fanfare of a presidential inauguration. Even before the hundred days he set as his target, the House passed nine of the ten measures in the contract. On April 7, Gingrich declared victory on prime-time television. In an April 18 news conference, Clinton was reduced to lamely asserting that he had not become politically superfluous, because "the Constitution makes me relevant."

The next day circumstances demonstrated that the bully pulpit can make the president a potent force. A massive bomb was detonated at an Oklahoma City federal building, killing 163 people. On April 23, Clinton delivered a moving address at a memorial service for the victims at the site of the destruction. A *Time* magazine poll conducted immediately after his remarks found that his approval level had soared from 49 percent a month earlier to 60 percent.[8]

Over the next several months, it was Gingrich's turn to miscalculate. He pushed through severe spending reductions on education, the environment, and Medicare. Clinton presented himself as the defender of those programs but added that he also favored a balanced budget. When Clinton vetoed the bills mandating the spending cuts, there was an impasse that led to two shutdowns of the federal government. Deprived of needed services, the public sided with Clinton, and Gingrich became deeply unpopular.

As the 1996 election approached, Clinton focused on traditionally Republican issues, calling for more police officers on the streets, stiffer sentences for criminals, and policies designed to reduce teen pregnancy. In a final act of repositioning, Clinton signed a sweeping welfare reform act, offending many liberal Democrats, but following through on his 1992 promise to "end welfare as we know it." Clinton was renominated without opposition. He was reelected with 49 percent of the popular vote to 40 percent for the Republican candidate, the profoundly uncharismatic Bob Dole, and 9 percent for Ross Perot. The Republicans retained control of Congress.

SECOND-TERM REVELATIONS

On Inauguration Day 1997, Clinton launched his second term with a call for a government that "lives within its means, and does more with less."[9] In the weeks that followed, he spelled out an extensive list of low-price-tag legislative initiatives relating to such matters as education, crime, the environment, and welfare. With a booming economy and appealing proposals, Clinton's approval levels over the course of 1997 were the highest of his presidency.

The year that followed was almost totally consumed by scandal and impeachment. Clinton's troubles in 1998 went back to the period three years earlier when he turned the political tables against Newt Gingrich by allowing the government to shut down rather than countenance GOP budget cuts. The White House was relying on unpaid volunteers to do the work of furloughed government employees during the shutdowns, among them a twenty-one-year-old intern named Monica Lewinsky. She and Clinton exchanged flirtatious glances, and she then took matters a step further by revealing her scanty undergarments.

In an act of breathtaking recklessness, Clinton invited Lewinsky to the Oval Office suite, where she performed oral sex on him for the first of ten times over an eighteen-month period. As might have been predicted, Lewinsky did not keep the encounters secret. She discussed them with her psychotherapist, her mother, a number of her friends, and an older co-worker named Linda Tripp. The latter secretly recorded their conversations and made the tapes available to the attorneys in Paula Jones's sexual harassment suit against Clinton and to independent counsel Kenneth Starr.[10]

A week before Clinton was scheduled to give his State of the Union address, reports of the Clinton-Lewinsky affair leaked to the press. He vehemently denied having had sexual relations with Lewinsky both in public statements and in a deposition to Paula Jones's attorneys. The media were awash with speculation about how he would perform when he gave his address.

He hit a home run. Making no reference to his personal circumstances, Clinton hailed the strength of the economy and the recent projections that there was likely to be a budget surplus by fiscal year 1999. Speaking with vigor and self-assurance, Clinton announced an array of proposals, including lowering the age of eligibility for Medicare to fifty-five, providing a number of new educational benefits, and taking steps to ensure the solvency of the social security system.

The address had a dramatically positive effect on public response to Clinton's conduct of the presidency. His approval level rose from 59 percent before his presentation to 67 percent following it. For the remainder of the year, whenever the public was asked to assess Clinton's job performance, large majorities responded favorably, even though the same respondents made it clear that they disapproved of his moral character.[11]

IMPEACHMENT AND ITS AFTERMATH

On receiving Linda Tripp's tapes, independent counsel Kenneth Starr expanded his three-and-a-half-year investigation to Clinton's relationship with Lewinsky. His concern, Starr insisted, was not with Clinton's personal morality, but with whether he had perjured himself by denying that he had been sexually involved with Lewinsky. Starr's office took testimony from Clinton's closest aides, his personal secretary, and even his Secret Service bodyguards, shrinking the zone of confidentiality that hedges the chief executive. In early August, Lewinsky was granted immunity from prosecution for denying her relationship with Clinton under oath and testified before a grand jury about their encounters.

On August 17, it was Clinton's turn to testify. In a videotaped deposition and on nationwide television later in the day, he confessed to his relationship with Lewinsky. Admitting "a critical lapse in judgment,"

Clinton acknowledged that his behavior with Lewinsky was "not appropriate" and that he had "misled people, including even my wife," in an effort to conceal his behavior.

On September 9, Starr submitted a report to Congress, stating eleven possible grounds for impeaching Clinton. Although the balance of forces in the Senate made it highly unlikely that Clinton could be convicted, the conservative Republicans who dominated the House were undeterred. On December 19, following highly partisan hearings, the House voted along party lines to adopt two articles of impeachment, charging Clinton with perjury and obstruction of justice.

Meanwhile, the economy flourished, and congressional Democrats rallied around Clinton, who continued to perform his presidential responsibilities, sometimes with striking effectiveness. In the final stage of the 1998 appropriations negotiations, Clinton endeared himself to his party by using the threat of another government shutdown to compel the Republican congressional majority to accept many of his legislative proposals. He also earned praise for his role in a marathon peace negotiation between representatives of Israel and the Palestinians, personally brokering a breakthrough agreement between the two sides in all-night bargaining sessions.

If ever there was a pyrrhic victory, it was the Republican success in impeaching Bill Clinton. In the first poll after the House vote, the public approval of Clinton's official performance soared to 73 percent, the highest rating of his presidency. By then, the astonishing outcome of the midterm election was in. The partisan balance remained the same in the Senate, but the Democrats gained five seats in the House—the first seat-gain by a party in control of the White House since 1934. House Republicans turned against Gingrich, who announced that he would step down as Speaker and resign from Congress.

Between January 7 and February 12, 1999, the nation was exposed to the spectacle of the chief justice of the United States presiding over the Senate, while House Republicans presented their case against Clinton. Neither article of impeachment received majority support, much less the two-thirds required to remove a president from office.

QUEST FOR A LEGACY

In mid-January, with the Senate trial still in progress, Clinton delivered another bravura State of the Union address, speaking with ease and self-confidence and drawing attention to the flourishing economy. He proposed a lengthy list of initiatives and advocated using a portion of the projected budget surplus to strengthen Social Security and Medicare. But the final two years in office of a lame duck president are not a propitious time for policy breakthroughs, and the 1999 congressional session produced only routine enactments.[12]

In Clinton's final year in office, the focus of the political community inevitably moved from lawmaking to presidential politics. With his customary energy, Clinton remained engaged to the end. He invested particular effort in an attempt to broker a peace agreement in the Middle East, committing to memory the most minute detail of the disagreements between Israel and the Palestine Liberation Organization, but he did not succeed. In his final month in office, Clinton went into high gear. Denying himself sleep, he toured the nation to give farewell speeches and issued a spate of executive orders and pardons of federal criminal offenders, short-circuiting the review processes for such actions. In short, the messiness of the end of his presidency paralleled that of its beginning.

SIGNIFICANCE

Public Communication   At his best, Clinton was an outstanding public communicator. He was at the top of his form when he was on the defensive and in contexts that evoked his Southern Baptist heritage, such as his 1995 address in Oklahoma City. At his worst, he was long-winded, unfocused, and "off message," which is to say that his rhetoric mirrored the rest of his leadership.

Clinton's rhetorical shortcomings were most evident early in his presidency, when he sometimes stepped on his own lines by making multiple statements in the same news cycle. He also was capable of discarding a prepared text and ad libbing his way into political trouble.

For example, in his September 1993 endorsement of New York's first African American mayor, David Dinkins, for reelection, Clinton offhandedly remarked that New Yorkers who voted against Dinkins might well be guilty of unconscious racism. The assertion was harmful to Dinkins, drawing fire even from some of his supporters.[13]

Organizational Capacity   The oxymoronic organization of the Clinton White House has been compared to a little boys' soccer team with no assigned positions and each player chasing the ball. The conclusion of veteran Washington reporter Elizabeth Drew was that the Clinton White House did not fit the existing models of presidential organization. It followed neither the "spokes in the wheel" principle, in which the president coordinates his own advisory system, nor the hierarchical model in which the president employs a strong chief of staff. Instead, Clinton's key aides moved freely from issue to issue, and Clinton spent much of his time in meetings in which participation was a function of who showed up.[14]

Despite the freedom that Clinton afforded his staff, he was not the kind of president who was beloved by his aides. His associates found him difficult to advise, because of the inconstancy of his policy positions. He also was subject to fits of anger, and became a source of embarrassment to those of his aides who stood behind his denial of sexual involvement with Monica Lewinsky. It is no wonder that the memoirs of Clinton's former aides are uniformly ambivalent about him.[15]

After the chaotic opening months of his presidency, Clinton managed to find staff members who were able to channel his centrifugal tendencies, for example his second chief of staff, Leon Panetta, and Panetta's successor, Erskine Bowles. Still, there was never a point at which Clinton established a principle of organization that conserved his energy and mitigated the tendency of his administration's policies to exist mainly in his own mind.

Political Skill   As one might expect of someone whose adult life was devoted to politics, Clinton was capable of impressive displays of political skill. He was also susceptible to astonishing missteps and miscalculations. The unevenness of Clinton's performance was a partial function of his readiness to change his policies in response to political exigencies and his tendency to overreach himself under favorable political circumstances.

The Clinton presidency was marked by numerous political successes. The most impressive of them occurred when he was on the defensive, as he was in 1995 when he bested the forces of Newt Gingrich. His most notable failure was the defeat of his 1993 health initiative, which is additionally instructive because it might have been avoided if Clinton had taken a lesson from Carter's effort to win support for his similarly complex and politically vulnerable energy initiative.

Vision No American president has exceeded Clinton in his grasp of policy specifics, especially in the domestic sphere, but his was a mastery that did not translate into a clearly defined point of view. Why that was the case is not fully evident, but several factors were at work. Clinton's intelligence enabled him to envisage complexity; his verbal facility permitted him to express that complexity; and his intensely political nature led him to modify his positions from context to context.

This is not to suggest that Clinton's policies lacked a broad pattern. He tended to take the middle ground on contested issues, and he had faith in government, particularly as a catalyst to private endeavor. There could be no greater contrast than that between a Bill Clinton, whose positions were ever open to modification, and a Ronald Reagan, who was vague about the details of policies but stood for a handful of broad verities.

Cognitive Style There can be no doubt about Clinton's impressive intelligence. He read omnivorously, alternating between demanding works on public policy and fiction, sometimes while listening to briefings or watching television. He was a sponge for facts and had an ability to synthesize complex material. On one occasion at Oxford, he was given two weeks to prepare an essay on political pluralism in the

Soviet Union. Consulting some thirty books and articles, he wrote a paper that his instructor considered a model of clarity and kept as a teaching tool. At Yale Law School Clinton was famed for skipping class, reading a friend's notes just before an examination, and writing a better exam than the note-taker.[16]

There was a less positive side to Clinton's cognitive style, however. While he was a far cry from a Jimmy Carter, whose tendency was to amass specifics, he also seemed to lack the ability of an Eisenhower to cut to the core of a problem or make a balanced net assessment of a complex issue. Instead, Clinton fit the description of the lawyer who masters issues with the speed of oil covering water, but sometimes does so at the same depth.

Emotional Intelligence   The politically gifted, emotionally challenged William Jefferson Clinton provides yet another indication of the fundamental importance of emotional intelligence in the modern presidency. Clinton's political gifts enabled him to thwart the Republican effort to remove him from office, but his psychic shortcomings were debilitating. Assertions about the impact of an incumbent or recent president are necessarily provisional, but Clinton seems certain to be recognized for moving the Democratic party to the center of the political spectrum and for many incremental policy departures. Yet he is also likely to be remembered as a politically talented underachiever, whose White House experience provides a reminder that in the absence of emotional soundness, the American presidency is a problematic instrument of democratic governance.

The acts of terrorism of September 11, 2001, mark a pivot point in the presidency of George W. Bush. Before the assaults on the World Trade Center and the Pentagon, Bush had seemed out of his depth as chief executive. Within days, he had become dramatically more presidential, steeping himself in policy deliberations and addressing the nation and world with force and vigor. Here he is shown exhorting rescue workers at the site of the destroyed World Trade Center, assuring them that "the people who knocked these buildings down will hear all of us soon."

(White House photo by Eric Draper)

CHAPTER 13

George W. Bush and the Politics of Agenda Control

INTERVIEWER: Can you name the president of Chechnya?

BUSH: No, can you?

INTERVIEWER: And the prime minister of India?

BUSH: The new prime minister of India is (pause) . . . No.

—GEORGE W. BUSH,
"POP QUIZ," NOVEMBER 4, 1999

Terrorist attacks can shake the foundations of our biggest buildings, but they cannot touch the foundation of America. These acts shatter steel, but they cannot dent the steel of American resolve.

—GEORGE W. BUSH,
ADDRESS TO THE AMERICAN PEOPLE, SEPTEMBER 11, 2001

We're never going to get people all in agreement about force and the use of force. But action—confident action that will yield positive results—provides . . . a slipstream into which reluctant nations and leaders can get behind and show themselves that . . . something positive has happened toward peace.

—GEORGE W. BUSH,
INTERVIEW WITH BOB WOODWARD,
IN WOODWARD, *Bush at War*, 2002

The presidency is said to be an office in which the incumbent may grow or merely swell. If ever there was a chief executive to whom the former applies, it is George W. Bush. Arriving at the White House with only modest experience in public affairs, Bush took a minimalist approach to his responsibilities before the terrorist acts of September 11, 2001. Rising to the challenge, he went on to preside with far greater authority and assertiveness over an administration that has gone to great lengths to put its stamp on the national and international policy agendas, but been highly controversial in the policies it advances.

FORMATIVE YEARS

George W. Bush was born on July 6, 1946, in New Haven, Connecticut, where his war-hero father was a Yale undergraduate.[1] In contrast to George H. W. Bush, whose claim to be a Texan is belied by his Eastern accent and diffident manner, George W. Bush is very much a product of the Lone Star State. Whereas the elder Bush attended a private day school in the wealthy New York suburb of Greenwich, Connecticut, the younger Bush went to public school in the West Texas town of Midland, where oil was the dominant economic force and the ambience was that of tract houses, little league baseball, and easy informality. Acknowledging the difference between his Connecticut-bred father and himself, Bush has commented that while his father is mild mannered and avoids confrontation, he has the brashness and directness of a typical Texan.[2]

In 1953, the Bush family was devastated by the death of George's three-year-old sister Robin from leukemia. The seven-year-old George, who had no idea that his sister was gravely ill, was stunned when he was taken out of school and told that his sister was dead. His mother sank into a depression. His father was frequently away from home on business, and the son sought to be his mother's consoler, playing the clown and developing the bantering manner that is his adult hallmark.[3]

After completing elementary school in Texas, George followed in his father's footsteps, attending two intellectually rarified schools in the Northeast—Phillips Academy in Andover, Massachusetts, and Yale University. He had unhappy experiences at both. At Andover, he wrote a composition about the wrenching experience of learning of his sister's death, but used an inappropriate word to refer to the tears he shed. He was deeply hurt when the instructor ignored the content of the paper and criticized him for the way it was written. At Yale, he was offended when the college chaplain commented that his father had been beaten by "a better man" in his 1964 run for the Senate. The ironic effect of Bush's exposure to Andover and Yale was to alienate him from what he came to think of as the "intellectual snobs" who set the tone of these institutions.

Bush was an indifferent student in prep school and college, but he stood out for his social skills and popularity. At Andover, he became the football team's head cheerleader and "high commissioner" of a tongue-in-cheek stickball league. At Yale, he won ready admission to a fraternity that was legendary for its parties and beer consumption after revealing that he could name all of the fifty-odd fellow applicants. (None of the others could name more than a half dozen.) Bush went on to become the fraternity's president and to win admission to Yale's most exclusive secret society, returning to Texas with friendships that were to serve him well when he ran for public office.

Bush's freshman year at Yale saw the beginning of the American military intervention in Vietnam. By his senior year, the campus was wracked with antiwar protest. The political ferment of the 1960s largely passed Bush by, but he was far from indifferent to politics. In 1964, the eighteen-year-old Bush took part in his father's race for the Senate, delighting in the hoopla and camaraderie of campaign politics. By his mid-thirties, he had worked on the campaigns of two other senatorial aspirants and participated in his father's unsuccessful campaigns for the Senate in 1970 and the Republican presidential nomination in 1980.

After Yale, Bush spent two years in the Texas Air National

Guard and went on to Harvard Business School, graduating in 1974 with an MBA. He then returned to Midland, first holding an entry-level position in the oil industry and then forming an oil exploration company with funds raised through family connections. In 1978, the congressman in the district that included Midland announced that he was retiring, and Bush entered the race to succeed him. He won the Republican nomination, but lost the general election to a conservative Democrat, who portrayed him as a carpetbagger from the Northeast and a representative of his party's moderate wing. Nevertheless, he received 47 percent of the vote in a traditionally Democratic congressional district and learned a lesson he took to heart when he re-entered electoral politics—that of refusing to be outflanked from the right.

There is another theme in Bush's early adulthood. For most of the two decades after he graduated from college, he was conspicuous as the underachieving son of a superachieving father. He drank to excess and had a devil-may-care lifestyle that was marked by periodic alcohol-related scrapes. Gradually, his life came together. In 1977, he married the level-headed librarian Laura Welch. In 1981, he became a father. During the next several years, he experienced a spiritual awakening and became a regular reader of the Bible. Then, after waking up with a fierce hangover on the morning of his fortieth birthday, he swore off alcohol, anchoring his resolve in his Christian faith.

PRE-PRESIDENTIAL POLITICAL CAREER

Oil prices plunged in the 1980s, and Bush's company went in the red. Because of favorable provisions in the tax code, he was able to sell it for $2.2 million to a firm specializing in takeovers. The sale coincided with the initial stage of his father's efforts to become the 1988 Republican presidential nominee. Bush moved his family to Washington and became codirector, along with the veteran political consultant Lee Atwater, of his father's campaign. Bush's account of the part he played in the campaign provides insight into his managerial philosophy:

> I was a loyalty enforcer and a listening ear. When someone wanted to talk to the candidate but couldn't, I was a good substitute; people felt that if they said something to me, it would probably get to my dad. It did only if I believed it was important for him to know. A candidate needs to focus on the big picture, his message and agenda, and let others worry about most of the details.[4]

After his father's election, Bush returned to Texas, where a promising business opportunity came his way. He was asked to organize an investment group to buy the Texas Rangers, a second-tier major league baseball team that had come on the market. Bush was an ideal fundraiser. He had never struck it rich in the oil business, but he had been successful in raising capital, and it did not hurt that his father was president of the United States. He assembled a consortium of investors that purchased the team, naming him its managing general partner. With new leadership and greater resources, the team prospered, hiring star players and finally making its way to the playoffs. Bush proved to be an excellent front man. He became a popular speaker at meetings of Texas business, civic, and athletic groups, and was regularly seen on television, rooting for the team from the sidelines. Before long he was a state celebrity.

Baseball was Bush's political springboard. It publicized him, demonstrated that he could manage a complex organization, and gave him financial independence. After his father was defeated for re-election in 1992, Bush felt free to resume his own political career. The next year, he entered the running to become the 1994 Republican opponent of Ann Richards, the state's feisty, popular Democratic governor. Assembling a strikingly professional campaign staff, he raised an impressive war chest and handily won his party's nomination.

Bush's next hurdle was the outspoken Richards, who had

famously declared at the 1988 Democratic National Convention that the senior George Bush had been born "with a silver foot in his mouth." Richards derided the younger Bush, calling him "Shrub." Rather than replying in kind, Bush ran an issue-driven campaign. Taking as a warning his father's failure to enunciate a clear policy vision during his time as president, Bush ran on a small number of explicitly stated issues that already had support in the Democratically controlled legislature—greater local control of education, welfare reform, stiffer penalties for juvenile offenders, and limitations on the right to litigate against businesses. He campaigned vigorously, stayed on message, and ignored Richards's provocations, winning with 53 percent of the two-party vote.

Bush conducted his governorship in a whirl of face-to-face negotiation and persuasion. Even before the election results were in, he forged a bond with the legislature's most influential Democrat. Upon taking office, he formally proposed the program on which he had campaigned. By the end of the first legislative session, he had advanced that program in dozens of meetings with lawmakers of both parties. All four of his signature measures were enacted. Although he had gone along with compromises in their provisions, Bush declared victory and went on to run for a second term in 1998.[5] He was re-elected with a record 69 percent of the vote, drawing strongly from such traditionally Democratic groups as women and minorities.

As governor, Bush was sweeping in his acts of delegation. A study of his Texas schedule found that when a report was delivered to him on a tragedy in which a number of Texas college students had died in a bonfire, he read neither the report itself nor its executive summary, leaving it to his aides to highlight a few paragraphs of its conclusions. Even in the sensitive realm of capital punishment, Bush relied heavily on the recommendations of his aides, reducing the time he spent on reviews of death sentences from thirty to fifteen minutes over the course of his governorship. There was a laid-back quality to his management of time as governor, including an extended midday break during which he worked out and had lunch.[6] It was by no means obvious from his gubernatorial style that he was burning to seek the presidency.

TO THE WHITE HOUSE

As the 2000 presidential primary season approached, it was evident that the Republican party needed a strong presidential candidate if it was not to go down in defeat as it had in 1992 and 1996. Bush's name recognition and Texas record made him an instant front-runner, a status that enabled him to raise an unprecedented $90 million in campaign funds. Bush suffered a stinging blow in the New Hampshire primary, when he was defeated by Arizona senator John McCain, but he bounced back, clinching the nomination in March with victories in California, New York, and seven other states. Vice President Al Gore locked in the Democratic nomination the same week, and the two men girded themselves for the longest presidential campaign in American history.

Just as he had in Texas, Bush took pains to enunciate a clear-cut program. As he put it in his campaign autobiography, "The first challenge of leadership . . . is to outline a clear vision and agenda."[7] Included in his program were proposals for sharply reduced taxes, military modernization, Social Security and health care reform, and measures targeted to disadvantaged groups that fell under what he referred to as "compassionate conservatism." Principal among them were a testing-based educational program designed to identify schools in which students were failing to learn basic skills and to enable their pupils to transfer to good schools, and a "faith-based initiative" that would channel federal funds through the church-based charities that provide many of the social services in high-poverty areas.[8]

Bush said nothing in the campaign that anticipated his administration's major military involvements in Afghanistan and Iraq, its commitment to rebuild those nations, and its later initiatives in the Middle East and Africa. Instead, he declared his opposition to a globally expansive foreign policy, criticizing the use of the American military in "nation building." The danger of an activist foreign policy, he declared, was that the United States would be disliked for its arrogance, whereas "if we're a humble nation, . . . they'll welcome us."[9]

Whatever the merits of Bush's campaign proposals, it was widely held that he was likely to be defeated by Gore. The vice president represented the incumbent administration in a period of prosperity, he had far more governmental experience than Bush, and he was a formidable debater. But the economy began to sag, Bush held his own in the presidential debates, and Gore ran an unimpressive campaign. As Election Day approached, the polls showed Bush and Gore running neck and neck. What resulted was one of the closest and most controversial election outcomes in the nation's history. Gore ran ahead in the popular vote by a fraction of 1 percent, and there was a close division in the all-important electoral vote.

The outcome of the election hinged on Florida, where Bush and Gore were in a dead heat and there was a bewildering array of controversies about the mechanics of the voting. There ensued a thirty-six-day impasse over the Florida vote count, which was broken by a five-to-four ruling of the United States Supreme Court that made Bush the winner. On the evening of December 13, Gore conceded. Within the hour, Bush made his victory speech, doing so in the chamber of the Texas House of Representatives. He had chosen that venue, he explained, "because it has been home to bipartisan cooperation," adding that "the spirit of cooperation we have seen in this hall is what is needed in Washington, D.C."[10]

A BLAND BEGINNING

Given the intensely controversial conclusion of the 2000 presidential campaign, Bush might have been expected to assume the presidency in a firestorm of contention. In fact, the political system's healing processes had set in. The media coverage of Bush's inauguration focused on the dignified pomp of the occasion, not the legitimacy of the process that led up to it. Bush seemed at ease as he took the oath of office, and the fourteen-minute inaugural address written by his talented speech writer Michael Gerson was free of apologetics.

The address was widely praised for its eloquence. Taking its theme from Bush's frequent campaign references to "compassion," it declared that "the ambitions of some Americans are limited by failing schools and hidden prejudice and the circumstances of their birth," promising to "reclaim America's schools, before ignorance and apathy claim more young lives." The speech enumerated the issues on which Bush campaigned, and went on to quote a rhetorical question asked of Thomas Jefferson by one of his contemporaries during the dark days of the American Revolution: "Do you not think an angel rides in the whirlwind and directs this storm?" It concluded with the questioner's assertion that "an angel still rides in the whirlwind and directs this storm."[11]

The effect of this moving imagery was blunted by Bush's delivery, which lacked force and was further weakened by his propensity to stumble over words and pause in mid-phrase rather than at logical breaking points. By the time Bush arrived at the address's peroration, his halting presentation made it obvious that he was reading a script, rather than speaking in a voice that was natural to him. Bush was more fluent on unscripted occasions, but then there was the risk that his lack of experience would lead him to misspeak, as he did in an April 26, 2001, interview in which he stated that the United States was committed to do "whatever it takes" to defend Taiwan from attack by the People's Republic of China. In fact, it had long been American policy to remain vague about how to respond to such a contingency, and Bush had not intended to signal a policy departure. The State Department was compelled to engage in damage control, saying that Bush had meant only to highlight the seriousness with which the United States took its relationship with Taiwan.[12]

There was another problem with Bush's early public communications—their infrequency. Bush never addressed the nation from the Oval Office until the night of September 11, 2001. He never convened a full-fledged, prime-time news conference until a month after that date. He periodically fielded questions from reporters, but did so in hastily convened exchanges with the White House press pool, avoiding pre-announced conferences in which he would have faced the heavyweights of the media. Bush also put little emphasis on his capacity as the nation's symbolic leader. Thus, he made no statement to the nation when the city of Cincinnati was wracked with racial unrest, and he did not join in the welcoming ceremony for the crew of a reconnaissance plane that had been held captive in China for eleven days. Three months into the Bush presidency, the *Washington Post*'s David Broder devoted a column to Bush's neglect of the bully pulpit, saying that the American people had been left without a "clear definition" of their new leader.[13]

Yet in other respects Bush exhibited impressive strengths—for instance, in organizing his presidency and advancing his program. He made his most significant organizational choice—even before the Republican National Convention made him his party's official nominee—by selecting as his running mate the Washington-wise, strategically shrewd Dick Cheney, someone who would compensate for his own lack of national experience rather than serving mainly to balance the ticket or share the burdens of campaigning.

With Cheney as a source of advice, Bush appointed an experienced White House staff and cabinet, not waiting until the resolution of the Florida electoral dispute to engage in transition planning. Bush's appointees included veterans of the Ford, Reagan, and first Bush presidencies, as well as two of his longtime Texas aides, political strategist Karl Rove and communications adviser Karen Hughes. His national security team was particularly well seasoned: Secretary of State Colin Powell had been chairman of the Joint Chiefs of Staff and national security adviser, Secretary of Defense Donald Rumsfeld had served before in the same capacity, and national security adviser Condoleezza Rice had been a White House foreign policy adviser.

In advancing his legislative agenda, Bush had notable successes not only by practicing the bipartisanship that he lauded in his victory speech, but also by dint of rigorous partisanship. On the bipartisan front, Bush began his presidency by launching what the media referred to as a "charm offensive," meeting with a wide range of Democrats. He put particular effort into wooing Massachusetts senator Edward Kennedy, whose cooperation was necessary to pass Bush's education bill, by inviting the Kennedy family to the White House for a screening of a film on John F. Kennedy's handling of the Cuban missile crisis and by naming the Justice Department building for Robert Kennedy. By the end of the year, Congress enacted an education bill with provisions favored by legislators on both sides of the aisle. In praising the outcome, Kennedy declared, "President Bush was there every step of the way."[14]

But earlier in the year, Bush had concentrated single-mindedly on mobilizing the congressional Republicans and a handful of Democrats to enact a record tax cut. Four months into his presidency, however, his administration's hard-edged partisanship boomeranged. On May 24, Vermont senator James Jeffords, a moderate Republican, announced that he was resigning from his party. Bush and the Republican congressional leaders had sought to punish the Vermont senator for voting for a smaller tax reduction than Bush had called for by eliminating a dairy program that was vital to his state. Jeffords's defection placed the Democrats in control of the closely divided Senate.

By the time of the fateful events of September 11, 2001, there had been periodic signs that Bush was growing into the job. In the episode in which an American reconnaissance aircraft was forced down by China, for example, his first response had been to issue a peremptory demand that the plane be returned and the crew released, but he backed off and remained patient while negotiations went on to release the crew. And in August, he gave a thoughtful address to the nation on the complex and controversial issue of government funding of embryonic stem-cell research, making it evident that he had begun to recognize the importance of rhetoric in presidential leadership. Still, there was a widespread view in the political community that he was not up to the demands of the nation's highest office.

TERROR AND TRANSFORMATION

Bush was visiting a Sarasota, Florida, elementary school to promote his administration's "No Child Left Behind" education bill on the morning of September 11, 2001, when he was informed that an airliner had crashed into the North Tower of the World Trade Center in New York City. When a second airliner flew into the South Tower fifteen minutes later, it became evident that the first collision had been no accident. By mid-morning, a third plane crashed into the Pentagon, and the twin towers of the World Trade Center collapsed. Before leaving the school, Bush read a statement declaring that "terrorism against our nation will not stand."[15]

Because there was concern that he would be targeted by terrorists, Bush was flown to an air force base in Louisiana, where he made another public statement, and then to the control center of the Strategic Air Command in Nebraska, where he presided by electronic means over a meeting of the National Security Council. At the meeting the director of the Central Intelligence Agency reported that the attacks were almost certainly the work of al-Qaeda, an Afghanistan-based terrorist organization that had been behind other acts of terrorism directed at the United States. Bush then returned to the White House, where he addressed the nation from the Oval Office, asserting that "these acts of mass murder were intended to frighten our nation into chaos and retreat[,] but they have failed," and that the United States would "make no distinction between the terrorists who committed these acts and those who harbor them."[16]

In the chaotic first day of the episode, Bush came across as less than completely self-assured. He read his statements from Florida and Louisiana mechanically and did not seem fully at ease as he delivered his September 11 address to the nation. He then underwent a transformation. On September 14, he delivered a deeply emotional tribute to the victims of the terrorist attacks at a memorial service at Washington's National Cathedral. He then flew to New York City, where he inspected the wreckage of the World Trade Center, using a bullhorn to address the rescue workers. When members of the audience shouted that they could not hear him, Bush replied, "I can hear you. The rest of the world hears you[,] and the people who knocked these buildings down will hear all of us soon!"[17]

In the weeks that followed, Bush became a compelling public presence. On September 20, he made a forceful presentation to Congress, giving the Taliban regime in Afghanistan an ultimatum to turn over the al-Qaeda leadership to the United States and close down its terrorist camps. Three weeks later, he gave a similarly effective address to the United Nations. Most impressive was his October 11 prime-time news conference in the East Room of the White House. Responding in depth to questions, he radiated a sense of composure and made evident his detailed mastery of what his administration had begun to refer to as the War on Terror.

Just as Bush's conduct of his responsibilities improved dramatically, so too did the American public's ratings of his job performance, which underwent a near perpendicular spike in the aftermath of September 11. In a Gallup Poll fielded the week before the attacks on the World Trade Center and the Pentagon, Bush's approval level was at low ebb for his presidency—51 percent. Two weeks later, it had soared to 90 percent, the record high in Gallup presidential approval ratings.

Meanwhile, members of the political community formed markedly more positive views of Bush's leadership qualities. Before September 11, even a good number of his supporters had not been persuaded that he was up to his responsibilities. Thereafter, even many of his critics concluded that he had been underestimated, a view that extended to other nations. On October 20, for example, a columnist for the influential *Frankfurter Allgemeine* commented that Bush had grown into his job "before our eyes," comparing him to another president who rose to the demands of his times following an unpromising start—Harry S. Truman.[18]

One reason Bush improved his mastery of policy in the weeks following September 11 was the depth of his immersion in policy deliberations. In the month between the bombings of the World Trade Center and the Pentagon and his bravura October 11 press conference, Bush met with his NSC twenty-four times. These meetings, moreover, were far from pro forma. In the September 12 meeting, for example, there was a sharp debate that foreshadowed the 2003 war in Iraq. Vice President Cheney and Defense Secretary Rumsfeld advocated attacking not just al-Qaeda, but also nations they viewed as sponsors of terrorism, notably Iraq. Secretary of State Powell disagreed, however, arguing that the American people would readily back action against the terrorists linked to the September 11 attacks, but would be puzzled by a proposal to attack Iraq. Bush put a halt to the debate, indicating that this was not the time to resolve that issue.[19]

In early October, the Afghan regime let it be known that it would not surrender the al-Qaeda leadership, and the United States and its ally Great Britain began an intensive bombing campaign. Later in the month, U.S. Special Forces entered Afghanistan and began to provide military support to the anti-Taliban Northern Alliance. By November 13, the Northern Alliance had occupied the Afghan capital of Kabul, and in early December, the last major Taliban stronghold surrendered. When the Gallup organization polled the public at the end of December, Bush's approval level was a towering 86 percent.

IRAQ AND THE ECONOMY

Bush had postponed a decision on whether to target Iraq in the War on Terror in the September 12, 2001, NSC meeting, but Iraq came into his cross-hairs in his January 2002 State of the Union address. Anticipating the doctrine of preemption that his administration would formally promulgate later in the year, Bush declared that he would not "wait on events" while "the world's most destructive weapons" were acquired by "the world's most dangerous regimes." One such regime, he specified, was Iraq, which he grouped with Iran and North Korea in what he described as an "axis of evil."[20]

Bush's speech sent out shock waves. Whereas his response to

September 11 had been favorably received, there was widespread criticism at home and abroad of his axis-of-evil locution. Some of it was prompted by a belief that Bush had lumped together nations that were very different in terms of whether and to what extent they posed threats; some was directed at the term "evil," which led critics to worry about whether the president's intense personal commitment to evangelical Christianity was leading him to advance an inappropriately moralistic foreign policy.

Despite the attention Bush's assertions about the global situation received, a good half of his address was devoted to his domestic program. "We have clear priorities," he declared, "and we must act at home with the same purpose and resolve we have shown overseas."[21] The actions he proposed included reform of Social Security, Medicare, and welfare, and passage of legislation designed to advance free trade and reduce the nation's reliance on oil imports. Above all, Bush promoted his preferred policy for stimulating the economy— further tax reduction. Acknowledging that the economy was in a recession, he declared that the "way out" was to provide "tax relief so people have more money to spend," invoking the controversial "supply-side" economic theory that his father had once derided as "voodoo economics."

Bush's address presaged two major preoccupations of the second and third years of his presidency: his efforts to come to terms with Iraq and stimulate the sluggish economy. Bush himself was sufficiently dissatisfied with his administration's performance on the economic front to accept the resignations of his secretary of the treasury and top economic adviser in December 2002. But neither his displeasure with his advisers nor the continuing weaknesses in the economy shook his confidence in the merits of reducing taxes, and by the spring of 2003 he had signed the third of the major tax cuts sponsored by his administration. In so doing, he was undeterred by the contention of budgetary specialists that he was depriving the government of the revenues that would be needed later in the decade to pay for the retirement needs of the first wave of the post–World War II baby boom generation.

Bush's reference to Iraq was the prelude to a procession of actions directed at Saddam Hussein's regime. Diplomacy prevailed in the fall of 2002, when the administration persuaded the United Nations Security Council to enact a resolution insisting that Iraq destroy any weapons of mass destruction it might have and admit United Nations inspectors to establish that it had done so. Early the following year, the administration turned to military action, attempting without success to persuade the Security Council to authorize the use of force on the grounds that Iraq had failed to comply with the U.N. demand. Then, in the face of substantial opposition at home and abroad, it launched an invasion of Iraq, proceeding with Great Britain as its principal ally.

The Anglo-American assault on Iraq began on March 20, 2003; on April 6 American troops took control of Baghdad, and on May 1 Bush announced the end of "major combat operations."[22] But the situation in Iraq remained highly unsettled, and the number of American troops killed in the guerilla action that followed Bush's declaration exceeded the number who died during the period of "major" fighting by the end of the summer of 2003. Meanwhile, the prospect for full economic recovery remained uncertain, and the American public's assessment of Bush's performance, which had surged during the war in Iraq, receded. Whatever the fate of his presidency, however, it was evident that George W. Bush had molded a distinctive and often strikingly effective leadership style.

SIGNIFICANCE

Public Communication   In the first eight months of his presidency, Bush seemed insensitive to the importance of public communication in presidential leadership. He appeared reluctant to address the public; when he did so, his delivery was unpersuasive; and when he was unscripted, was error-prone. In the wake of the acts of terror of September 11, 2001, Bush became a rhetorical activist, addressing the public regularly, forcefully, and sometimes eloquently and handling himself far more effectively in extemporaneous contexts.

As the immediacy of the crisis receded, Bush sometimes slipped into his former plodding manner, especially when he read routine remarks, but he remained effective in major addresses. Meanwhile, his ad-lib communications continued to be more effective than they had been in the pre-9/11 period. Bush also developed a punchy, vernacular style of stump speaking that undoubtedly contributes to his sustained high approval ratings.

There are distinct limitations to Bush's ability to win support, for reasons that fall as much under the heading of "vision" as "public communication." His rhetorical manner, coupled with the content of those of his messages in which he asserts his determination to take such controversial actions as the intervention in Iraq, has produced a visceral aversion toward him for many American liberals, an antipathy that is widely shared elsewhere in the world. In a sense, Bush has proven to be a mirror image of Bill Clinton, who was as passionately disliked by some of Bush's most fervent supporters and viewed very favorably by many of his opponents.

Organizational Capacity   Organizational leadership is one of the strengths of the nation's first MBA president. Bush has chosen strong associates; he excels at rallying his subordinates; and he encourages diversity of advice. Because avoiding public disagreement is a watchword of the Bush administration, its deliberative processes are not well documented. What evidence there is points to a presidency in which bureaucratic politics simmer beneath the surface, most notably in foreign affairs, where there has been a scarcely veiled conflict between the supporters of Secretary of Defense Rumsfeld and Secretary of State Powell. An unknown in the George W. Bush adviser system is the extent to which the prudent George H. W. Bush provides his son with off-the-record advice. The senior Bush has commented that "historians will be very interested" in what he and the younger Bush discuss, but "they've got to wait."[23]

Preliminary insights into the inner workings of the Bush presidency can be gained from Bob Woodward's account of the administration's post–September 11 decision making. Woodward reports, for example, that Powell and Rumsfeld expressed their disagreements more sharply at meetings from which Bush was absent than in those at which he was present, which suggests that Bush may sometimes be shielded from instructive debate. Woodward also describes instances on August 5 and September 2, 2002, in which Powell arranged to meet privately with Bush and national security adviser Rice in order to register his disagreement with the hawkish proposals of Rumsfeld and Vice President Cheney.[24] There was a similar instance on September 2, 2003, in which Powell circumvented the administration's hawks by meeting with Bush to make the case for seeking a United Nations–sanctioned military force in Iraq, having established that he had the agreement of the chairman of the Joint Chiefs of Staff.[25] The shortcoming of policy making by end run is that it places a premium on an adviser's bureaucratic skills and not just the merits of his or her recommendations.

Such practices would have been anathema to the modern president who was most gifted at organizational leadership, Dwight Eisenhower. "I know of only one way in which you can be sure you have done your best to make a wise decision," the former supreme allied commander once remarked: "That is to get all of the responsible policy makers with their different viewpoints in front of you, and listen to them debate. I do not believe in bringing them in one at a time, and therefore being more impressed by the most recent one you hear than the earlier ones."[26]

Political Skill   Much like his Texas predecessors Sam Rayburn and Lyndon Johnson, the congenitally gregarious George W. Bush is a political natural, especially when it comes to face-to-face politics. It is sometimes argued that Bush tends to view politics in rigidly black-and-white terms, but this is belied by the flexibility of his political tactics. Thus he worked easily with the Democratic majority in the Texas legislature during his governorship, but in Washington alternated between rigorous partisanship and cross-party coalition building as circumstances permitted.

Unlike Rayburn and Johnson, Bush is not a creature of Washington politics, but he has compensated for that limitation by appointing highly experienced subordinates, including the same director of congressional relations that his father had employed. Still, Bush and his aides have sometimes been less than sure-footed in the international arena. This was particularly evident in the lead-up to the Iraq war, when the Bush administration relied on shifting arguments and blatant economic inducements in its unsuccessful efforts to win broad support for immediate military action.

Vision When it comes to the "vision thing," George W. Bush is the virtual antithesis of his highly pragmatic father, whom he has faulted for not building on the momentum of victory in the 1991 Gulf War to rack up domestic accomplishments on which he could campaign for re-election. George W. Bush *does* have the "vision thing," not because he is an aficionado of policy, but because he holds that if a leader does not set his own goals, others will set them for him. The question in the case of the younger Bush is the viability of his vision, whether that of relying on tax cuts to stimulate the economy or of mounting a war in Iraq in the face of domestic and international opposition. The ultimate result of these policies remains to be seen.

Cognitive Style Bush's ostensible cognitive failings are a staple of late-night television humor, but it is evident from his remarks on matters that engage him that he has ample native intelligence. In the words of one member of Congress, who remarked on Bush's far greater mastery of policy after September 11, "He's as smart as he wants to be."[27] To the extent that Bush's presidential performance suffers from his cognitive style, his problem may be that of lacking intellectual curiosity, a shortcoming that blunts a president's sensitivity to emerging issues.

There also are cognitive implications to Bush's management style, which leads him to rely heavily on subordinates to structure his options. Having been a front man in his business career, his tendency is to do better at outlining his administration's positions than elucidating their subtleties. In this he contrasts with a leader with whom he periodically shares a podium, British prime minister Tony Blair. At a March 27, 2003, joint "press availability," for example, Bush and Blair responded to questions about how long the fighting in Iraq would continue. Bush was laconic and uninformative, contenting himself with such assertions as "however long it takes," whereas Blair was expansive and analytic, reviewing the roots of the conflict, its global ramifications, and its likely aftermath. All told, Blair rather than Bush provided a model of the intellectual suppleness one might hope for in the American chief executive.[28]

Emotional Intelligence   By the litmus of emotional intelligence, the heavy-drinking, young George W. Bush was too volatile and unreliable to be a promising prospect for a responsible public position. It would not be surprising if a man who had abused alcohol until early middle age and had abruptly gone on the wagon proved to be an emotional tinder box, but Bush's pre-presidential job and his early presidency were not marred by emotional excesses. Woodward's investigation is again instructive. As it turns out, there are no episodes reported in *Bush at War* in which Bush is shown to have acted out of uncontrolled passion. Indeed, Bush explained that he expected national security adviser Rice "to take the edge off" any such impulses on his part, adding that "she's good at that."[29] In the case of Iraq, an extensive interview granted to NBC news anchor Tom Brokaw not long after the fall of Baghdad is illuminating. Bush came across as thoughtful and good humored, neither boasting at the rapidity of the military victory nor revealing defensiveness in the face of his administration's many critics. In short, whatever the merits of his actions, his emotions appear to have been well in hand.

CHAPTER 14

Lessons from the Modern Presidency

The executive branch of our government is like a chameleon. To a startling degree it reflects the character and personality of the President.

—CLARK M. CLIFFORD, 1972

The highly personalized nature of the modern American presidency makes the strengths and weaknesses of the White House incumbent of the utmost importance. It places a premium on the ability of chief executives to get the most out of their strong points and compensate for their limitations. It also places a great value on the ability of Americans to select presidents with attributes that serve well in the Oval Office. Two premises underlie this review of the modern presidential experience: presidents who steep themselves in the record of their predecessors will be better equipped for their responsibilities as a result of doing so; and members of the public who are able to place presidential contenders in a historical context will be able to make wiser electoral choices.

In seeking to provide such a context, I avoided two common approaches to assessing American presidents. I have abstained from judging the ends that presidents pursue so as better to focus on their means. I have avoided ranking presidents, because there is at least as much to be learned from their failures and limitations as from their successes and strengths. Each of the preceding chapters consists of two narratives: an account of its subject's background, leadership style, and White House actions, followed by a commentary on the implications of his leadership qualities for the conduct of the presidency. I conclude with summary observations about each subject and general remarks on the qualities that shape presidential performance.

SUMMING UP THE PRESIDENTS

- Of all of the modern chief executives, Franklin Roosevelt lends himself least well to a balance sheet of positive and negative qualities. FDR had towering strengths in the realms of rhetoric, superb political skills, and an unequalled capacity to radiate optimism and confidence. He provides endless positive lessons, but even he is a source of warnings. His chaotic organizational arrangements made the influence of his subordinates as much a function of their bureaucratic wiles as the merits of their recommendations. His weakness as a conceptualizer contributed to the incoherence of his administration's effort to combat the Depression. Even his astonishing self-assurance had a negative side, sometimes leading him to act on untested intuitions.

  Whatever his limitations, it would be difficult to overstate the historical importance of Franklin Roosevelt. Consider a possibility that nearly become a reality. Just two weeks before Roosevelt was to take office, a gunman sprayed his car with bullets, narrowly missing him. If Roosevelt's would-be assassin had found his mark, the next president would have been Vice President-elect John Nance Garner. Few public figures were less well equipped for restoring public confidence than the crusty Garner, who is best known for equating the vice presidency to a pitcher of warm spit. There is no sure way of knowing what would have transpired if the United States had been deprived of the political genius of FDR. It is far from impossible that it would have succumbed to authoritarian rule, or even dissolved as a political entity, as the Soviet Union did in 1991.

• Harry Truman had an exemplary capacity to energize and rally his subordinates in an administration that had to contend with a highly unfavorable political environment. He also deserves attention for his ability to remain on an even keel, despite his often-turbulent emotions. Truman provides an example of the broker politician at his best in his actions relating to the enactment of the Marshall Plan. When it comes to rhetoric and vision, however, Truman is a negative role model. He illustrates the costs of a defective communication style and a situation-determined approach to presidential leadership.

• Dwight Eisenhower is the Clark Kent of the American presidency. He was once assumed to have been a well-intentioned political innocent, but he emerges from the historical record as a self-consciously oblique political sophisticate with a highly distinctive leadership style. Eisenhower had a firm sense of self-worth that was not bound up in his presidency—he had made his historical mark by V-E Day. He has the most to offer future presidents in the domains of policy vision and organization of the presidency. His greatest deficiency was in public communication. Eisenhower's failure to persuade the public and the political community that the United States should not enter into a missile race with the Soviet Union underscores the shortcomings of a political style that places little weight on the teaching and preaching functions of the presidency.

• John Kennedy's forte was public communication. A less publicly persuasive chief executive would have been unable to maintain public support in the face of such setbacks as the debacle at the Bay of Pigs and the erection of the Berlin Wall. Kennedy's personal qualities also set a high standard. His keen intelligence and sense of historical perspective made for thoughtful, well-informed policy choices. He also was striking for the emotional detachment he brought to his public actions. Despite his private excesses, Kennedy was measured and clear-headed in his official capacity.

Kennedy also is a source of negative lessons. He squandered Eisenhower's organizational legacy, discarding an advisory mechanism that could have been of inestimable value for later presidencies. Kennedy's lack of an overarching policy vision led him to muddle through in the vital relationship with the Soviet Union. By posing an unintended threat to the men in the Kremlin, he contributed to a spiral of misunderstanding that culminated in the near nuclear disaster of the Cuban missile crisis.

Following Kennedy there were the emotionally impaired Lyndon Johnson and Richard Nixon, under whom the nation experienced Vietnam and Watergate. In the absence of that succession of traumas, the tenor of American politics in the final quarter of the twentieth century would have been far more conducive to effective governance.

- Lyndon Johnson's most positive lessons bear on political skill. Presidents who study Johnson's often pyrotechnic political maneuvers will be the recipient of a graduate education in political operations. Future presidents also would be advised to take LBJ as a source of warnings. Especially instructive are the qualities that led Johnson to commit over a half-million American troops to the jungles of Vietnam between 1965 and 1968. Because he was deficient in organizational capacity, he presided over an advisory process that failed to provide him with a rigorous assessment of the pros and cons of alternative courses of action. Because he was tone-deaf when it came to policy content, his political skill enhanced his ability to pursue a bankrupt course of action.

- The presidential leadership of Richard Nixon provides an illustration of the superficiality of efforts to rank chief executives. In a 1996 survey of presidential greatness conducted by Arthur Schlesinger, Jr., a panel of authorities placed Nixon in the lowest of six performance categories.[1] That assessment might lead later presidents to conclude that they had nothing to learn from Nixon. Yet it would be difficult to imagine a more positively, as well as negatively, instructive chief executive. Nixon's stunning international achievements illustrate the value of strategic vision in presidential leadership. His self-destructive qualities demonstrate the capacity of a dysfunctional psyche to sabotage even the most proficient political leader.

- Enter the underappreciated Gerald Ford. Presidents and presidential advisers who dismiss the Ford experience will miss out on a rich set of precedents about how to manage the presidency. More fundamentally, they will fail to take account of the personal strengths of a chief executive who had an impressive capacity to withstand the pressures of office. Future presidents cannot simply will emotional balance on themselves, but they are likely to approach their job with greater ease if they attend to the presidents who were not intimidated by their office.

- The presidency of Jimmy Carter is informative as a limiting case. No president has been as reluctant as Carter to engage in the normal process of political give and take. No presidency provides a fuller catalogue of avoidable shortfalls than his. The exception is Camp David. By negotiating a peace agreement between Israel and Egypt, Carter provides a reminder that presidents need not simply respond to circumstances. They can make opportunity their servant, engaging in acts of political creativity.

- Ronald Reagan was a Jimmy Carter in reverse. He was a fluent public communicator with an ingratiating behind-the-scenes manner, who stood for a handful of broad verities. Reagan also was astonishingly uninformed about the specifics of his programs. The positive lessons of the Reagan presidency relate to its professionalism in public communication and political management. Its warnings derive from Reagan's cognitive limitations and his hands-off management

215

style, which spawned rivalries and conflict in his inner circle. Competent aides are essential in the modern presidency, but when it comes to effective organization of the presidency the buck stops in the Oval Office.

- George H. W. Bush also was his predecessor's antithesis. He failed to take advantage of the rhetorical potentialities of the presidency, and he was fundamentally reactive in his stance toward public affairs. However, he was the master of the specifics of politics and policy, and he worked closely and skillfully with his aides and political counterparts, especially in international affairs. Such a competent custodian president can thrive under favorable political and economic conditions, but is likely to flounder in the face of adversity. If the Bush presidency had been marked by larger themes, and if Bush had better communicated what he did accomplish, he might well have occupied the Oval Office through January 1997.

- Then there is Bill Clinton, whose political aspirations seem almost to have been incubated in the womb. Clinton had already formulated a precise strategy for seeking the presidency at age twenty-six, when he confided to a fellow McGovern campaign worker that he planned to return to Arkansas after law school and run for governor with a view to gaining the national prominence that would enable him to seek the presidency.[2] It is a tribute to Clinton's resiliency and political prowess that he succeeded in serving two presidential terms. It is a commentary on his weaknesses that this talented political leader did not have more to show for his time in office.

- Lastly there is George W. Bush, whose first two-and-a-half years in office are likely to assure him more space in future history books than eight years in the White House will for Bill Clinton. Although Bush has much less mastery of the inner workings of policies than his predecessor, he far exceeds Clinton (and many other modern presidents) in his propensity to set goals and be tireless in their pursuit. This was his practice before he threw himself more intensively into his responsibilities after September 11 and it remained so thereafter. Like Truman before him, Bush illustrates the proposition that the presidency is an office in which it is possible to grow in competence and effectiveness.

THE QUALITIES THAT BEAR ON PRESIDENTIAL PERFORMANCE

Effectiveness as a Public Communicator   For an office that places so great a premium on the presidential pulpit, the modern presidency has been surprisingly lacking in effective public communicators. Most presidents have not addressed the public with anything approximating the professionalism of countless educators, members of the clergy, and radio and television broadcasters. Roosevelt, Kennedy, and Reagan—and Clinton at his best—are the shining exceptions.

Chief executives who find the most able of the presidential communicators daunting should be relieved to learn that their eloquence was in part the product of effort and experience. Roosevelt, Kennedy, and Reagan took part in drafting their speeches and rehearsed their presentations. In 1910, when Eleanor Roosevelt first heard her husband give a speech, she was taken aback by his long pauses and slow delivery. "I was worried for fear that he would never go on," she recalled.[3] When Kennedy was a freshman congressman, he had a diffident, self-effacing public manner. And for all of Reagan's professionalism, he did not perfect the podium manner of his political years until the 1950s, when his film career drew to a close and he found employment on the speaking circuit.

One president who allowed himself to be fazed by an accomplished predecessor was George H. W. Bush, who seems to have concluded that since he could not compare with Reagan as a communicator, he should be his near antithesis. Bush used the White House briefing room for his public communications, only rarely addressing the nation from the Oval Office, and he instructed his speechwriters to temper his prose. Bush's initial three years of high public approval provide a reminder that formal addresses are not the only way for a president to remain in the good graces of the public. His defeat highlights the costs of a leadership style that gives short shrift to the teaching and preaching side of presidential leadership.

Organizational Capacity   A president's capacity as an organizer includes his ability to forge a team and get the most out of it, minimizing the tendency of subordinates to tell their boss what they sense he wants to hear. It also includes a quite different matter: his proficiency at creating effective institutional arrangements. There is an illuminating postpresidential indicator of a president's success as a team builder—the way that he is remembered by alumni of his administration. Veterans of the Truman, Eisenhower, Kennedy, Ford, and George H. W. Bush presidencies have nothing but praise for their erstwhile chiefs. In contrast, few Johnson, Carter, and Clinton lieutenants emerged from their White House service with unmixed views of the president they served. Most ambivalent are the former aides of Richard Nixon, a number of whom went to prison for their actions in his service.

Presidents also differ in their ability to avail themselves of a rich and varied fare of advice and information. FDR encouraged diversity in the recommendations that reached him by pitting his assistants against one another. Kennedy's method was to charge his brother Robert and his alter ego Theodore Sorensen with scrutinizing the proposals of his other advisers for flaws and pitfalls. The modern president with by far the greatest and most demanding organizational experience was Eisenhower, who had a highly developed view of the matter. "I know of only one way in which you can be sure you have done your best to make a wise decision," he declared in a 1967 interview:

> That is to get all of the [responsible policymakers] with their different viewpoints in front of you, and listen to them debate. I do not believe in bringing them in one at a time, and therefore being more impressed by the most recent one you hear than the earlier ones. You must get courageous men of strong views, and let them debate with each other.[4]

218

Not all of the modern presidents have been open to vigorous give and take. Nixon and Reagan were uncomfortable in the presence of face-to-face disagreement. Johnson's Texas-sized personality had a chilling effect on some of his subordinates. His NSC staff member Chester Cooper recalled recurrent fantasies of facing down LBJ at NSC meetings when Johnson sought his concurrence on a matter relating to Vietnam by replying, "I most definitely do not agree." But when LBJ turned to him and asked, "Mr. Cooper, do you agree?" Cooper found himself replying, "Yes, Mr. President, I agree."[5]

The capacity to design effective institutional arrangements has been in even scarcer supply than effective public communication in the modern presidency. In this department, Eisenhower was in a class of his own. The most emulation-worthy of his departures was the set of arrangements that framed his administration's national security deliberations. Each week the top planners in the bodies represented in the NSC hammered out option papers stating the policy recommendations of their agencies. The disagreements were clearly delineated and set before the NSC, where they were the object of sharp, focused debate. The result was as important for preparing Eisenhower's foreign policy team to work together as it was for grounding it in the issues bearing on unfolding global contingencies.

Political Skill　The classic statement of the centrality of political skill to presidential performance is Richard E. Neustadt's *Presidential Power,* which has been described as the closest approximation to Machiavelli's writings in the literature of American politics.[6] The question Neustadt addresses is how the chief executive can put his stamp on public policy in the readily stalemated American political system. Neustadt's prescription is for the president to use the powers of his office assertively, build and maintain public support, and establish a reputation among fellow policymakers as a skilled, determined political operator. If there ever was reason to doubt Neustadt's diagnosis, it was eliminated by the presidential experience of Jimmy Carter.

Lyndon Johnson seemed almost to have taken his methods from the pages of *Presidential Power.* Within hours after Kennedy's assassi-

nation, Johnson had begun to muster support for major domestic policy departures. He exhibited will as well as skill, cultivating his
political reputation by keeping Congress in session until Christmas
1963 in order to prevail in one of his administration's first legislative
contests. His actions won him strong public support, making it apparent to his opposite numbers on Capitol Hill that it would be politically
costly to ignore his demands.

Vision "Vision" is a term with a variety of connotations. One is the
capacity to inspire. In this the rhetorically gifted presidents—
Kennedy, Reagan, and above all FDR—excelled. In the narrower
meaning employed here, "vision" refers to preoccupation with the
content of policies, an ability to assess their feasibility, and the pos-
session of a set of overarching goals. Here the standouts are Eisenhower, Nixon, and to a lesser extent Ronald Reagan, whose views
were poorly grounded in specifics. Vision also encompasses consistency of viewpoint. Presidents who stand firm are able to set the
terms of policy discourse. In effect they serve as anchors for the rest
of the political community.

George H. W. Bush was not alone in lacking "the vision thing." He
falls in a class of presidential pragmatists that includes the bulk of the
modern chief executives. The costs of vision-free leadership include
internally inconsistent programs, policies that have unintended consequences, and sheer drift. When it comes to vision, the senior Bush
could not have been more different from his son, George W. Bush, for
whom having an explicit agenda is a watchword. Ironically, the
younger Bush's vision led him in potentially problematic directions,
most strikingly in the case of the war in Iraq, in which a short-run military victory was followed by a continuing pattern of guerilla warfare
against the American occupying force. In short, the first Bush suffered
for his lack of vision, and the second Bush may prove to suffer *because*
of his policy vision.

Cognitive Style Presidents vary widely in their cognitive styles.
Jimmy Carter had an engineer's proclivity to reduce issues to what he
perceived to be their component parts. That style served him well in

the 1978 Camp David negotiations, but it was ill suited for providing his administration with a sense of direction. Carter's cognitive qualities contrast with the kind of strategic intelligence that cuts to the heart of a problem, as Eisenhower did when he introduced his administration's deliberations on Dien Bien Phu with the incisive observation that the jungles of Indochina would "absorb our divisions by the dozens."[7]

Another example of strategic intelligence is to be had from a chief executive who will never grace Mount Rushmore: Richard Nixon. Two years before entering the White House, Nixon laid down the goals of moving the United States beyond its military involvement in Vietnam, establishing a balance of power with the Soviet Union and an opening with China. By the final year of his first term, he had accomplished his purposes.

Nixon's first-term successes contrast with the paucity of major accomplishments in the two White House terms of the first presidential Rhodes scholar, Bill Clinton. Clinton possessed a formidable ability to absorb and process ideas and information, but his mind was more synthetic than analytic, and his political impulses sometimes led him to substitute mere rationalization for reasoned analysis.

Two presidents who were marked by cognitive limitations were Harry Truman and Ronald Reagan. Truman's uncritical reading of works of popular history made him susceptible to false historical analogies. Reagan was notorious for his imperfect understanding of a number of his policy initiatives. That both presidents had major policy accomplishments shows that intelligence and information as measured by standardized tests is not the sole cause of presidential effectiveness.

Emotional Intelligence   Four of the twelve modern presidents stand out as fundamentally free of distracting emotional perturbations: Eisenhower, Ford, George H. W. Bush, and George W. Bush. Four others were marked by emotional undercurrents that did not significantly impair their leadership: Roosevelt, Truman, Kennedy, and Reagan. That leaves Johnson, Nixon, Carter, and Clinton, all of whom were emotionally handicapped. The vesuvian LBJ was subject to mood swings of clinical proportions. Jimmy Carter's rigidity was a significant impediment to his White House performance. The defective impulse control of Bill Clinton led him into actions that ensued in his impeachment.

Richard Nixon was the most emotionally flawed of the presidents considered here. His anger and suspiciousness were of Shakespearean proportions. He more than any other president summons up the classic notion of a tragic hero who is defeated by the very qualities that brought him success. It has been argued that the tortured psyche of a Nixon is a precondition of political creativity. This was the view of Elliot Richardson, who held that if Nixon's "rather petty flaws" had been taken away, "you would probably have removed that very inner core of insecurity that led to his rise."[8] Richardson's claim is a variant of the proposition that the inner torment of a Van Gogh is the price of his creativity, but other great painters were free of Van Gogh's self-destructiveness, and the healthy-minded Eisenhower was as gifted as Nixon in the positive aspects of leadership. Great political ability does sometimes derive from troubled emotions, but the former does not justify the latter in the custodian of the most destructive military arsenal in human experience.

CODA

In the world of imagination it is possible to envisage a cognitively and emotionally intelligent chief executive, who happens also to be an inspiring public communicator, a capable White House organizer, and the possessor of exceptional political skill and vision. In the real world, human imperfection is inevitable, but some imperfections are more disabling than others. Many of the modern presidents have performed adequately without being brilliant orators. Only a few chief executives have been organizationally competent. A minimal level of political skill is a precondition of presidential effectiveness, but political skill is widely present in the handful of individuals who rise to the political summit. Vision is rarer than skill, but only Lyndon Johnson was disastrously deficient in the realm of policy.

Finally there are thought and emotion. The importance of cognitive strength in the presidency should be self-evident. Still, Presidents

222

Johnson, Nixon, Carter, and Clinton had impressive intellects and defective temperaments. They reversed Justice Holmes's characterization of FDR. Clinton's foibles made him an underachiever and national embarrassment. Carter's defective temperament contributed to making his time in office a period of lost opportunity. Johnson and Nixon presided over major policy breakthroughs, but also over two of the most unhappy episodes of the twentieth century. All four presidential experiences point to the following moral: Beware the presidential contender who lacks emotional intelligence. In its absence all else may turn to ashes.

Background on the Modern Presidency*

FRANKLIN DELANO ROOSEVELT, 32D PRESIDENT (1933–1945)

Life

Birthdate: 30 January 1882
Birthplace: Hyde Park, N.Y.
Parents: James Roosevelt, Sara Delano
Religion: Episcopalian
College Education: Harvard College
Wife: (Anna) Eleanor Roosevelt
Date of Marriage: 17 March 1905
Children: Anna Eleanor, James, Franklin, Elliott, Franklin Delano, John Aspinwall
Political Party: Democratic
Other Positions Held:
   Member, New York Senate (1910–1913)
   Assistant Secretary of the Navy (1913–1920)
   Governor of New York (1929–1933)
Date of Inauguration: 4 March 1933
End of Term: 12 April 1945 (died in office)
Date of Death: 12 April 1945
Place of Death: Warm Springs, Ga.
Place of Burial: Hyde Park, N.Y.

*Adapted from *The Presidents: A Reference History,* 2d ed., Henry F. Graff, ed. (New York: Scribners, 1996).

Elections

CANDIDATE	PARTY	ELECTORAL VOTE	POPULAR VOTE
Election of 1932			
Franklin D. Roosevelt	Democratic	472	57.4%
Herbert C. Hoover	Republican	59	39.7%
Norman Thomas	Socialist	0	2.2%
Election of 1936			
Franklin D. Roosevelt	Democratic	523	60.8%
Alfred M. Landon	Republican	8	36.5%
William Lemke	Union	0	1.9%
Election of 1940			
Franklin D. Roosevelt	Democratic	449	54.8%
Wendell Willkie	Republican	82	44.8%
Election of 1944			
Franklin D. Roosevelt	Democratic	432	53.5%
Thomas E. Dewey	Republican	99	46.0%

Political Composition of Congress

73d Congress (1933–1935)
Senate: Dem. 60; Rep. 35; other 1
House: Dem. 310; Rep. 117; others 5

74th Congress (1935–1937)
Senate: Dem. 69; Rep. 25; others 2
House: Dem. 319; Rep. 103; others 10

75th Congress (1937–1939)
Senate: Dem. 76; Rep. 16; others 4
House: Dem. 331; Rep. 89; others 13

76th Congress (1939–1941)
Senate: Dem. 69; Rep. 23; others 4
House: Dem. 261; Rep. 164; others 4

77th Congress (1941–1943)
Senate: Dem. 66; Rep. 28; others 2
House: Dem. 268; Rep. 162; others 5

78th Congress (1943–1945)
Senate: Dem. 58; Rep. 37; other 1
House: Dem. 218; Rep. 208; others 4

79th Congress (1945–1947)
Senate: Dem. 56; Rep. 38; other 1
House: Dem. 242; Rep. 190; others 2

Appointments

Vice Presidents:
  John Nance Garner (1933–1941)
  Henry A. Wallace (1941–1945)
  Harry S. Truman (1945)

Cabinet Members:
  Cordell Hull, secretary of state (1933–1944)
  Edward R. Stettinius, Jr., secretary of state (1944–1945)
  W. H. Woodin, secretary of the treasury (1933)
  Henry Morgenthau, Jr., secretary of the treasury (1934–1945)
  George H. Dren, secretary of war (1933–1936)
  Harry H. Woodring, secretary of war (1936–1940)
  Henry L. Stimson, secretary of war (1940–1945)
  Homer S. Cummings, attorney general (1933–1939)
  Frank Murphy, attorney general (1939–1940)
  Robert H. Jackson, attorney general (1940–1941)
  Francis Biddle, attorney general (1941–1945)
  James A. Farley, postmaster general (1933–1940)
  Frank C. Walker, postmaster general (1941–1945)
  Claude A. Swanson, secretary of the navy (1933–1939)
  Charles Edison, secretary of the navy (1939)
  Frank Knox, secretary of the navy (1940–1944)
  James V. Forrestal, secretary of the navy (1944–1945)
  Harold L. Ickes, secretary of the interior (1933–1945)
  Henry A. Wallace, secretary of agriculture (1933–1940)
  Claude R. Wickard, secretary of agriculture (1940–1945)
  Daniel C. Roper, secretary of commerce (1933–1938)
  Harry L. Hopkins, secretary of commerce (1938–1940)
  Jesse H. Jones, secretary of commerce (1940–1945)
  Henry A. Wallace, secretary of commerce (1945)
  Frances Perkins, secretary of labor (1933–1945)

Supreme Court Appointments:
  Hugo L. Black (1937–1971)
  Stanley F. Reed (1938–1957)
  Felix Frankfurter (1939–1962)
  William O. Douglas (1939–1975)
  Frank Murphy (1940–1949)
  James F. Byrnes (1941–1942)
  Harlan Fiske Stone, chief justice (1941–1946) (promoted from associate
    justice)

Robert H. Jackson (1941–1954)
Wiley B. Rutledge (1943–1949)

Key Events

1933 Roosevelt inaugurated (4 Mar.); called for the use of "broad Executive power" and stated that "the only thing we have to fear is fear itself." Announced Good Neighbor policy to improve relations with Latin America. On 5 Mar. called a special session of Congress to meet 9 Mar. Declared a 4-day bank holiday, suspending all financial transactions, government as well as private. Launched "Hundred Days" program of legislative enactments: Emergency Banking Relief Act (9 Mar.), Civilian Conservation Corps (31 Mar.), Agricultural Adjustment Act (12 May), Federal Emergency Relief Act (12 May), Federal Securities Act (17 May), Tennessee Valley Authority (18 May), National Industrial Recovery Act (16 June), Civil Works Administration (8 Nov.); U.S. comes off gold standard (30 Apr.); U.S. recognizes U.S.S.R. (16 Nov.); with ratification of Twenty-First Amendment, Prohibition ends (5 Dec.).

1934 Export-Import Bank established (2 Feb.); Securities and Exchange Act passes (6 June); Federal Communications Commission established (19 June). Democrats gain 9 seats in Senate and 9 in House in congressional elections (6 Nov.).

1935 A second New Deal announced by Roosevelt (4 Jan.) for social reform: Soil Conservation Act (27 Apr.), Works Progress Administration (11 May), National Labor Relations Act (5 July), Social Security Act (14 Aug.), Public Utilities Act (28 Aug.). Supreme Court in a 9–0 decision declared NRA unconstitutional (27 May). Roosevelt signed Neutrality Act of 1935, the first of several such acts, forbidding U.S. citizens from traveling on belligerent vessels except at their own risk, and prohibiting export of arms and munitions to belligerents (31 Aug.).

1936 Roosevelt signs second neutrality bill (29 Feb.), banning loans to countries at war; Merchant Marine Act (26 June) creates U.S. Maritime Commission.

1937 Roosevelt's Inaugural Address (20 Jan.) listed progress made but saw the need for further social reform, with "one-third of a nation ill-housed, ill-clad, ill-nourished." Proposed a bill to reorganize the Supreme Court by adding members for justices who did not retire at age seventy (5 Feb). Described by critics as "court packing." Neutrality Act (1 May) prohibits export of arms and ammunition to belligerent nations and the use of U.S. ships for carrying munitions and war materials into belligerent zones; U.S. Senate rejects "court-packing" plan by Roosevelt (22 July).

1938 House Committee to investigate Un-American Activities formed (26 May); Civil Aeronautics Act passed (23 June), establishes Civil Aeronautics Authority to supervise nonmilitary air transport; Fair Labor Standards (Wages and Hours) Act passes (25 June).

1939 At opening of New York World's Fair, Roosevelt becomes first president to be televised (30 Apr.); Executive Office of the President established (1 July); U.S. proclaims neutrality in European hostilities (5 Sept.); Roosevelt declares limited national emergency (8 Sept.); Neutrality Act of 1939 passes (4 Nov.) authorizing "cash and carry" sale of arms to belligerents.

1940 U.S. population 131,669,275
National Defense Research Committee established (15 June) with Vannevar Bush as chairman; embargo on exports of scrap iron and steel to non-Western Hemisphere nations except Great Britain (26 Sept.); Roosevelt reelected for record third term (5 Nov.); Office of Production Management established (20 Dec.); Roosevelt calls for production effort to make U.S. "arsenal of democracy" (29 Dec.).

1941 Lend-Lease bill passes (11 Mar.), for lending goods and services to democratic countries in return for services; secret U.S.-British talks in Washington, D.C. (27 Jan.–29 Mar.), produce war plan ABC-1 and set "Germany first" priority in event of war with Germany and Japan; Roosevelt declares unlimited national emergency (27 May); German and Italian consulates ordered closed (6 June); Atlantic Charter formulated (14 Aug.) by Roosevelt and Churchill outlining war aims; Japanese attack (7 Dec.) on Pearl Harbor cripples Pacific fleet; U.S. enters World War II with declarations of war on Japan (8 Dec.) and Germany (11 Dec.).

1942 U.S. signs U.N. Declaration (1 Jan.); Roosevelt orders (19 Feb.) relocation of Japanese-Americans to interior internment camps; first Moscow Conference (12–15 Aug.): U.S., Soviet Union, and Great Britain decide not to open second front in Europe; Manhattan Project to develop atomic bomb placed under command of Leslie R. Groves (31 Aug.).

1943 Casablanca Conference (14–24 Jan.): Roosevelt and Churchill decide that war would be fought to "unconditional surrender"; first Cairo Conference (22–26 Nov.): Roosevelt and Churchill confer with Chiang Kai-shek regarding war in Far East.

1944 Operation Overlord (D day): massive Allied landings (6 June) on Normandy beaches; Bretton Woods Conference (1–22 July) establishes International Monetary Fund; Dumbarton Oaks Conference (21 Aug.–7 Oct.) establishes basis for U.N. Charter.

1945 Yalta Conference (4–11 Feb.): Roosevelt, Churchill, and Stalin plan defeat of Germany; United Nations Conference (25 Apr.–26 June) in San Francisco drafts U.N. Charter; death of Roosevelt (12 Apr.).

HARRY S. TRUMAN, 33D PRESIDENT (1945–1953)

Life
Birthdate: 8 May 1884
Birthplace: Lamar, Mo.

Parents: John Anderson Truman, Martha Ellen Young
Religion: Baptist
College Education: None
Wife: Elizabeth Virginia ("Bess") Wallace
Date of Marriage: 28 June 1919
Child: Margaret
Political Party: Democratic
Other Positions Held:
    Judge, Jackson County (Mo.) Court (1922–1924; 1926–1934)
    U.S. Senator (1935–1945)
    Vice President (1945)
Date of Inauguration: 12 April 1945 (succeeded to presidency on death of
    Franklin D. Roosevelt)
End of Term: 20 January 1953
Date of Death: 26 December 1972
Place of Death: Kansas City, Mo.
Place of Burial: Independence, Mo.

Elections

CANDIDATE	PARTY	ELECTORAL VOTE	POPULAR VOTE
Election of 1948			
Harry S. Truman	Democratic	303	49.5%
Thomas E. Dewey	Republican	189	45%
J. Strom Thurmond	States' Rights	39	2.4%
Henry A. Wallace	Progressive	0	2.4%

Did Not Run in Election of 1952

Political Composition of Congress

79th Congress (1945–1947)
Senate: Dem. 56; Rep. 38; other 1
House: Dem. 242; Rep. 190; others 2

80th Congress (1947–1949)
Senate: Rep. 51; Dem. 45
House: Rep. 245; Dem. 188, other 1

81st Congress (1949–1951)
Senate: Dem. 54; Rep. 42
House: Dem. 263; Rep. 171; other 1

82d Congress (1951–1953)
Senate: Dem. 49; Rep. 47
House: Dem. 234; Rep. 199; other 1

Appointments

Vice President:
  Alben W. Barkley (1949–1953)

Cabinet Members:
  Edward R. Stettinius, Jr., secretary of state (1945)
  James F. Byrnes, secretary of state (1945–1947)
  George C. Marshall, secretary of state (1947–1949)
  Dean G. Acheson, secretary of state (1949–1953)
  Henry Morgenthau, Jr. secretary of the treasury (1945)
  Frederick M. ("Fred") Vinson, secretary of the treasury (1945–1946)
  John W. Snyder, secretary of the treasury (1946–1953)
  Henry L. Stimson, secretary of war (1945)
  Robert P. Patterson, secretary of war (1945–1947)
  Kenneth C. Royall, secretary of war (1947)
  James V. Forrestal, secretary of defense (1947–1949)
  Louis A. Johnson, secretary of defense (1949–1950)
  George C. Marshall, secretary of defense (1950–1951)
  Robert A. Lovett, secretary of defense (1951–1953)
  Francis Biddle, attorney general (1945)
  Tom C. Clark, attorney general (1945–1949)
  J. Howard McGrath, attorney general (1949–1952)
  James P. McGranery, attorney general (1952–1953)
  Frank C. Walker, postmaster general (1945)
  Robert E. Hannegan, postmaster general (1945–1947)
  Jesse M. Donaldson, postmaster general (1947–1953)
  James V. Forrestal, secretary of the navy (1945–1947)
  Harold L. Ickes, secretary of the interior (1945–1946)
  Julius A. Krug, secretary of the interior (1946–1949)
  Oscar L. Chapman, secretary of the interior (1949–1953)
  Claude R. Wickard, secretary of agriculture (1945)
  Clinton P. Anderson, secretary of agriculture (1945–1948)
  Charles F. Brannan, secretary of agriculture (1948–1953)
  Henry A. Wallace, secretary of commerce (1945–1946)
  W. Averell Harriman, secretary of commerce (1946–1948)
  Charles Sawyer, secretary of commerce (1948–1953)
  Frances Perkins, secretary of labor (1945)
  Lewis B. Schwellenbach, secretary of labor (1945–1948)
  Maurice J. Tobin, secretary of labor (1948–1953)

Supreme Court Appointments:
  Harold H. Burton (1945–1958)
  Frederick M. ("Fred") Vinson, chief justice (1946–1953)
  Tom C. Clark (1949–1967)
  Sherman Minton (1949–1956)

Key Events

1945 Truman becomes president upon death of Roosevelt (12 Apr.); Germany surrenders (27 May); European Advisory Commission (5 June) establishes German occupation zones; Potsdam Conference (17 July–2 Aug.): Truman, Stalin, and Churchill plan future of postwar Europe; U.S. drops atomic bombs on Hiroshima (6 Aug.) and Nagasaki (9 Aug.); Japan surrenders (15 Aug.), ending World War II.

1946 Atomic bomb tests at Bikini Atoll in Pacific (1 July); Philippines given independence (4 July); Atomic Energy Act (1 Aug.) passes control of atomic energy to new Atomic Energy Commission. Truman dismisses Henry A. Wallace as secretary of commerce (29 Sept.).

1947 Truman Doctrine (12 Mar.): first U.S. attempt to contain Communism; aid to Greece and Turkey approved (22 May); Marshall Plan proposed (5 June) to aid Europe in postwar economic recovery; National Security Act passes (26 July), establishing National Security Council and Central Intelligence Agency; Department of Defense supersedes Department of War and Department of the Navy. Republicans win control of Congress for first time in 14 years, gaining 13 seats in the Senate and 56 in the House (5 Nov.). Henry Wallace announces formation of a third party called the Progressive Party (28 Dec.).

1948 Truman sends Congress a 10-point program on civil rights to end segregation in public schools and accommodations, and reduce discrimination in employment (2 Feb.); signs European Recovery Act, providing $17 billion (3 Apr.); challenges Republican-controlled 80th Congress to act on his anti-inflation bill (5 Aug.); begins a cross-country speaking tour taking him 21,928 miles, and to almost 200 cities (17 Sept.); wins presidency in a 4-candidate election (2 Nov.).

1949 North Atlantic Treaty Organization established (24 Aug.) by U.S., Canada, and 10 European nations; a complete reconstruction of the White House begins (12 Dec.). Truman announces that Soviet Union has perfected an atomic bomb (23 Sept.); Chinese Communists victorious in their struggle with the Nationalists (8 Dec.).

1950 U.S. population: 150,697,361

U.S. recalls (14 Jan.) consular officials from China after consulate general seized in Peking; H-bomb production authorized (31 Jan.); NSC-68 memorandum calls for massive increase in military spending to face Soviet threat (April); North Koreans cross 38th parallel into South Korea (25 June), provoking Korean War; U.N. command in Korea formed (7 July) with Gen. MacArthur designated commander (8 July); amphibious Inchon landing (15 Sept.) leads to recapture of Seoul (26 Sept.).

1951 Twenty-Second Amendment limits presidential terms (26 Feb.); Julius and Ethel Rosenberg found guilty (29 Mar.) as spies and sentenced to death (executed 1953); MacArthur removed in Korea by Truman over strategy disagreements (11 Apr.); armistice negotiations begin (10 July).

1952 Reconstructed White House ready for occupancy (27 Mar.); Truman seizes steel mills (8 Apr.) to prevent strike; seizure ruled unconstitutional (2 June); Eisenhower elected president (4 Nov.).

1953 Truman makes his Farewell Address to the American people on radio and television (15 Jan.).

DWIGHT DAVID EISENHOWER, 34TH PRESIDENT (1953–1961)

Life

Birthdate: 14 October 1890
Birthplace: Denison, Tex.
Parents: David Jacob Eisenhower, Ida Elizabeth Stover
Religion: Presbyterian
College Education: United States Military Academy
Wife: Marie ("Mamie") Geneva Doud
Date of Marriage: 1 July 1916
Children: Doud Dwight, John Sheldon Doud
Political Party: Republican
Other Positions Held:
    Brigadier General, U.S. Army (1941–1942)
    Major General, U.S. Army (1942–1943)
    General, U.S. Army, and Supreme Allied Commander (1943–1945)
    General of the Army (1944–1952; 1961–1969)
    Chief of Staff, U.S. Army (1945–1948)
    President, Columbia University (1948–1953)
    Supreme Commander, NATO forces in Europe (1951–1952)
Date of Inauguration: 20 January 1953
End of Term: 20 January 1961
Date of Death: 28 March 1969
Place of Death: Washington, D.C.
Place of Burial: Abilene, Kans.

Elections

CANDIDATE	PARTY	ELECTORAL VOTE	POPULAR VOTE
Election of 1952			
Dwight D. Eisenhower	Republican	442	55.1%
Adlai E. Stevenson	Democratic	89	44.4%
Election of 1956			
Dwight D. Eisenhower	Republican	457	57.6%
Adlai E. Stevenson	Democratic	73	42.1%

Ineligible to Run in Election of 1960

Political Composition of Congress

83d Congress (1953–1955)
Senate: Rep. 48; Dem. 47; other 1
House: Rep. 221; Dem. 211; other 1

84th Congress (1955–1957)
Senate: Dem. 48; Rep. 47; other 1
House: Dem. 232; Rep. 203

85th Congress (1957–1959)
Senate: Dem. 49; Rep. 47
House: Dem. 233; Rep. 200

86th Congress (1959–1961)
Senate: Dem. 64; Rep. 34
House: Dem. 283; Rep. 153

Appointments

Vice President:
Richard M. Nixon (1953–1961)

Cabinet Members:
John Foster Dulles, secretary of state (1953–1959)
Christian A. Herter, secretary of state (1959–1961)
George M. Humphrey, secretary of the treasury (1953–1957)
Robert B. Anderson, secretary of the treasury (1957–1961)
Charles E. Wilson, secretary of defense (1953–1957)
Neil H. McElroy, secretary of defense (1957–1959)
Thomas S. Gates, secretary of defense (1959–1961)
Herbert Brownell, Jr., attorney general (1953–1957)
William P. Rogers, attorney general (1958–1961)
Arthur E. Summerfield, postmaster general (1953–1961)
Douglas McKay, secretary of the interior (1953–1956)
Frederick A. Seaton, secretary of the interior (1956–1961)
Ezra Taft Benson, secretary of agriculture (1953–1961)
Sinclair Weeks, secretary of commerce (1953–1958)
Frederick H. Mueller, secretary of commerce (1959–1961)
Martin P. Durkin, secretary of labor (1953)
James P. Mitchell, secretary of labor (1953–1961)
Oveta Culp Hobby, secretary of health, education, and welfare (1953–1955)
Marion B. Folsom, secretary of health, education, and welfare (1955–1958)
Arthur S. Flemming, secretary of health, education, and welfare
    (1958–1961)

Supreme Court Appointments:
Earl Warren, chief justice (1953–1969)
John M. Harlan (1955–1971)
William J. Brennan, Jr. (1956–1990)
Charles E. Whittaker (1957–1962)
Potter Stewart (1958–1981)

Key Events

1953   Department of Health, Education, and Welfare established; hostilities halted in Korea (26 July). Soviet Union explodes a hydrogen bomb (12 Aug.).

1954   Communist Viet Minh besiege French forces at Dien Bien Phu in French Indochina (13 Mar.); fortress falls (7 May). McCarthy-Army Hearings (22 Apr.–17 June): investigation by Sen. Joseph McCarthy into charges army was lax in ferreting out Communist spies; *Brown v. Board of Education of Topeka, Kansas* bans racial segregation in schools (17 May); Southeast Asia Treaty Organization formed (8 Sept.) by 8 nations.

1955   Eisenhower holds first televised news conference (19 Jan.); military advisers dispatched to South Vietnam to train army (23 Feb.); Supreme Court orders desegregation "with all deliberate speed" (31 May); Eisenhower suffers heart attack (24 Sept.); hospitalized for 2 months.

1956   1st transatlantic cable in operation (25 Sept.); Suez Crisis: Israeli invasion of Gaza Strip and the Sinai (29 Oct.) is followed by British and French attacks on Egypt; U.S. leads efforts for a cease-fire (in effect 2 Nov.). Eisenhower reelected for a second term (6 Nov.)

1957   Arkansas National Guard called in (4 Sept.) to bar black students from integrating Little Rock High School; federal court orders Guardsmen removed; federal troops sent in (24 Sept.) and Arkansas National Guard put under federal command; Civil Rights Act (9 Sept.): first since Reconstruction, establishes Civil Rights Commission; Soviets launch *Sputnik 1* (4 Oct.) and *Sputnik 2* (3 Nov.), first artificial satellites.

1958   Presidential assistant Sherman Adams denies before a House investigating committee that he had intervened with federal agencies on behalf of industrialist Bernard Goldfine (17 Jun.); Adams resigns (22 Sept.). Eisenhower signs National Defense Education Act, which establishes a $295 million loan fund for college students (2 Sept.). Democrats gain 15 seats in Senate and 48 in House in midterm election (4 Nov.).

1959   Alaska (3 Jan.) and Hawaii (21 Aug.) admitted as states; Communist Fidel Castro seizes power in Cuba (Jan.); St. Lawrence Seaway opens (25 Apr.); Soviet Premier Nikita Khrushchev engages in "Kitchen Debate" with Vice President Nixon during 10-day tour of U.S. (Sept.).

1960   U.S. Population: 179,323,175
        Congress approves voting rights act (21 Apr.) and civil rights act (6 May); U.S. U-2 reconnaissance plane shot down over U.S.S.R. (1 May); Kennedy and Nixon on television engage in first presidential candidate

debates (26 Sept., 7, 13, and 21 Oct.); Kennedy elected president (8 Nov.).

1961 Eisenhower delivers Farewell Address urging vigilance against dangers to nation's liberties implicit in a vast military-industrial establishment (17 Jan.).

JOHN FITZGERALD KENNEDY, 35TH PRESIDENT (1961–1963)

Life

Birthdate: 29 May 1917
Birthplace: Brookline, Mass.
Parents: Joseph Patrick Kennedy, Rose Fitzgerald
Religion: Roman Catholic
College Education: Harvard College
Wife: Jacqueline Lee Bouvier
Date of Marriage: 12 September 1953
Children: Caroline Bouvier, John Fitzgerald, Patrick Bouvier
Political Party: Democratic
Other Positions Held:
    Member, U.S. House of Representatives (1947–1953)
    U.S. Senator (1953–1960)
Date of Inauguration: 20 January 1961
End of Term: 22 November 1963 (assassinated by Lee Harvey Oswald)
Date of Death: 22 November 1963
Place of Death: Dallas, Tex.
Place of Burial: Arlington, Va.

Elections

CANDIDATE	PARTY	ELECTORAL VOTE	POPULAR VOTE
Election of 1960			
John F. Kennedy	Democratic	303	49.9%
Richard M. Nixon	Republican	219	49.6%

Political Composition of Congress

87th Congress (1961–1963)
Senate: Dem. 65; Rep. 35
House: Dem. 263; Rep. 174

88th Congress (1963–1965)
Senate: Dem. 67; Rep. 33
House: Dem. 258; Rep. 177

Appointments

Vice President:
Lyndon B. Johnson (1961–1963)

Cabinet Members:
Dean Rusk, secretary of state (1961–1963)
C. Douglas Dillon, secretary of the treasury (1961–1963)
Robert S. McNamara, secretary of defense (1961–1963)
Robert F. Kennedy, attorney general (1961–1963)
J. Edward Day, postmaster general (1961–1963)
John A. Gronouski, Jr., postmaster general (1963)
Stewart L. Udall, secretary of the interior (1961–1963)
Orville L. Freeman, secretary of agriculture (1961–1963)
Luther H. Hodges, secretary of commerce (1961–1963)
Arthur J. Goldberg, secretary of labor (1961–1962)
W. Willard Wirtz, secretary of labor (1962–1963)
Abraham A. Ribicoff, secretary of health, education and welfare
(1961–1962)
Anthony J. Celebrezze, secretary of health, education, and welfare
(1962–1963)

Supreme Court Appointments:
Byron R. White (1962–1993)
Arthur J. Goldberg (1962–1965)

Key Events

1961 Twenty-Third Amendment ratified (3 Apr.), granting District of Columbia the vote in presidential elections; Bay of Pigs invasion (17 Apr.): failed CIA-backed invasion of Cuba by Cuban exiles; Cmdr. Alan B. Shepard in first U.S. manned suborbital space flight (5 May); Kennedy meets with Soviet premier Khrushchev in Vienna (3–4 Jun.); East Germany erects the Berlin Wall (13 Aug.).

1962 Lt. Col. John Glenn is first American in orbit (20 Feb.); first U.S. communications satellite launched (July); federal troops and Mississippi National Guard assist in admitting black student James Meredith into University of Mississippi (30 Sept.–10 Oct.); Cuban missile crisis: buildup of Soviet missiles in Cuba revealed (22 Oct.), Cuba quarantined, U.S.S.R. removes missiles.

1963 U.S., U.S.S.R., and Great Britain agree (25 July) on nuclear test ban treaty, barring all but underground tests; 200,000 people demonstrate for equal rights for blacks in Washington (28 Aug.); hot-line communications installed between Moscow and White House (30 Aug.); South Vietnamese president Diem assassinated (2 Nov.); Kennedy assassinated in Dallas by Lee Harvey Oswald (22 Nov.).

LYNDON BAINES JOHNSON, 36TH PRESIDENT (1963–1969)

Life

Birthdate: 27 August 1908
Birthplace: Stonewall, Tex.
Parents: Sam Ealy Johnson, Jr., Rebekah Baines
Religion: Disciples of Christ
College Education: Southwest Texas State Teachers College
Wife: Claudia Alta ("Lady Bird") Taylor
Date of Marriage: 17 November 1934
Children: Lynda Bird, Luci Baines
Political Party: Democratic
Other Positions Held:
    Member, U.S. House of Representatives (1937–1949)
    U.S. Senator (1949–1961; Democratic Leader, 1953–1961)
    Vice President (1961–1963)
Date of Inauguration: 22 November 1963 (succeeded to presidency on death
    of John F. Kennedy)
End of Term: 20 January 1969
Date of Death: 22 January 1973
Place of Death: San Antonio, Tex.
Place of Burial: Johnson City, Tex.

Elections

CANDIDATE	PARTY	ELECTORAL VOTE	POPULAR VOTE
Election of 1964			
Lyndon B. Johnson	Democratic	486	61.1%
Barry M. Goldwater	Republican	52	38.5%

Did Not Run in Election of 1968

Political Composition of Congress

88th Congress (1963–1965)
Senate: Dem. 67; Rep. 33
House: Dem. 258; Rep. 177

89th Congress (1965–1967)
Senate: Dem. 68; Rep. 32
House: Dem. 295; Rep. 140

90th Congress (1967–1969)
Senate: Dem. 64; Rep. 36
House: Dem. 246; Rep. 187

Appointments

Vice President:
 Hubert H. Humphrey (1965–1969)

Cabinet Members:
 Dean Rusk, secretary of state (1963–1969)
 C. Douglas Dillon, secretary of the treasury (1963–1965)
 Henry H. Fowler, secretary of the treasury (1965–1968)
 Joseph W. Barr, secretary of the treasury (1968–1969)
 Robert S. McNamara, secretary of defense (1963–1968)
 Clark M. Clifford, secretary of defense (1968–1969)
 Robert F. Kennedy, attorney general (1963–1964)
 Nicholas deB. Katzenbach, attorney general (1965–1966)
 Ramsey Clark, attorney general (1967–1969)
 John A. Gronouski, Jr., postmaster general (1963–1965)
 Lawrence F. O'Brien, postmaster general (1965–1968)
 W. Marvin Watson, postmaster general (1968–1969)
 Stewart L. Udall, secretary of the interior (1963–1969)
 Orville L. Freeman, secretary of agriculture (1963–1969)
 Luther H. Hodges, secretary of commerce (1963–1965)
 John T. Connor, secretary of commerce (1965–1967)
 Alexander B. Trowbridge, secretary of commerce (1967–1968)
 C. R. Smith, secretary of commerce (1968–1969)
 W. Willard Wirtz, secretary of labor (1963–1969)
 Anthony J. Celebrezze, secretary of health, education, and welfare
  (1963–1965)
 John W. Gardner, secretary of health, education, and welfare (1965–1968)
 Wilbur J. Cohen, secretary of health, education, and welfare (1968–1969)
 Robert C. Weaver, secretary of housing and urban development
  (1966–1968)
 Robert C. Wood, secretary of housing and urban development (1969)
 Alan S. Boyd, secretary of transportation (1966–1969)

Supreme Court Appointments:
 Abe Fortas (1965–1969)
 Thurgood Marshall (1967–1991)

Key Events

1963 Johnson becomes eighth president to come into office upon death of a president (22 Nov.).

1964 Johnson addresses Congress (3 Jan.), calling for a "War on Poverty"; signs the Civil Rights Bill of 1964, the most sweeping legislation of its kind in American history (3 July); Gulf of Tonkin resolution (7 Aug.) authorizes Johnson to "repel any army attack" in Vietnam and number of U.S. forces increases through 1968; War on Poverty bill passes (11

Aug.); Warren Commission report (27 Sept.) concludes Oswald was lone assassin of Kennedy; Johnson elected president (3 Nov.).

1965 Johnson delivers State of the Union Address detailing his "Great Society" proposals for the nation (4 Jan.); Viet Cong attack U.S. forces at Pleiku, and Johnson orders U.S. air raids on North Vietnam (7 Feb.); signs the Elementary and Secondary Education Bill at Johnson City, Texas (11 Apr.) (during its first year, federal government spends over $1 billion under its auspices); announces open-ended military commitment to defend South Vietnam (27 July); signs Medicare act providing medical care for the aged (30 July); signs Voting Rights Act eliminating literacy tests and other restrictive registration devices that were designed to keep African Americans from the polls (6 Aug.).

1966 In State of the Union message, Johnson declares that U.S. can afford its international commitments while building a Great Society (Jan.). Robert C. Weaver confirmed as secretary of newly created department of housing and urban development, first African American to hold a cabinet position. Johnson undertakes a 17-nation Asia-Pacific trip to discuss Vietnam and other related matters with U.S. allies in region (17 Oct.–2 Nov.).

1967 Riots by blacks (July) put down by federal troops and National Guardsmen; Twenty-Fifth Amendment ratified, dealing with presidential disability and succession (10 Feb.); Thurgood Marshall becomes first African American named a justice of the Supreme Court (13 June).

1968 Tet Offensive by North Vietnamese (30 Jan.); Johnson announces that he will not seek another term (31 Mar.); Martin Luther King, Jr., assassinated (4 Apr.) by James Earl Ray; peace talks on Vietnam open in Paris (10 May); Sen. Robert F. Kennedy assassinated (5 June) by Sirhan Sirhan; U.S. bombing halted in Vietnam (31 Oct.); Nixon elected president (5 Nov.).

RICHARD MILHOUS NIXON, 37TH PRESIDENT (1969–1974)

Life
Birthdate: 9 January 1913
Birthplace: Yorba Linda, Calif.
Parents: Francis Anthony Nixon, Hannah Milhous
Religion: Quaker
College Education: Whittier College; Duke University Law School
Wife: Thelma Catherine ("Pat") Ryan
Date of Marriage: 21 June 1940
Children: Patricia ("Tricia"), Julie
Political Party: Republican

Other Positions Held:
  Member, U.S. House of Representatives (1947–1951)
  U.S. Senator (1951–1953)
  Vice President (1953–1961)
Date of Inauguration: 20 January 1969
End of Term: 9 August 1974 (resigned office)
Date of Death: 22 April 1994
Place of Death: New York, N. Y.
Place of Burial: Yorba Linda, Calif.

Elections

CANDIDATE	PARTY	ELECTORAL VOTE	POPULAR VOTE
Election of 1968			
Richard Nixon	Republican	301	43.4%
Hubert H. Humphrey	Democratic	191	42.7%
George C. Wallace	Amer. Independent	46	13.5%
Election of 1972			
Richard Nixon	Republican	520	60.6%
George S. McGovern	Democratic	17	37.5%

Political Composition of Congress

91st Congress (1969–1971)
Senate: Dem. 57; Rep. 43
House: Dem. 245; Rep. 189

92d Congress (1971–1973)
Senate: Dem. 54; Rep. 44; others 2
House: Dem. 254; Rep. 180

93d Congress (1973–1975)
Senate: Dem. 56; Rep. 42; others 2
House: Dem. 239; Rep. 192; other 1

Appointments

Vice Presidents:
  Spiro T. Agnew (1969–1973)
  Gerald R. Ford (1973–1974)

Cabinet Members:
  William P. Rogers, secretary of state (1969–1973)
  Henry A. Kissinger, secretary of state (1973–1974)
  David M. Kennedy, secretary of the treasury (1969–1971)
  John B. Connally, Jr., secretary of the treasury (1971–1972)

George P. Shultz, secretary of the treasury (1972–1974)
William E. Simon, secretary of the treasury (1974)
Melvin R. Laird, secretary of defense (1969–1973)
Elliot L. Richardson, secretary of defense (1973)
James R. Schlesinger, secretary of defense (1973–1974)
John N. Mitchell, attorney general (1969–1972)
Richard G. Kleindienst, attorney general (1972–1973)
Elliot L. Richardson, attorney general (1973)
William B. Saxbe, attorney general (1974)
Wilton M. Blount, postmaster general (1969–1971)
Walter J. Hickel, secretary of the interior (1969–1970)
Rogers C. B. Morton, secretary of the interior (1971–1974)
Clifford M. Hardin, secretary of agriculture (1969–1971)
Earl L. Butz, secretary of agriculture (1971–1974)
Maurice H. Stans, secretary of commerce (1969–1972)
Peter G. Peterson, secretary of commerce (1972–1973)
Federick B. Dent, secretary of commerce (1973–1974)
George P. Shultz, secretary of labor (1969–1970)
James D. Hodgson, secretary of labor (1970–1973)
Peter J. Brennan, secretary of labor (1973–1974)
Robert H. Finch, secretary of health, education, and welfare (1969–1970)
Elliot L. Richardson, secretary of health, education, and welfare (1970–1973)
Caspar W. Weinberger, secretary of health, education, and welfare (1973–1974)
George W. Romney, secretary of housing and urban development (1969–1973)
James T. Lynn, secretary of housing and urban development (1973–1974)
John A. Volpe, secretary of transportation (1969–1973)
Claude S. Brinegar, secretary of transportation (1973–1974)

Supreme Court Appointments:
Warren Earl Burger, chief justice (1969–1986)
Harry A. Blackmun (1970–1994)
Lewis F. Powell, Jr. (1972–1987)
William H. Rehnquist (1972–)

Key Events

1969 Nixon inaugurated (20 Jan.); declares that "the greatest honor history can bestow is the title peacemaker"; travels to London, Paris, Bonn, Brussels, Berlin, and Rome (23 Feb.–3 March), heralding a return to a foreign policy stressing relations with Europe; meets with South Vietnamese President Thieu on Midway Island to initiate policy of "Vietnamizing" the Vietnam War (8 Jun.); flies to the South Pacific for splashdown of *Apollo XI* (moon landing) spacecraft on first leg of an around-the-world diplomatic mission (23 July); announces the "Nixon

Doctrine" stating that the U.S. would keep all existing commitments in Asia, but not undertake any more (24 July); in a televised speech, Nixon calls for "the great silent majority of Americans" to support his policy of gradual "Vietnamization" of the Vietnam fighting (3 Nov.).

1970 U.S. population: 203, 235, 298

U.S.-South Vietnamese incursion into Cambodian territory to attack alleged communist sanctuaries (29 Apr.); student protests erupt throughout U.S.; Nixon calls campus radicals "bums"; at Ohio's Kent State University National Guard troops open fire on demonstrators killing four (4 May); Republicans lose 9 House seats, gain 2 in Senate (3 Nov.). By year's end U.S. troops in Vietnam down to 340,000.

1971 *New York Times* begins publishing the classified *Pentagon Papers* study of the Vietnam War, leading Nixon to form the secret "plumbers" group to prevent such leaks; Kissinger secretly visits China (9–10 Jul.); in a televised speech, Nixon announces he will travel to the People's Republic of China (Jul. 15).

1972 Nixon visits Peking (21 Feb.), Moscow (22 May), first for a U.S. president; North Vietnamese attack in force across demilitarized zone (30 Mar.) and U.S. bombs Hanoi and Haiphong (15 Apr.); break-in of Democratic National Party Headquarters at Watergate (17 June); ABM Treaty between U.S. and U.S.S.R. enters into force (3 Oct.); Nixon re-elected (7 Nov.).

1973 Supreme Court rules in *Roe v. Wade* (Jan.) that states cannot categorically ban abortion; cease-fire effective in Vietnam (28 Jan.); China and U.S. agree (22 Feb.) to establish liaison offices in each country; Vice President Agnew resigns (10 Oct.), pleading no contest to tax-evasion charges; Gerald Ford becomes first appointed vice president (12 Oct.); ban by Middle East oil nations on exports to U.S. (19–21 Oct., lifted 18 Mar. 1974); War Powers Act (7 Nov.) sets 60-day limit on presidential commitment of troops unless Congress authorizes continued action.

1974 House Judiciary Committee recommends 3 articles of impeachment against Nixon (24–30 July); Nixon resigns (9 Aug.).

GERALD RUDOLPH FORD, 38TH PRESIDENT (1974–1977)

Life

Birthdate: 14 July 1913
Birthplace: Omaha, Nebr.
Parents: Leslie Lynch King, Dorothy Ayer Gardner
Religion: Episcopalian
College Education: University of Michigan; Yale University Law School
Wife: Elizabeth ("Betty") Bloomer Warren

Date of Marriage: 15 October 1948
Children: Michael Gerald, John ("Jack") Gardner, Steven Meigs, Susan
    Elizabeth
Political Party: Republican
Other Positions Held:
    Member, U.S. House of Representatives (1949–1973; Republican Leader,
    1965–1973)
    Vice President (1973–1974)
Date of Inauguration: 9 August 1974 (succeeded to presidency on
    resignation of Richard Nixon)
End of Term: 20 January 1977
Resides in Rancho Mirage, Calif.

Elections

Defeated in Election of 1976 by Jimmy Carter

Political Composition of Congress

93d Congress (1973–1975)
Senate: Dem. 56; Rep. 42; others 2
House: Dem. 239; Rep. 192; other 1

94th Congress (1975–1977)
Senate: Dem. 61; Rep. 37; others 2
House: Dem. 291; Rep. 144

Appointments

Vice President:
Nelson A. Rockefeller (1974–1977)

Cabinet Members:
Henry A. Kissinger, secretary of state (1974–1977)
William E. Simon, secretary of the treasury (1974–1977)
James R. Schlesinger, secretary of defense (1974–1975)
Donald H. Rumsfeld, secretary of defense (1975–1977)
William B. Saxbe, attorney general (1974–1975)
Edward H. Levi, attorney general (1975–1977)
Rogers C. B. Morton, secretary of the interior (1974–1975)
Stanley K. Hathaway, secretary of the interior (1975)
Thomas S. Kleppe, secretary of the interior (1975–1977)
Earl L. Butz, secretary of agriculture (1974–1976)
John A. Knebel, secretary of agriculture (1976–1977)
Frederick B. Dent, secretary of commerce (1974–1975)
Rogers C. B. Morton, secretary of commerce (1975)
Elliot L. Richardson, secretary of commerce (1976–1977)

Peter J. Brennan, secretary of labor (1974–1975)
John T. Dunlop, secretary of labor (1975–1976)
William J. Usery, Jr., secretary of labor (1976–1977)
Caspar W. Weinberger, secretary of health, education, and welfare
    (1974–1975)
F. David Mathews, secretary of health, education and welfare (1975–1977)
James T. Lynn, secretary of housing and urban development (1974–1975)
Carla Anderson Hills, secretary of housing and urban development
    (1975–1977)
Claude S. Brinegar, secretary of transportation (1974–1975)
William T. Coleman, Jr., secretary of transportation (1975–1977)

Supreme Court Appointments:
John Paul Stevens (1975–)

Key Events

1974 Ford becomes president upon resignation of Nixon (9 Aug.); pardons
      Nixon (8 Sept.); testifies before House Judiciary Committee about cir-
      cumstances surrounding the pardon (18 Oct.).
1975 U.S. civilians evacuated from Saigon (29 Apr.), Communists overrun
      country; *Mayaguez* incident (15 May): merchant ship is rescued from
      Cambodians by U.S. navy and marines; Rockefeller Commission re-
      veals (10 June) illegal CIA operations.
1976 United States celebrates bicentennial (4 July); *Viking 2* lands on Mars
      (3 Sept.); President Ford escapes 2 assassination attempts (5, 22 Sept.);
      Ford's first debate with Carter on domestic and economic policy (23
      Sept.); in second debate on foreign policy and defense, says, "There is
      no Soviet domination of Eastern Europe" (6 Oct.); defeated by Carter
      in general election (2 Nov.).

JAMES EARL ("JIMMY") CARTER, 39TH PRESIDENT (1977–1981)

Life
Birthdate: 1 October 1924
Birthplace: Plains, Ga.
Parents: James Earl Carter, (Bessie) Lillian Gordy
Religion: Baptist
College Education: United States Naval Academy
Wife: Rosalynn Smith
Date of Marriage: 7 July 1946
Children: John William ("Jack"), James Earl ("Chip"), Donnel Jeffrey
    ("Jeff"), Amy Lynn
Political Party: Democratic

Other Positions Held:
    Member, Georgia Senate (1963–1967)
    Governor of Georgia (1971–1975)
Date of Inauguration: 20 January 1977
End of Term: 20 January 1981
Resides in Atlanta, Ga.

Elections

CANDIDATE	PARTY	ELECTORAL VOTE	POPULAR VOTE
Election of 1976			
Jimmy Carter	Democratic	297	50.1%
Gerald R. Ford	Republican	240	47.9%

Defeated in Election of 1980 by Ronald Reagan

Political Composition of Congress

95th Congress (1977–1979)
Senate: Dem. 61; Rep. 38; other 1
House: Dem. 292; Rep. 143

96th Congress (1979–1981)
Senate: Dem. 58; Rep. 41; other 1
House: Dem. 276; Rep. 157

Appointments

Vice President:
    Walter F. Mondale (1977–1981)

Cabinet Members:
    Cyrus R. Vance, secretary of state (1977–1980)
    Edmund S. Muskie, secretary of state (1980–1981)
    W. Michael Blumenthal, secretary of the treasury (1977–1979)
    G. William Miller, secretary of the treasury (1979–1981)
    Harold Brown, secretary of defense (1977–1981)
    Griffin B. Bell, attorney general (1977–1979)
    Benjamin R. Civiletti, attorney general (1979–1981)
    Cecil D. Andrus, secretary of the interior (1977–1981)
    Bob S. Bergland, secretary of agriculture (1977–1981)
    Juanita M. Kreps, secretary of commerce (1977–1979)
    Philip M. Klutznick, secretary of commerce (1980–1981)
    Ray Marshall, secretary of labor (1977–1981)
    Joseph A. Califano, Jr., secretary of health, education, and welfare
        (1977–1979)

Particia Roberts Harris, secretary of health, education, and welfare
 (1979–1981)
Particia Roberts Harris, secretary of housing and urban development
 (1977–1979)
Moon Landrieu, secretary of housing and urban development (1979–1981)
Brock Adams, secretary of transportation (1977–1979)
Neil Goldschmidt, secretary of transportation (1979–1981)
James R. Schlesinger, secretary of energy (1977–1979)
Charles W. Duncan, secretary of energy (1979–1981)
Shirley M. Hufstedler, secretary of education (1979–1981)

Supreme Court Appointments:
None

Key Events

1977 Carter inaugurated (20 Jan.); pardons approximately 10,000 Vietnam
 draft evaders (21 Jan.); gives televised "fireside chat" from the White
 House library wearing cardigan sweater (2 Feb.); appears before a town
 meeting in Clinton, Mass. (5 Mar.); announces commitment to withdraw American ground forces in Korea within 4 or 5 years (9 Mar.); announces plan to reconsider congressionally approved dams and water
 projects to determine whether spending is justified. Soviet Union rejects
 U.S. arms limitation proposals (30 Mar.); Bert Lance resigns as budget
 director because of continuing assertions of impropriety regarding his
 position as head of Georgia bank (21 Sept.); Carter postpones 12-day
 foreign trip to seek enactment of his energy program (7 Nov.).
1978 Congress votes (18 Apr.) to turn over Panama Canal to Panama in
 1999; Camp David summit with Begin and Sadat ends with signing of a
 framework for Mideast peace (5–17 Sept.); Carter calls for voluntary
 wage and price controls to bring down inflation (24 Oct.); signs wa-
 tered-down Energy Bill (9 Nov.)
1979 Nuclear reactor accident at Three Mile Island, Pa. (28 Mar.); Carter
 and Soviet premier Brezhnev embrace and sign SALT II treaty in Vienna
 (18 Jun.); Carter cancels a planned vacation (1 July) and returns to his
 desk to prepare an address to Congress calling for a "bold, forceful"
 energy program; calls off address (4 July) and engages in extensive consultations with leaders from all walks of American life (6–11 July);
 gives speech on "crisis of confidence" of the American people (15 July);
 shakes up cabinet, accepting resignations of 4 members (19–20 July);
 63 Americans taken hostage at U.S. embassy in Tehran, Iran (4 Nov.);
 Soviet Union invades Afghanistan (27 Dec.).
1980 U.S. population: 226, 504, 825
 U.S. retaliates against Soviet invasion of Afghanistan with grain em-
 bargos (4 Jan.); military mission fails (24 Apr.) in attempt to rescue
 American hostages in Iran, with 8 killed and 5 wounded; Reagan elected
 president (4 Nov.).

RONALD WILSON REAGAN, 40TH PRESIDENT (1981–1989)

Life

Birthdate: 6 February 1911
Birthplace: Tampico, Ill.
Parents: John Edward ("Jack") Reagan, Nelle Clyde Wilson
Religion: Episcopalian
College Education: Eureka College
First Wife: Jane Wyman (divorced 1949)
Date of First Marriage: 24 January 1940
Children from First Marriage: Maureen Elizabeth, Michael Edward
    (adopted)
Second Wife: Nancy Davis
Date of Second Marriage: 4 March 1952
Children from Second Marriage: Patricia ("Patti") Ann, Ronald ("Skip")
    Prescott
Political Party: Republican
Other Positions Held:
    President, Screen Actors Guild (1947–1952; 1959–1960)
    Governor of California (1967–1975)
Date of Inauguration: 20 January 1981
End of Term: 20 January 1989
Resides in Bel Air, Los Angeles, Calif.

Elections

CANDIDATE	PARTY	ELECTORAL VOTE	POPULAR VOTE
Election of 1980			
Ronald Reagan	Republican	489	50.9%
Jimmy Carter	Democratic	49	41.2%
John B. Anderson	Independent	0	7.9%
Election of 1984			
Ronald Reagan	Republican	525	59.2%
Walter Mondale	Democratic	13	40.8%

Ineligible to Run in Election of 1988

Political Composition of Congress

97th Congress (1981–1983)
Senate: Rep. 53; Dem. 46; other 1
House: Dem. 242; Rep. 189

98th Congress (1983–1985)
Senate: Rep. 54; Dem. 46
House: Dem. 268; Rep. 167

99th Congress (1985–1987)
Senate: Rep. 53; Dem. 47
House: Dem. 253; Rep. 182

100th Congress (1987–1989)
Senate: Dem. 55; Rep. 45
House: Dem. 258; Rep. 177

Appointments

Vice President:
George H. W. Bush (1981–1989)

Cabinet Members:
Alexander M. Haig, secretary of state (1981–1982)
George P. Shultz, secretary of state (1982–1989)
Donald T. Regan, secretary of the treasury (1981–1985)
James A. Baker III, secretary of the treasury (1985–1988)
Nicholas F. Brady, secretary of the treasury (1988–1989)
Caspar W. Weinberger, secretary of defense (1981–1987)
Frank C. Carlucci, secretary of defense (1987–1989)
William French Smith, attorney general (1981–1985)
Edwin Meese III, attorney general (1985–1988)
Richard L. Thornburgh, attorney general (1988–1989)
James G. Watt, secretary of the interior (1981–1983)
William P. Clark, secretary of the interior (1983–1985)
Donald P. Hodel, secretary of the interior (1985–1989)
John R. Block, secretary of agriculture (1981–1986)
Richard E. Lyng, secretary of agriculture (1986–1989)
Malcolm Baldrige, secretary of commerce (1981–1987)
C. William Verity, Jr., secretary of commerce (1987–1989)
Raymond J. Donovan, secretary of labor (1981–1985)
William E. Brock III, secretary of labor (1985–1987)
Ann D. McLaughlin, secretary of labor (1987–1989)
Samuel R. Pierce, Jr., secretary of housing and urban development (1981–1989)
Andrew L. Lewis, secretary of transportation (1981–1983)
Elizabeth H. Dole, secretary of transportation (1983–1987)
James H. Burnley IV, secretary of transportation (1987–1989)
James B. Edwards, secretary of energy (1981–1982)
Donald P. Hodel, secretary of energy (1982–1985)
John S. Herrington, secretary of energy (1985–1989)

Terrel H. Bell, secretary of education (1981–1985)
William J. Bennett, secretary of education (1985–1988)
Lauro F. Cavazos, secretary of education (1988–1989)
Richard S. Schweiker, secretary of health and human services (1981–1983)
Margaret M. Heckler, secretary of health and human services (1983–1985)
Otis R. Bowen, secretary of health and human services (1985–1989)

Supreme Court Appointments:
Sandra Day O'Connor (1981–)
William H. Rehnquist, chief justice (1986–) (promoted from associate
    justice)
Antonin Scalia (1986–)
Anthony M. Kennedy (1988–)

Key Events

1981 In Inaugural Address as 40th president of the U.S., Reagan declares
      that in the current economic crisis "government is not the solution to
      our problem; government is the problem." Reagan survives assassina-
      tion attempt (30 Mar.); space shuttle *Columbia* launched, the first
      reusable spacecraft (12 Apr.); Reagan appoints Sandra Day O'Connor
      first woman justice of the Supreme Court (7 July); largest tax cut in na-
      tion's history passes (29 July); federal air traffic controllers strike and
      are dismissed by Reagan (5 Aug.).

1982 Reagan rules out new taxes in second State of the Union address (26
      Jan.); acknowledges that a balanced budget by 1984 is not achievable
      (6 Feb.); unveils proposed 1983 budget with projected deficit; Soviet
      leader Leonid Brezhnev dies of heart attack at age 75 (2 Nov.). Two
      days later Yuri Andropov elected to replace him as General Secretary of
      the Communist Party's Central Committee.

1983 In address to convention of Protestant Evangelicals in Orlando,
      Florida, Reagan refers to Soviet Union as an Evil Empire (Mar. 5); seeks
      public support in nationally televised address for the Strategic Defense
      Initiative (SDI), which he describes as a revolutionary new technology
      with the promise of rendering nuclear missiles obsolete (23 Mar.); de-
      nounces Soviet Union for "Korean Air Line massacre" in nationally
      televised speech, but avoids any major retaliation (5 Sept.); orders U.S.
      marines to invade Grenada in response to request by Organization of
      Eastern Caribbean States to restore law and order to the island (25
      Oct.).

1984 Reagan calls for improved relations with Soviet Union (16 Jan.); Soviet
      Communist Party General Secretary Andropov dies (9 Feb.), Konstan-
      tin Chernenko succeeds him; Reagan meets Soviet foreign minister An-
      dre Gromyko in White House, the first such meeting of his presidency
      (28 Aug.); reelected to a second term (6 Nov.).

1985 Reagan announces that White House chief of staff James Baker III and treasury secretary Donald Regan will exchange jobs (8 Jan.); in second inaugural address (20 Jan.) stresses importance of controlling size of government and defends SDI (20 Jan.). Soviet General Secretary Chernenko dies (10 Mar.); Bush and Shultz attend funeral in Moscow carrying summit invitation to Chernenko's successor, Mikhail Gorbachev. Reagan-Gorbachev summit held in Geneva, Switzerland (19–20 Nov.); Reagan refuses to compromise on SDI but promises to share its technology with Soviets.

1986   Reagan expresses desire of U.S. to reduce nuclear arsenal and achieve better understanding with Soviet Union in videotaped New Year's message broadcast on Soviet TV (1 Jan.); gives enthusiastic endorsement to sweeping changes in income tax code approved by Senate Finance Committee (11 May); attends summit meeting with Gorbachev in Reykjavik (11–12 Oct.). Democrats recapture Senate 55-45 despite vigorous campaign by president on behalf of Republican candidates (4 Nov.); *New York Times* and *Washington Post* report secret contacts between U.S. and Iranian officials in both Iran and Europe for more than a year (5–6 Nov.); in televised address (13 Nov.), Reagan acknowledges for first time that U.S. had sent "defensive weapons and spare parts" to Iran but denies weapons were part of an arms-for-hostages deal; Iran-contra scandal emerges (3 Nov.); former senator John Tower appointed to head commission to review Iran-contra affair (2 Dec.).

1987   Tower Commission issues report blaming Reagan for allowing himself to be misled by White House staff who organized sale of arms to Iran and pursued secret war against Nicaraguan government and chief of staff Donald Regan for letting situation get out of control; Reagan cleared of cover-up charges (26 Feb.); Reagan accepts Regan's resignation (27 Feb.). Reagan-Gorbachev summit held in Washington (8–10 Dec.), marked by signing of Intermediate-Range Nuclear Forces (INF) Treaty (8–10 Dec.).

1988   Reagan pledges vigorous final year of his presidency in State of the Union message; speaks of a turnaround in international relations with democracy everywhere on the move (28 Jan.); Gorbachev announces all Soviet troops to leave Afghanistan (8 Feb.); Senate votes 93-5 to ratify INF treaty (27 May). Reagan meets Gorbachev in Moscow in 4th summit; criticizes Soviet record on human rights and religious freedom; two leaders exchange formal documents ratifying INF treaty (29 May-2 Jun.); George Bush wins U.S. presidential election (8 Nov.); Gorbachev at U.N. announces 500,000 troops cut and meets with Reagan and Bush at Governor's Island in New York (7 Dec.).

1989   Reagan delivers Farewell Address (11 Jan.), saying, "I won a nickname: 'The Great Communicator.' But I never thought it was my style or the words I used that made a difference—it was the content."

GEORGE HERBERT WALKER BUSH, 41ST PRESIDENT (1989–1993)

Life
Birthdate: 12 June 1924
Birthplace: Milton, Mass.
Parents: Prescott Sheldon Bush, Dorothy Walker
Religion: Episcopalian
College Education: Yale College
Wife: Barbara Pierce
Date of Marriage: 6 January 1945
Children: George Walker, Robin, John Ellis ("Jeb"), Neil Mallon, Marvin
    Pierce, Dorothy Pierce
Political Party: Republican
Other Positions Held:
    Member, U.S. House of Representatives (1967–1971)
    Ambassador to United Nations (1971–1973)
    Chairman, Republican National Committee (1973–1974)
    Chief U.S. Liaison, People's Republic of China (1974–1975)
    Director, Central Intelligence Agency (1976–1977)
    Vice President (1981–1989)
Date of Inauguration: 20 January 1989
End of Term: 20 January 1993
Resides in Houston, Tex.

Elections

CANDIDATE	PARTY	ELECTORAL VOTE	POPULAR VOTE
Election of 1988			
George H. W. Bush	Republican	426	53.4%
Michael S. Dukakis	Democrat	111	45.6%

Defeated in Election of 1992 by Bill Clinton

Political Composition of Congress

101st Congress (1989–1991)
Senate: Dem. 55; Rep. 45
House: Dem. 260; Rep. 175

102d Congress (1991–1993)
Senate: Dem. 56; Rep. 44
House: Dem. 267; Rep. 167; other 1

Appointments

Vice President:
  J. Danforth ("Dan") Quayle (1989–1993)

Cabinet Members:
  James A. Baker III, secretary of state (1989–1992)
  Lawrence S. Eagleburger, secretary of state (1992–1993)
  Nicholas F. Brady, secretary of the treasury (1989–1993)
  Richard B. Cheney, secretary of defense (1989–1993)
  Richard L. Thornburgh, attorney general (1989–1991)
  William Barr, attorney general (1991–1993)
  Manuel Lujan, Jr,. secretary of the interior (1989–1993)
  Clayton K. Yeutter, secretary of agriculture (1989–1991)
  Edward R. Madigan, secretary of agriculture (1991–1993)
  Robert A. Mosbacher, secretary of commerce (1989–1992)
  Barbara A. Franklin, secretary of commerce (1992–1993)
  Elizabeth H. Dole, secretary of labor (1989–1991)
  Lynn Martin, secretary of labor (1991–1993)
  Jack F. Kemp, secretary of housing and urban development
     (1989–1993)
  Samuel K. Skinner, secretary of transportation (1989–1992)
  Andrew H. Card, secretary of transportation (1992–1993)
  James Watkins, secretary of energy (1989–1993)
  Lauro F. Cavazos, secretary of education (1989–1990)
  Lamar Alexander, secretary of education (1991–1993)
  Louis W. Sullivan, secretary of health and human services (1989–1993)
  Edward J. Derwinski, secretary of veterans affairs (1989–1992)

Supreme Court Appointments:
  David H. Souter (1990–)
  Clarence Thomas (1991–)

Key Events

1989 Bush, in Inaugural Address (20 Jan.), calls on Americans "to make
      kinder the face of the nation and gentler the face of the world"; orders
      a "pause" in diplomacy with Moscow (13 Feb.); begins 3-nation tour
      of Asia with a 3-day visit to Japan to attend funeral of Emperor Hiro-
      hito; then visits China and speaks with leaders about opening up for-
      eign investment (23–27 Feb.); announces he is suspending high-level
      contacts with China in protest over crackdown on student activists;
      later secretly sent envoy to Beijing (20 June); meets with U.S.S.R. for-
      eign minister Eduard Shevardnadze on SDI, summit meeting for 1990,
      and obstacles to Strategic Arms Limitation Treaty (START) (21 Sept.);
      meets with Gorbachev in shipboard summit near Malta; discusses op-
      tions for speeding up arms control negotiations between U.S. and So-

viet Union (2–3 Dec.); intervenes in Panama, overthrowing government of Manuel Noriega (20 Dec.).

1990 U.S. population: 248,709,873

Bush declares in State of the Union address that there is "a new era in the world's affairs," but insists on continuing U.S. strategic defense modernization and SDI (31 Jan.); attends summit in Washington with Gorbachev and signs agreements on strategic arms reduction, chemical weapons, trade, and other matters (31 May–3 June); vetoes Family and Medical Leave Act, requiring companies over a certain size to grant employees time off to care for sick or newborn children (29 Jun.); Iraq invades Kuwait (2 Aug.); in Moscow, Secretary of State James Baker III and Soviet foreign minister Shevardnadze jointly condemn Iraq's invasion (3 Aug.); Bush meets with Gorbachev in Helsinki and agrees to cooperate to end Iraqi aggression (9 Sept.), East and West Germany unite (3 Oct.); U.N. passes Security Resolution 678 authorizing use of force in the Persian Gulf (27 Nov.).

1991 Persian Gulf War begins with air attack on Baghdad (16 Jan.); ground assault phase follows (24 Feb.); organized Iraqi resistance crumbles within 48 hours; Bush orders cease-fire after 100 hours of fighting (27 Feb.); Bush and Gorbachev sign START treaty in Moscow, announcing their co-sponsorship of a Middle East peace conference (29 July–1 Aug.); hardliners stage unsuccessful coup against Gorbachev (18–21 Aug.); Gorbachev resigns, and the U.S.S.R. ceases to exist (25 Dec.).

1992 Congress passes Bush-sponsored Americans with Disability Act, most sweeping civil rights enactment since 1964 (26 Jan.); Bush and Russian president Boris Yeltsin issue statement officially ending cold war (1 Feb.); riots erupt in Los Angeles over police beating of a black motorist (29 Apr.–4 May); unemployment rises to 7.8%, highest level since 1983; Bush defeated for reelection by Arkansas governor Bill Clinton (3 Nov.).

WILLIAM JEFFERSON ("BILL") CLINTON, 42D PRESIDENT (1993–2001)

Life

Birthdate: 19 August 1946
Birthplace: Hope, Ark.
Parents: William Jefferson Blythe III, Virginia Cassidy
Religion: Baptist
College Education: Georgetown University; Rhodes Scholar, Oxford University, England; Yale University Law School
Wife: Hillary Diane Rodham
Date of Marriage: 11 October 1975
Child: Chelsea

Political Party: Democratic
Other Positions Held:
    Law Professor, University of Arkansas (1973–1976)
    Attorney General of Arkansas (1977–1979)
    Governor of Arkansas (1979–1981; 1983–1992)
Date of Inauguration: 20 January 1993
Resides in Washington, D.C., and Little Rock, Ark.

Elections

CANDIDATE	PARTY	ELECTORAL VOTE	POPULAR VOTE
Election of 1992			
Bill Clinton	Democratic	370	43%
George H. W. Bush	Republican	168	37%
H. Ross Perot	Independent	0	19%
Election of 1996			
Bill Clinton	Democratic	379	49%
Bob Dole	Republican	159	41%
H. Ross Perot	Independent	0	8%

Political Composition of Congress

103d Congress (1993–1995)
Senate: Dem. 56; Rep. 44
House: Dem. 258; Rep. 176; other 1

104th Congress (1995–1997)
Senate: Rep. 52; Dem. 48
House: Rep. 230; Dem. 204; other 1

105th Congress (1997–1999)
Senate: Rep. 55; Dem. 45
House: Rep. 227; Dem. 207; other 1

106th Congress (1999–2001)
Senate: Rep. 55; Dem. 45
House: Rep. 223; Dem. 211; other 1

Appointments

Vice President:
    Albert A. Gore, Jr. (1993–2001)

Cabinet Members:
    Warren M. Christopher, secretary of state (1993–1997)
    Madeleine K. Albright, secretary of state (1997–2001)

Lloyd M. Bentsen, Jr., secretary of the treasury (1993–1994)
Robert E. Rubin, secretary of the treasury (1995–1999)
Lawrence H. Summers, secretary of the treasury (1999–2001)
Les Aspin, Jr., secretary of defense (1993–1994)
William J. Perry, secretary of defense (1994–1997)
William S. Cohen, secretary of defense (1997–2001)
Janet Reno, attorney general (1993–2001)
Bruce Babbitt, secretary of the interior (1993–2001)
Mike Espy, secretary of agriculture (1993–1994)
Dan Glickman, secretary of agriculture (1994–2001)
Ronald H. Brown, secretary of commerce (1993–1996)
Mickey Kantor, secretary of commerce (1996–1997)
William M. Daley, secretary of commerce (1997–2000)
Norman Y. Mineta, secretary of commerce (2000–2001)
Robert B. Reich, secretary of labor (1993–1997)
Alexis M. Herman, secretary of labor (1997–2001)
Donna E. Shalala, secretary of health and human services (1993–2001)
Henry G. Cisneros, secretary of housing and urban development (1993–1997)
Andrew M. Cuomo, secretary of housing and urban development (1997–2001)
Federico F. Peña, secretary of transportation (1993–1997)
Rodney E. Slater, secretary of transportation (1997–2001)
Hazel R. O'Leary, secretary of energy (1993–1997)
Federico F. Peña, secretary of energy (1997–1998)
Bill Richardson, secretary of energy (1998–2001)
Richard W. Riley, secretary of education (1993–2001)
Jesse Brown, secretary of veterans affairs (1993–1997)
Togo D. West, Jr., secretary of veterans affairs (1998–2000)
Hershel W. Gober, secretary of veterans affairs (2000–2001)

Supreme Court Appointments:
Ruth Bader Ginsburg (1993–)
Stephen G. Breyer (1994–)

Key Events

1993   Clinton sworn in as 42nd president (20 Jan.); withdraws nomination of his first choice for attorney general after learning she hired an illegal alien as domestic help; his second choice withdraws for similar reasons; he then appoints Janet Reno. After storm of protest at Clinton's announcement of a new military policy under which homosexuals will no longer be discharged from the military, he modifies it to a policy of "Don't ask, don't tell" (Jan.–Feb.); Congress passes Clinton's $500 million deficit reduction measure on a party-line vote, cutting spending and raising taxes on the wealthy (5–6 Aug.). Israel and Palestine Liberation Organization sign a peace accord on the White House lawn (13 Sept.). Clinton unveils plan for universal health care (22 Sept.); signs North American Free Trade Agreement (NAFTA) (8 Dec.).

1994   Independent counsel named to investigate allegations of wrongdoing by Clintons in the 1980s, including their role in the Whitewater Development Corporation (20 Jan.). Clinton replaces Thomas McLarty III as chief of staff with OMB Director Leon Panetta, as part of an extensive shuffling of his staff (27 Jun.). White House and congressional leaders concede that Clinton health care reform proposal is dead (26 Aug.). Clinton signs a $30.2 billion anticrime package providing for 100,000 new police officers, expanding the death penalty, and banning the sale of certain assault weapons (13 Sept.); Republicans win control of Congress for the first time in 40 years (8 Nov.).

1995   Sidestepping Congress, Clinton uses his own emergency authority to lend up to $20 billion to Mexico to keep it from defaulting on government-issued bonds (31 Jan.); in his first prime-time news conference in 8 months, Clinton declares he is not irrelevant in the face of the new Republican majority in Congress (18 Apr.). Congress passes a compromise 7-year budget plan that would cut spending by nearly $900 billion, cut taxes by $245 billion, and hold down increases in Medicare and other social programs (29 Jun.). Repudiating his own earlier budget, Clinton says that the Republican goal of wiping out the deficit by 2002 is attainable, but insists on scaling back proposed cuts in education, health, and environmental programs (19 Oct.). The federal government suspends nonessential services in a shutdown lasting 6 days (14 Nov.). Clinton vetoes the Republican balanced-budget bill (6 Dec.). In ensuing impasse, government shuts down for a second time (16 Dec.).

1996   Congress votes to end government shutdown, and Clinton offers a plan to balance budget within 7 years, but with smaller tax cuts than demanded by Republicans (5–6 Jan.). Under threat of sanctions, China begins enforcing the accord on intellectual property rights for foreign software, music, and videos it signed more than a year earlier (19 Jun.). Clinton spends spring and summer proposing low-cost solutions to social problems, such as curfews for teenagers, uniforms in schools, fighting truancy and violence on television, and a national registry for sex offenders. Sweeping reform of welfare system enacted (22 Aug.). Clinton reelected to second term (5 Nov.).

1997   In second inauguration address (20 Jan.) Clinton called for "government that is smaller, lives within its means, and does more with less"; in weeks that follow, spells out an extensive list of low-price-tag legislative initiatives relating to such matters as education, crime, the environment, and welfare. Clinton and the Republican congressional leadership agree on plan to balance the federal budget by year 2002 (2 May).

1998   Allegations leaked to press that Clinton has had an affair with White House intern Monica Lewinsky; Clinton repeatedly denies charge (21, 22, and 26 Jan.); in State of the Union message, Clinton hails economy's strength, pointing to recent projections of a budget surplus by fiscal year 1999, and announcing an array of new proposals (27 Jan.). Clinton's approval level rises from 59% before his presentation to 67% following it. Confessing to "a critical lapse in judgment," Clinton admits that he behaved toward Lewinsky in a manner that was "not appropriate" and that he had misled his wife and the American people (17 Aug.). Independent Counsel Kenneth Starr submits a report to Congress, stating 11 possible grounds for impeaching Clinton (9 Sept.); House votes along party lines to adopt 2 articles of impeachment, charging Clinton with perjury and obstruction of justice for attempting to cover up his affair with Lewinsky (19 Dec.). Democrats gain seats in Congress, the first such midterm gain by a party holding the White House since 1934 (6 Nov.).

1999   Senate deliberates on articles of impeachment voted by the House; Clinton acquitted (7 Jan.–12 Feb.). With Senate trial in progress, Clinton delivers State of the Union address (19 Jan.), drawing attention to the booming economy, and proposing that a significant portion of the projected budget surplus be used to strengthen social security and Medicare. As part of a NATO effort to halt repression of ethnic Albanians in Kosovo by forces under the control of Serbian president Slobodan Milosevic, U.S. enters into a successful 11-week bombing campaign in the former Yugoslavia (27 Mar.).

2000   Clinton delivers his final State of the Union address, asserting that "the state of our union is the strongest it has ever been" and calling on Congress to pass a variety of new programs, including education initiatives, health care reforms, and gun control (27 Jan.); marks the 107th consecutive month of economic expansion, the longest economic boom in U.S. history (1 Feb.). Hillary Rodham Clinton formally announces her campaign for the U.S. Senate (6 Feb.). Clinton presents a $1.84 trillion budget proposal to Congress, including increased investment in some programs, targeted tax cuts, and provisions to reduce the national debt; a surplus is expected for the third consecutive year (7 Feb.). Clinton announces the release of $125 million in emergency heating-oil aid for low-income families in the Northeast (16 Feb.). A U.S. District Court judge rules that Clinton violated the federal Privacy Act in March of 1998 when he released letters written by Kathleen Willey, a former White House volunteer who had accused the president of making unwanted sexual advances (29 Mar.). U.S. immigration agents seize 6-year-old Cuban boy Elian Gonzalez Brotons from the home of Florida relatives in order to return him to his father in Cuba (22 April); the boy had been rescued at sea after his mother died in a failed attempt to reach U.S. shores. Clinton vetoes a bill to create a permanent storage site for tons of nuclear waste near Yucca Mountain, Nevada (25 April); unemployment rate falls to a 30-year low of 3.9% (5 May); Arkansas Supreme Court Committee on Professional Conduct recommends that Clinton's law license be revoked because of misleading testimony under oath in the Paula Jones sexual harassment lawsuit (22 May). Two-week summit between Israeli prime minister Ehud Barak and Palestinian leader Yasir Arafat arranged by Clinton and held at Camp David ends in deadlock (25 July). Clinton gives final speech as president to Democratic National Convention (14 August); announces he will not authorize construction of a national missile defense system because of technical flaws and diplomatic concerns (1 Sept.). Independent Counsel Robert Ray clears the Clintons of criminal wrongdoing in the Arkansas Whitewater land deal (20 Sept.). Clinton orders the release of 30 million barrels of oil from the nation's Strategic Petroleum Reserve in an attempt to combat low levels of home heating oil inventories (22 Sept.); signs bill granting China permanent normal trade relations, one of the last major foreign policy initiatives of his administration (10 Oct.). Seventeen U.S. sailors are killed and 39 wounded in a terrorist attack when bombers explode a small boat next to the USS *Cole*, a Navy destroyer stopped for refueling in Yemen (12 Oct.). First Lady Hillary Rodham Clinton elected to the Senate from New York (7 Nov.). Presidential election remains undecided and is not resolved until a U.S. Supreme Court ruling (13 Dec.)

2001 Clinton makes a televised farewell address to the nation (18 Jan.); agrees to a plea bargain with Independent Counsel Robert Ray in which Ray drops plans to indict the president for perjury and obstruction of justice, in exchange for an admission of giving false testimony in the Paula Jones lawsuit; Clinton also agrees to surrender his Arkansas law license for 5 years and pay a $25,000 fine (19 Jan.). On his last day in office, Clinton issues 141 pardons and commutes 36 sentences (20 Jan.); among the figures pardoned are Marc Rich and Pincus Green, commodities traders who had fled to Switzerland to escape tax-evasion and other charges; the pardons are severely criticized by members of both parties; federal prosecutors and a Senate panel investigate why regular procedures were not followed in the Rich pardon and examine the role of Rich's ex-wife, a major Democratic Party fund-raiser.

GEORGE WALKER BUSH, 43D PRESIDENT (2001–)

Life

Birthdate: 6 July 1946
Birthplace: New Haven, Conn.
Parents: George Herbert Walker Bush, Barbara Pierce
Religion: Methodist
College Education: Yale University; Harvard Business School
Wife: Laura Welch
Date of Marriage: 5 November 1977

Children: Barbara, Jenna
Political Party: Republican
Other Positions Held:
  Founder and CEO, Bush Exploration and Gas Co. (1975–1987)
  Senior Advisor, Bush Presidential Campaign (1988)
  Managing General Partner, Texas Rangers (1989–1994)
  Governor of Texas (1994–2000)
Date of Inauguration: 20 January 2001

Elections

CANDIDATE	PARTY	ELECTORAL VOTE	POPULAR VOTE
Election of 2000			
George W. Bush	Republican	271	47.8%
Albert Gore	Democrat	266	48.4%
Ralph Nader	Green	0	2.7%

Political Composition of Congress

107th Congress (2001–2003)
Senate: Dem. 50; Rep. 49; other 1
          (after Senator Jeffords's switch to Independent)
House: Rep. 223; Dem. 210; other 2

108th Congress (2003–2005)
Senate: Rep. 51; Dem. 48; other 1
House: Rep. 229; Dem. 205; other 1

Appointments

Vice President:
  Richard B. Cheney (2001–)

Cabinet Members:
  Colin Powell, secretary of state (2001–)
  Paul H. O'Neill, secretary of the treasury (2001–2003)
  John W. Snow, secretary of the treasury (2003–)
  Donald H. Rumsfeld, secretary of defense (2001–)
  John Ashcroft, attorney general (2001–)
  Gale A. Norton, secretary of the interior (2001–)
  Ann M. Veneman, secretary of agriculture (2001–)
  Donald L. Evans, secretary of commerce (2001–)
  Elaine Chao, secretary of labor (2001–)
  Tommy Thompson, secretary of health and human services (2001–)
  Mel Martinez, secretary of housing and urban development (2001–)
  Norman Y. Mineta, secretary of transportation (2001–)
  Spencer Abraham, secretary of energy (2001–)

Roderick R. Page, secretary of education (2001–)
Anthony J. Principi, secretary of veterans affairs (2001–)
Thomas Ridge, secretary of homeland security (2003–)

Supreme Court Appointments:
None

Key Events

2001   Bush inaugurated, promising to reform schools, cut taxes, shore up
Social Security and Medicare, and strengthen the country's defenses
(20 Jan.); signs an executive order creating the new White House
Office of Faith-Based and Community Initiatives (29 Jan.); presents his
budget proposal, including large tax cuts, to Congress (27 Feb.).
China detains the crew of a U.S. spy plane that made an emergency
landing on Hainan Island after colliding with a Chinese fighter jet; the
crew is finally released eleven days later (1–12 April). Senator Jim
Jeffords of Vermont announces plans to leave the Republican Party,
shifting control of the Senate to the Democrats (24 May). In a televised address, Bush announces he will permit federal funding of
research on human embryonic stem cells under limited conditions (9
Aug.). Hijackers fly commercial jetliners into the World Trade Center
towers in New York City and into the Pentagon; a fourth jet crashes
in a rural Pennsylvania field; Bush addresses the nation from the Oval
Office, saying that terrorist attacks "can shake the foundations of our
biggest buildings, but they cannot touch the foundation of America"
(11 Sept.). Bush calls the attacks "acts of war" (12 Sept.); speaks at
National Cathedral as part of a "National Day of Prayer and Re-
membrance" and rallies rescue workers at the site of the World Trade
Center; Congress votes to authorize "all necessary and appropriate
force" to retaliate against terrorists (14 Sept.). Bush addresses a joint
session of Congress, outlining his campaign against terrorism and
announcing a new cabinet-level agency, the Office of Homeland
Security (20 Sept.). U.S. and British forces launch airstrikes against
Afghanistan's ruling Taliban regime and the al-Qaeda terrorist network (7 Oct.); by December, all major Afghan cities have fallen to U.S.
or Northern Alliance troops, and Hamid Karzai is sworn in as head of
an interim government; al-Qaeda forces retreat to mountain cave
complexes. Bush holds the first formal prime-time news conference of
his presidency (11 Oct.). Bush addresses the U.N. General Assembly
on the pursuit of Osama bin Laden and his terrorist network (10
Nov.); authorizes the use of military tribunals to try foreign nationals
accused of terrorism (13 Nov.); signs legislation federalizing air security workers (19 Nov.). After a three-day summit (13–15 Nov.), Bush
and Russian president Vladimir Putin agree to cut their nuclear arsenals; they reach no consensus about U.S. plans to develop a missile
defense shield; Bush announces that the U.S. will withdraw from

the 1972 Antiballistic Missile Treaty, marking the first time in the nuclear era that the U.S. has withdrawn from a major arms control treaty.

2002 Bush signs sweeping education reform measure requiring new math and reading tests (8 Jan.); delivers first State of the Union address, calling North Korea, Iran, and Iraq an "axis of evil" (29 Jan.). A new system of color-coded terrorism alerts is unveiled (12 Mar.). Bush signs landmark campaign finance legislation, but calls it "flawed" (27 Mar.); takes major foreign trips to Asia (Feb.), Latin America (Mar.), and Europe (May). With Russia's Vladimir Putin, Bush signs a sweeping arms control treaty (24 May). Bush calls pre-emptive action against potential enemies a "new doctrine" (14 June). In a speech at the U.N. General Assembly, Bush asserts that world leaders must force Saddam Hussein to destroy his weapons of mass destruction or action to depose him will be "unavoidable" (12 Sept.); Congress approves the use of U.S. military force against Iraq (11 Oct.). Republicans regain control of the Senate and add 6 seats to their margin in the House (5 Nov.). U.N. Security Council unanimously approves a new resolution warning of "serious consequences" if Iraq fails to comply with strict new weapons inspections (8 Nov.). Amid signs of continued economic difficulty, Treasury Secretary Paul O'Neill and senior economic adviser Larry Lindsey resign (6 Dec.).

2003 Bush renominates candidates for federal appeals and district courts who had been rejected or blocked by Democrat-controlled Senate (7 Jan.); proposes a $670-billion tax-cut package, including the elimination of the tax on stock dividends (7 Jan.). Chief U.N. Weapons Inspector Hans Blix makes a series of reports to the U.N. Security Council on inspectors' efforts to uncover evidence that Iraq is developing chemical, biological, or nuclear weapons (9 Jan.; 27 Jan.; 14 Feb.); North Korea announces its withdrawal from the 1970 Treaty on the Nonproliferation of Nuclear Weapons (10 Jan.). Senate confirms Tom Ridge as secretary of the new Homeland Security Department (22 Jan). Bush delivers his State of the Union address to Congress, highlighting the economy, his tax-cut proposal, Medicare overhaul, increased contributions to fighting AIDS in Africa, the prospect of war with Iraq, and the crimes of Saddam Hussein (28 Jan.). The space shuttle *Columbia* breaks apart as it re-enters Earth's atmosphere, killing its seven crew members (1 Feb.). North Korea announces the resumption of "normal operations" at its nuclear reactor at Yongbyon (5 Feb.); Colin Powell addresses an open session of the U.N. Security Council, detailing intelligence information about threats posed by Iraq, including its weapons programs and ties to terrorist organizations (5 Feb.). The U.S. and Britain offer a draft resolution to the Security Council declaring that Iraq has missed its last chance to disarm peacefully (24 Feb.); the U.S. amends its proposal, setting a deadline of March 17, with France promising to veto any resolution authorizing force (7 Mar.). Bush, British prime minister Blair, and

Spanish prime minister Jose Maria Aznar declare that their diplomatic efforts to win support for the use of force against Iraq will end in 24 hours (16 Mar.); in a nationally televised speech, Bush issues an ultimatum giving Saddam Hussein and his sons 48 hours to leave Iraq or face war (17 Mar.). U.S. forces begin the conflict in Iraq by launching air strikes against targets in Baghdad (19 Mar.); Bush announces the beginning of the war in a televised address (19 Mar.); the ground war in Iraq begins as U.S.-led forces cross from Kuwait into Iraq (20 Mar.); troops move rapidly toward Baghdad, but encounter harassment from small bands of Iraqi fighters, complicating efforts to secure supply lines (20–27 Mar.); the U.S. opens a northern front (26 Mar.); the al-Jazeera television network broadcasts videotapes of captured U.S. soldiers (23–24 Mar.); demonstrations against the war occur around the world (20–31 Mar.). Bush and Tony Blair meet to discuss the future of Iraq (7–8 April); U.S. forces take control of most of Baghdad, as thousands of residents take to the streets to destroy images of Saddam Hussein; widespread looting is reported (9 April). Bush and Tony Blair address the Iraqi people on a television channel previously controlled by Saddam Hussein's regime (10 April); Bush declares the end of Saddam Hussein's regime (15 April). The U.S. and North Korea hold direct talks in Beijing, China (23–25 April); the U.S., Russia, the European Union, and the United Nations formally publish a "road map" for Israeli-Palestinian peace that includes the creation of an independent Palestinian state in 2005 (30 April). In a nationally televised address from an aircraft carrier, the USS *Abraham Lincoln*, Bush declares that combat operations in Iraq have ended (1 May); four al-Qaeda suicide bombing attacks against Westerners in Riyadh, Saudi Arabia, kill 34 people, including 9 attackers (12–13 May). Bush signs a package of $330 billion in tax cuts and $20 billion in federal aid to the states, calling it "aggressive action to strengthen the foundation of our economy"; Bush and Tony Blair encounter growing criticism over the failure to find weapons of mass destruction in Iraq (29 May–4 June); deadly attacks on U.S. forces in Iraq rise (18–25 June); the Bush administration acknowledges that the president relied on faulty intelligence when he claimed in his State of the Union address that Iraq had attempted to buy uranium from Africa and admits that the claim "should not have been included" in the speech (7 July).

PRESIDENTIAL JOB APPROVAL *(SOURCE: GALLUP POLL)*

		HIGH	LOW	AVERAGE
Roosevelt				
	Jan. 1942:	84		*
	Nov. 1938:		54	
Truman				
	Jun. 1945:	87		*
	Feb. 1952:		22	
Eisenhower				
	Dec. 1956:	79		65
	Jul. 1960:		49	
Kennedy				
	May 1961:	83		71
	Sep. 1963:		56	
Johnson				
	Feb. 1964:	79		56
	Aug. 1968:		35	
Nixon				
	Nov. 1969:	67		
	Jan. 1973:	67		48
	Jul. 1974:		24	
	Aug. 1974:		24	
Ford				
	Aug. 1974:	71		
	Jan. 1975:		37	47
	Mar. 1975:		37	
Carter				
	Mar. 1977:	75		47
	Jun. 1979:		28	
Reagan				
	May 1981:	68		
	May 1986:	68		52
	Jan. 1983:		35	
Bush				
	Feb. 1991:	89		61
	Jul. 1992:		29	
Clinton				
	Dec. 1998:	73		55
	Jun. 1993:		37	
Bush				
	Sep. 2001 (21–22):	90		—
	Sep. 2001 (7–10):		51	

*Polling too irregular to compute meaningful averages for Roosevelt and Truman.

CHAPTER 1
The Presidential Difference

1. For documentation of the two episodes, see John P. Burke and Fred I. Greenstein with the collaboration of Larry Berman and Richard Immerman, *How Presidents Test Reality: Decisions on Vietnam, 1954 and 1965* (New York: Russell Sage Foundation, 1989).
2. Richard E. Neustadt, *Presidential Power: The Politics of Leadership* (New York: Wiley, 1960), and James David Barber, *The Presidential Character: Predicting Success in the White House* (Englewood Cliffs, N.J.: Prentice Hall, 1972).
3. Max Weber, "Politics as a Vocation," in *From Max Weber: Essays in Sociology*, ed. H. H. Gerth and C. Wright Mills (New York: Oxford University Press, 1956, originally published in 1919), 115. Daniel Goleman, *Emotional Intelligence* (New York: Bantam Books, 1995).
4. *A Discussion with Gerald R. Ford: The American Presidency* (Washington, D.C.: American Enterprise Institute, 1977), 3.
5. Clinton Campaign Speech at Pleasant Grove Baptist Church, March 13, 1992 (C-Span Archives).
6. "Remarks on Signing the Line Item Veto Act and an Exchange with Reporters," April 9, 1996, in *Public Papers of the Presidents: William J. Clinton, 1996* (Washington, D.C.: U.S. Government Printing Office, 1997).

CHAPTER 2
Franklin D. Roosevelt

1. Geoffrey C. Ward, *Before the Trumpet: Young Franklin Roosevelt, 1881–1905* (New York: Harper & Row, 1985), 243.
2. William Hopkins, oral history interview, John F. Kennedy Presidential Library, Boston, Massachusetts.
3. For the texts of the fireside chats, see Russell D. Buhite and David W. Levy, *FDR's Fireside Chats* (Norman, Okla.: University of Oklahoma Press, 1992). Roosevelt's remark about rationing his talks appears in a May 20,

1935, letter to the journalist Ray Stannard Baker, which is reproduced in *FDR: His Personal Letters: 1928–1945* (New York: Duell, Sloan, Pearce, 1950), 3: 144–145.

4. Leo C. Rosten, *The Washington Correspondents* (New York: Harcourt Brace, 1937), 49.

5. Arthur Schlesinger, Jr., *The Coming of the New Deal* (Boston: Houghton Mifflin, 1959), 528.

6. Robert Sherwood, *Roosevelt and Hopkins: An Intimate History* (New York: Harper, 1948), 9; Harold Ickes, *The Secret Diary of Harold Ickes: The Inside Struggle* (New York: Simon & Schuster, 1953–1954), 659.

7. Samuel I. Rosenman, *Working with Roosevelt* (New York: Harper & Row, 1952), 468.

8. Schlesinger, *The Coming of the New Deal*, 522–523.

9. I draw particularly on the account of the Hundred Days by Kenneth S. Davis, *FDR: The New Deal Years, 1933–1937: A History* (New York: Random House, 1986), chaps. 3, 4.

10. The quarterback analogy is from Roosevelt's April 19, 1933, press conference. *Complete Presidential Press Conferences of Franklin D. Roosevelt* (New York: Da Capo Press, 1972), 1: 156–158. On Roosevelt's about-face on deposit insurance, see Frank Freidel, *Franklin D. Roosevelt: Launching the New Deal* (Boston: Little, Brown, 1973), 442–443.

11. George Martin, *Madam Secretary: Francis Perkins* (Boston: Houghton Mifflin, 1976), 435.

12. For a fuller account, see Warren Kimball, *The Most Unsordid Act: Lend Lease, 1939–1941* (Baltimore, Md.: Johns Hopkins University Press, 1969).

13. For a review of the literature on Roosevelt's wartime diplomacy, see Mark A. Stoler, "A Half Century of Conflict: Interpretations of U.S. World War II Diplomacy," *Diplomatic History* 18 (1994): 375–403.

14. Warren F. Kimball, ed., *Churchill and Roosevelt: The Complete Correspondence: 1. Alliance Emerging* (Princeton, N.J.: Princeton University Press, 1984), 421.

15. Quoted by Frances Perkins in *The Roosevelt I Knew* (New York: Viking, 1946), 83–85.

16. Milovan Djilas, *Conversations with Stalin* (New York: Harcourt, Brace & World, 1962), 73.

17. In 1970, the Bureau of the Budget was renamed the Office of Management and Budget. For a fuller account, see Larry Berman, *The Office of Management and Budget and the Presidency: 1921–1979* (Princeton, N.J.: Princeton University Press, 1979).

18. Raymond Moley, *After Seven Years* (New York: Harper & Brothers, 1939), 48.

19. On the economics of the New Deal, see Stanley Lebergott, *The Americans: An Economic Record* (New York: Norton, 1982), 453–465.

20. Geoffrey C. Ward, *A First-Class Temperament: The Emergence of Franklin Roosevelt* (New York: Harper & Row, 1989), xv.

21. Davis, *FDR: The New Deal Years,* 319–320.
22. On Roosevelt's last year, see Robert H. Ferrell, *The Dying President: Franklin D. Roosevelt: 1944–1945* (Columbia, Mo.: University of Missouri Press, 1998), 138–152. For the assertion by a Roosevelt aide that he "must have been psychoanalyzed by God," see John Gunther, *Roosevelt in Retrospect* (New York: Harper, 1950), 33.

CHAPTER 3
Harry S. Truman

1. On the routinization of charisma, see H. H. Gerth and C. Wright Mills, eds., *From Max Weber: Essays in Sociology* (New York: Oxford University Press, 1956), 53–54, 297.
2. On Truman's shifting reputation, see Geoffrey S. Smith, "'Harry, We Hardly Know You,'" *American Political Science Review* 70 (1976): 560–582, and Daniel Yergin, "Harry Truman—Revived and Revised," *New York Times Magazine,* October 24, 1976. For a book that exemplifies the latter-day idealization of Truman, see David McCullough's Pulitzer Prize-winning *Truman* (New York: Simon & Schuster, 1992).
3. The phrase "small ego" appears on page 43 of Alonzo L. Hamby, "An American Democrat: A Reevaluation of the Personality of Harry S. Truman," *Political Science Quarterly* 106 (1991): 1–55. Any unattributed quotations in this chapter are from Hamby's *Man of the People: A Life of Harry S. Truman* (New York: Oxford University Press, 1995).
4. Remarks at Camp Pike, Arkansas, August 1933, County Judge File, Truman Library, Independence, Missouri.
5. *Time,* April 30, 1945, 17–19. For Truman's Gallup poll ratings see *The Gallup Opinion Index,* Report No. 182 (October–November 1980). All of the Gallup statistics reported in this book are from that report, George C. Edwards III, *Presidential Approval: A Sourcebook* (Baltimore, Md.: Johns Hopkins University Press, 1990), and in information provided by Gallup.
6. For detailed documentation, see Robert James Maddox, *From War to Cold War: The Education of Harry S. Truman* (Boulder, Colo.: Westview Press, 1988).
7. Robert H. Ferrell, ed., *Off the Record: The Private Papers of Harry S. Truman* (New York: Harper & Row, 1980), 31.
8. Leslie R. Groves, *Now It Can Be Told: The Story of the Manhattan Project* (New York: Harper & Row, 1962), 265. See also J. Samuel Walker, "The Decision to Use the Bomb: A Historiographical Update," *Diplomatic History* 14 (1970): 97–114. For the revisionist view on Truman's use of nuclear weapons, see Gar Alperovitz, *Atomic Diplomacy: Hiroshima and Potsdam, the Use of the Atomic Bomb and the American Confrontation with Soviet Power* (New York: Elisabeth Sifton Books, 1985).

9. Robert J. Donovan, *Conflict and Crisis: The Presidency of Harry S. Truman, 1945–1948* (New York: Norton, 1977), 116.

10. For a full reconstruction of this confused and confusing episode, see ibid., chaps. 19, 23.

11. On Acheson's speech, see Robert J. Donovan, *Tumultuous Years: The Presidency of Harry S. Truman: 1949–1954* (New York: Norton, 1982), 136–138, 200, 221.

12. Dean Acheson, *Present at the Creation: My Years at the State Department* (New York: Norton, 1969), 730.

13. Donovan, *The Tumultuous Years*, 370–371. Robert H. Ferrell has edited a number of collections of Truman's private reflections and fulminations, including *Off the Record: The Private Papers of Harry S. Truman* and *The Autobiography of Harry S. Truman* (Boulder, Colo.: Colorado Associated University Press, 1980).

14. On the Truman White House, see Francis H. Heller, ed., *The Truman White House: The Administration of the Presidency: 1945–1953* (Lawrence, Kans.: Regents Press of Kansas, 1980), and Ken Hechler, *Working with Truman: A Personal Memoir of the White House Years* (New York: Putnam, 1982). On the changes in the Executive Office of the President in Truman's time, see Richard E. Neustadt's "Presidency and Legislation: The Growth of Central Clearance," *American Political Science Review* 43 (1954): 641–671, and "Presidency and Legislation: Planning the President's Program," *American Political Science Review* 44 (1955): 980–1021. See also Larry Berman, *The Office of Management and Budget and the Presidency, 1921–1979* (Princeton, N.J.: Princeton University Press, 1979).

15. Harry S. Truman, *Memoirs*, Vol. 1, *Year of Decisions* (Garden City, N.Y.: Doubleday, 1955), 125.

16. For evidence from the archives of the former Soviet Union indicating that Acheson's speech may have emboldened Stalin to authorize the invasion of South Korea, see John Lewis Gaddis, *We Now Know: Rethinking Cold War History* (New York: Oxford University Press, 1997), 72–73. Sidney Hook's distinction between eventful and event-making leaders appears in his *The Hero in History* (New York: John Day, 1943).

17. Clifford J. Garry, "President Truman and Peter the Great's Will," *Diplomatic History* 4 (1980): 371–385.

CHAPTER 4
Dwight D. Eisenhower

1. On polls of historians about presidential greatness, see Robert K. Murray and Tim H. Blessing, *Greatness in the White House: Rating the Presidents from George Washington Through Ronald Reagan*, 2d ed. (University Park, Pa.: Pennsylvania State University Press, 1994).

2. Richard E. Neustadt, *Presidential Power: The Politics of Leadership* (New

York: Wiley, 1960). The most recent of several expansions of Neustadt's classic was published by the Free Press in 1990. The account of Eisenhower's leadership in this chapter builds on Fred I. Greenstein, *The Hidden-Hand Presidency: Eisenhower as Leader* (New York: Basic Books, 1982; 2d ed. with a new preface, Baltimore, Md.: Johns Hopkins University Press, 1994).

3. For a detailed account, see Greenstein, *The Hidden-Hand Presidency,* 155–227.

4. The discarded introduction to *Crusade in Europe* appears in the file containing the manuscript of that work, Eisenhower Library, Abilene, Kansas.

5. John Osborne, "White House Watch: Gabbing with (Bryce) Harlow," *New Republic,* May 13, 1978, 12–14. Harlow was a speechwriter and legislative liaison aide of Eisenhower.

6. On the importance of the effective use of the transition between election and inauguration, see James P. Pfiffner, *The Strategic Presidency: Hitting the Ground Running,* 2d ed. (Lawrence, Kans.: University Press of Kansas, 1996). Also see Charles O. Jones, *Passages to the Presidency: From Campaigning to Governing* (Washington, D.C.: Brookings Institution Press, 1998).

7. Robert H. Ferrell, ed., *The Eisenhower Diaries* (New York: Norton, 1981), 202.

8. The quotation from Kennan appears in *Project Solarium: A Collective Oral History,* February 27, 1988, transcript of John Foster Dulles Centennial Conference, Seeley Mudd Library, Princeton University. (The policy exercise was given the name Project Solarium for the room in the White House in which it was hatched.)

9. On Eisenhower's national security strategy, see John Lewis Gaddis, *Strategies of Containment: A Critical Appraisal of Postwar American National Security Policy* (New York: Oxford University Press, 1984), Robert R. Bowie and Richard H. Immerman, *Waging Peace: How Eisenhower Shaped an Enduring Cold War Strategy* (New York: Oxford University Press, 1998), and Meena Bose, *Shaping and Signaling Presidential Policy: The National Security Decision Making of Eisenhower and Kennedy* (College Station, Tex.: Texas A&M Press, 1998).

10. The account that follows is drawn from John Burke and Fred I. Greenstein, with Larry Berman and Richard Immerman, *How Presidents Test Reality* (New York: Russell Sage Foundation, 1988), chaps. 2–5.

11. Ibid., 32.

12. Peter J. Roman, *Eisenhower and the Missile Gap* (Ithaca, N.Y.: Cornell University Press, 1995).

13. Robert A. Divine, *The Sputnik Challenge: Eisenhower's Response to the Soviet Satellite* (New York: Oxford University Press, 1993), xiv–xvi.

14. Eisenhower's public communication style is discussed in Bose, *Shaping and Signaling Presidential Policy.*

15. On the Kennedy missile buildup, see Desmond Ball, *Politics and Force Lev-*

els: The Strategic Missile Program of the Kennedy Administration (Berkeley: University of California Press, 1980). According to a recent estimate, the combined nuclear arsenals of the United States, Russia, China, Great Britain, and France totaled 36,000 warheads. William M. Arkin, Robert S. Norris, and Joshua Handler, *Taking Stock: Worldwide Nuclear Deployments, 1998* (Washington, D.C.: National Resources Defense Council, 1998).

16. Robert R. Bowie, Columbia University Oral History, quoted in Greenstein, *The Hidden-Hand Presidency*, 33–34. Bowie was the head of the State Department policy planning staff.

17. Richard M. Nixon, *Six Crises* (Garden City, N.Y.: Doubleday, 1962), 158–159.

CHAPTER 5

John F. Kennedy

1. John Fitzgerald Kennedy, *Why England Slept* (New York: Funk, 1940).

2. James N. Giglio, "Past Frustrations, New Opportunities: Researching the Kennedy Presidency at the Kennedy Library," *Presidential Studies Quarterly* 22 (Spring 1992): 371–379.

3. John Fitzgerald Kennedy, *Profiles in Courage* (New York: Harper, 1956).

4. "Looking at the Kennedy Presidency 35 Years Later," *The Public Perspective: A Roper Center Review of Public Opinion and Polling* 9 (October–November 1988): 11.

5. For critiques of Kennedy as a cold warrior, see Thomas G. Paterson, ed. *Kennedy's Quest for Victory: American Foreign Policy, 1961–1963* (New York: Oxford University Press, 1989). For a balanced review of the literature on Kennedy and foreign affairs, see Burton I. Kaufman, "John F. Kennedy as World Leader: A Perspective on the Literature," *Diplomatic History* 17 (Summer 1993): 447–469. For a work that synthesizes the ideological and psychosexual criticisms that have been leveled at Kennedy, see Thomas C. Reeves, *A Question of Character: A Life of John F. Kennedy* (New York: Free Press, 1991).

6. This thesis is most fully developed in Reeves, *A Question of Character.*

7. For a richly documented account of the Kennedy–Khrushchev relationship, see Michael Beschloss, *The Crisis Years: Kennedy and Khrushchev, 1960–1963* (New York: HarperCollins, 1991).

8. Ibid., 20.

9. "Annual Message to Congress on the State of the Union," January 30, 1961, in *Public Papers of the Presidents of the United States: John F. Kennedy, 1961* (Washington, D.C.: U.S. Government Printing Office, 1962), 23.

10. Beschloss, *The Crisis Years,* 65.

11. Ibid., 68–70.

12. Arthur Schlesinger, Jr., *The Age of Roosevelt: The Coming of the New Deal*

(Boston: Houghton Mifflin, 1959). Richard E. Neustadt, *Presidential Power: The Politics of Leadership* (New York: Wiley, 1960).

13. "Remarks at the Rudolph Wilde Platz, Berlin," June 26, 1963, in *Public Papers of the Presidents: John F. Kennedy, 1963* (Washington, D.C.: U.S. Government Printing Office, 1964), 524.

14. The occasion was a fund-raising dinner for the Democratic party. "Remarks at the Inaugural Anniversary Dinner," January 20, 1962, in *Public Papers of the Presidents: John F. Kennedy, 1962* (Washington, D.C.: U.S. Government Printing Office, 1963), 40–41.

15. Bose, *Shaping and Signaling Presidential Policy,* 74.

16. Robert F. Kennedy, *Thirteen Days: A Memoir of the Cuban Missile Crisis* (New York: Norton, 1971), 109. Also See Richard E. Neustadt and Ernest R. May, *Thinking in Time: The Uses of History for Decision Makers* (New York: Free Press, 1986), 17–33.

17. Beschloss, *The Crisis Years,* 9–10.

CHAPTER 6
Lyndon B. Johnson

1. The description of Johnson appears in Robert Dallek, *Lone Star Rising: Lyndon Johnson and His Times, 1908–1960* (New York: Oxford University Press, 1991), 351. Unless otherwise indicated, quotations in this chapter are from that work and the author's companion volume, *Flawed Giant: Lyndon Johnson and His Times, 1961–1973* (New York: Oxford University Press, 1998). The statements of Johnson's associates are by Joseph A. Califano, Jr., *The Triumph and Tragedy of Lyndon Johnson: The White House Years* (New York: Simon & Schuster, 1991); George Reedy, quoted in Dallek, *Lone Star Rising,* 352; and John B. Connally, Jr., *The American Experience: LBJ,* Public Broadcasting Corporation, 1991.

2. "Address Before a Joint Session of Congress," November 27, 1963, in *Public Papers of the Presidents: Lyndon B. Johnson, 1963–64* (Washington, D.C.: U.S. Government Printing Office, 1965).

3. James Sundquist, *Politics and Policy: The Eisenhower, Kennedy, and Johnson Years* (Washington, D.C.: Brookings Institution, 1968), 111–154.

4. On the first episode see Lyndon Baines Johnson, *Vantage Point: Perspectives on the Presidency, 1963–1969* (New York: Holt, Rinehart & Winston, 1971), 39–40. On the second see John D. Pomfret, "The Rail Settlement: A Triumph for Mediation," *New York Times,* April 27, 1964.

5. "Man of the Year," *Time,* January 1, 1965.

6. Sundquist, *Politics and Policy,* 212; Johnson, *Vantage Point,* 206–212.

7. E. L. Kensworthy, "Most in Congress Relieved by President's Course," *New York Times,* July 29, 1965. "The President's News Conference of July 18, 1965," in *Public Papers of the Presidents: Lyndon B. Johnson, 1965* (Washington, D.C.: U.S. Government Printing Office, 1966), 388.

8. "Annual Message to Congress on the State of the Union," January 12,

1966, in *Public Papers of the Presidents: Lyndon B. Johnson, 1966* (Washington, D.C.: U.S. Government Printing Office, 1967).

9. Richard Allen Moore oral history interview, Richard B. Russell Papers, Richard B. Russell Library, Athens, Georgia.

10. "Address to the Nation," March 31, 1968, in *Public Papers of the Presidents: Lyndon B. Johnson, 1968* (Washington, D.C.: U.S. Government Printing Office, 1969).

11. The best-known statement of the view that American intervention in Vietnam was contextually determined is Leslie H. Gelb with Richard K. Betts, *The Irony of Vietnam: The System Worked* (Washington, D.C.: Brookings Institution, 1979).

12. "Senators Divided on Vietnam Stand: Frustration and Uncertainty Prevail as Debate Nears," *New York Times,* January 7, 1965. George H. Gallup, *The Gallup Poll: Public Opinion, 1935–1971* (New York: Random House, 1972), 1921–1922. "Remarks in Oklahoma at the Dedication of the Eufala Dam," in *Public Papers, 1963–64,* 1126. Unless otherwise indicated, the account that follows is taken from John Burke and Fred I. Greenstein, with Larry Berman and Richard Immerman, *How Presidents Test Reality: Decisions on Vietnam, 1954 and 1965* (New York: Russell Sage Foundation, 1988), and Larry Berman, *Planning a Tragedy: The Americanization of the War in Vietnam* (New York: Norton, 1982).

13. Quoted in Larry Berman, "Lyndon Johnson: Paths Chosen and Opportunities Lost," in *Leadership in the Modern Presidency,* ed. Fred I. Greenstein (Cambridge, Mass.: Harvard University Press, 1988), 151.

14. Ibid., 152–153.

15. Michael R. Beschloss, ed., *Taking Charge: The Johnson White House Tapes, 1963–1964* (New York: Simon & Schuster, 1997), 370.

16. Isaiah 1:18.

17. Alfred Steinberg, *Sam Johnson's Boy: A Close-up of the President from Texas* (New York: Macmillan, 1968), 500.

18. Beschloss, *Taking Charge,* 529.

CHAPTER 7

Richard M. Nixon

1. Harlow served with Nixon in the Eisenhower administration and was his first-term director of congressional relations. Bryce Harlow, "The Man and the Political Leader," in Kenneth W. Thompson, ed., *The Nixon Presidency: Twenty-Two Intimate Perspectives of Richard M. Nixon* (Latham, Md.: University Press of America, 1987), 7–10.

2. Richard Hofstadter, *The Paranoid Style in American Politics and Other Essays* (New York: Knopf, 1965).

3. Bela Kornitzer, *The Real Nixon: An Intimate Biography* (Chicago: Rand McNally, 1960), 57, 61–66.

4. Unless otherwise indicated, direct quotations in this section are taken from

Stephen Ambrose, *Nixon,* 3 vols. (New York: Simon & Schuster, 1987–1991). On Nixon's congressional campaigns, also see Irwin F. Gellman, *The Contender: Richard Nixon: The Congressional Years, 1946–1952* (New York: Free Press, 1999).

5. "New Faces in the House," *Time,* November 18, 1946, 16.

6. Richard M. Nixon, "Asia After Viet Nam," *Foreign Affairs* 46 (October 1967): 111–125.

7. Raymond Price, *With Nixon* (New York: Viking Press, 1977), 29.

8. John Lewis Gaddis, *Strategies of Containment: A Critical Appraisal of Postwar American National Security Policy* (New York: Oxford University Press, 1982), 289–297.

9. "Address to the Nation on the War in Vietnam," in *Public Papers of the Presidents, Richard Nixon, 1969* (Washington, D.C.: U.S. Government Printing Office, 1970), 901–909.

10. Stephen E. Ambrose, *Nixon,* Vol. 2, *The Triumph of a Politician: 1962–1972* (New York: Simon & Schuster, 1989), 320. In 1999, former Nixon aide Alexander M. Butterfield reported that much of that deluge of mail had been instigated by the Nixon White House. George Lardner, Jr., "Butterfield: Response to Nixon's Silent Majority Speech was Contrived," *Washington Post,* January 23, 1999.

11. Barbara Kellerman, *The Political Presidency: The Practice of Leadership* (New York: Oxford University Press, 1984), 79.

12. Final Report of the Committee on the Judiciary, House of Representatives, "Minority Views of Messrs. Hutchinson, Smith, Sandman, Wiggins, Dennis, Mayne, Lott, Moorhead, Maraziti and Latta," 1975, 482.

13. Richard M. Nixon, *RN: The Memoirs of Richard Nixon* (New York: Grosset & Dunlap, 1978), 411.

14. Ehrlichman interview, *Biography: Richard Nixon: Man and President* (New York: Arts and Entertainment Network video, 1996).

15. The foreign affairs specialist quoted is Harold H. Saunders (letter to the author, November 12, 1997).

16. Leonard Garment, *Crazy Rhythm: My Journey from Brooklyn, Jazz, and Wall Street to Nixon's White House, Watergate, and Beyond* (New York: Times Books, 1997), 85.

17. The first two assertions are by Elmer Bobst and Hobart Lewis, respectively, members of Nixon's small circle of personal friends. They are quoted in Dom Bonafede, "President's Inner Circle of Friends Serves as an Influential 'Kitchen Cabinet,'" *National Journal,* January 22, 1972, 132. The third, which is by Haldeman, appears in Gerald S. Strober and Deborah H. Strober, *Nixon: An Oral History of His Presidency* (New York: HarperCollins, 1994), 181.

18. H. R. Haldeman with Joseph DiMona, *The Ends of Power* (New York: Times Books, 1978), 62.

CHAPTER 8
Gerald R. Ford

1. Gerald R. Ford, *A Time to Heal: The Autobiography of Gerald R. Ford* (New York: Harper & Row, 1979), 53.
2. See Robert L. Peabody's "Party Leadership Change in the United States House of Representatives," *American Political Science Review* 61 (September 1967) and *Leadership in Congress: Succession, Stability, and Change* (Boston: Little, Brown, 1976), 110–148.
3. "The Public Record of Gerald R. Ford," *CQ Weekly Report*, October 20, 1972, 2762. A. James Reichley, *Conservatives in an Age of Change: The Nixon and Ford Administrations* (Washington, D.C.: Brookings Institution, 1981), 281.
4. "Address upon Assuming the Presidency," in *Public Papers of the Presidents: Gerald Ford, 1974* (Washington, D.C.: U.S. Government Printing Office, 1975), 1:1.
5. Roger B. Porter, "A Healing Presidency," in *Leadership in the Modern Presidency*, ed. Fred I. Greenstein (Cambridge, Mass.: Harvard University Press, 1988), 206–207.
6. The remaining respondents in each instance expressed no opinion. George H. Gallup, *The Gallup Poll: Public Opinion 1972–1977* (Wilmington, Del.: Scholarly Resources, 1978), 347.
7. *Facts on File Yearbook: 1974* (New York: Facts on File, 1975), 747–777. *The Gallup Opinion Index* (October–November 1980): 17.
8. Ford, *A Time to Heal*, 159.
9. Robert T. Hartmann, *Palace Politics: An Inside Account of the Ford Years* (New York: McGraw-Hill, 1980), 261.
10. Ford, *A Time to Heal*, 186.
11. Roger B. Porter, *Presidential Decision Making: The Economic Policy Board* (New York: Cambridge University Press, 1980).
12. James Cannon, *Time and Chance: Gerald Ford's Appointment with History* (New York: HarperCollins, 1994), 394.
13. Ford, *A Time to Heal*, 133.
14. The interview, with Associated Press reporter Saul Pett, conducted on October 21, 1974, and published in the *Los Angeles Times* on October 27, 1974, is excerpted in *Facts on File Yearbook: 1974*, 891.
15. The passages quoted from Alan Greenspan appear in *The President and the Council of Economic Advisors: Interviews with CEA Chairman*, ed. Erwin C. Hargrove and Samuel A. Morley (Boulder, Colo.: Westview Press, 1984), 416–419. Malkiel's comments are in a July 29, 1999, memorandum to the author.
16. Henry Kissinger, *Years of Renewal* (New York: Simon & Schuster, 1999), 171–172.

CHAPTER 9
Jimmy Carter

1. Douglas Brinkley, *The Unfinished Presidency: Jimmy Carter's Journey Beyond the White House* (New York: Viking, 1998); John Whiteclay Chambers II, "Jimmy Carter's Public Policy Ex-Presidency," *Political Science Quarterly* 113 (1998): 405–435.
2. Jimmy Carter, *Why Not the Best?* (Nashville, Tenn.: Broadman Press, 1975), 12.
3. Ibid., 60.
4. Ibid., 87.
5. Leslie Wheeler, *Jimmy Who? An Examination of Presidential Candidate Jimmy Carter: The Man, His Career, His Stand on Issues* (Woodbury, N.J.: Barrons, 1976), 115.
6. Ibid., 217.
7. Aaron Wildavsky and Jack Knott, "Jimmy Carter's Theory of Governing," *Wilson Quarterly* (Winter 1977): 49–67.
8. "Playboy Interview: Jimmy Carter: A Candid Conversation with the Democratic Candidate for the Presidency," *Playboy* (November 1976): 86.
9. Thomas P. O'Neill with William Novak, *Man of the House: The Life and Political Memoirs of Speaker Tip O'Neill* (New York: Random House, 1987), 297–329.
10. For a perceptive commentary on Carter's failure to set policy priorities, see David S. Broder, "Lack of Strategy in the Carter Camp," *Washington Post,* June 8, 1977.
11. Jimmy Carter, *Keeping Faith: Memoirs of a President* (New York: Bantam Books, 1982), 171.
12. "Energy and National Goals," in *Public Papers of the Presidents of the United States: Jimmy Carter, 1979* (Washington, D.C.: U.S. Government Printing Office, 1980), 1235.
13. "High Marks on Early Exams," *Time,* April 4, 1977; Peter Goldman, Eleanor Clift, and Thomas M. DeFrank, "Jimmy So Far," *Newsweek,* May 2, 1977, 48; *The Gallup Opinion Index* (October-November 1980): 14.
14. James Fallows, "The Passionless Presidency: The Trouble with the Jimmy Carter Administration," *Atlantic Monthly* (May 1979): 33–47.
15. Ibid., 42.
16. Ibid.
17. Don Oberdorfer, *The Two Koreas: A Contemporary History* (Reading, Mass.: Addison-Wesley, 1997), 84–115.

CHAPTER 10
Ronald Reagan

1. Unless otherwise indicated, the sources of this chapter are the two excellent biographical studies of Reagan and his presidency by *Washington Post* reporter Lou Cannon: *Reagan* (New York: G. P. Putnam's Sons, 1982) and

President Reagan: The Role of a Lifetime (New York: Simon & Schuster, 1991).

2. "A Time for Choosing," October 27, 1964, in Paul D. Erickson, *Reagan Speaks: The Making of an American Myth* (New York: New York University Press, 1985), 124–138.

3. Robert Dallek, *Ronald Reagan: The Politics of Symbolism* (Cambridge, Mass: Harvard University Press, 1984), 39–40.

4. Cannon, *President Reagan.*

5. Michael K. Deaver, *Behind the Scenes* (New York: Morrow, 1987), 165–166; Donald T. Regan, *For the Record: From Wall Street to Washington* (New York: Harcourt Brace Jovanovich, 1988), 142; David A. Stockman, *The Triumph of Politics: Why the Reagan Revolution Failed* (New York: Harper & Row, 1986), 419.

6. Martin Anderson, *Revolution* (New York: Harcourt Brace Jovanovich, 1988), 283–286, 291–292.

7. Hugh Heclo and Rudolf G. Penner, "Fiscal and Political Strategy in the Reagan Administration: 1981–1982," in *The Reagan Presidency: An Early Assessment,* ed. Fred I. Greenstein (Baltimore, Md.: Johns Hopkins University Press, 1983), 39.

8. *New York Times,* November 26, 1986, 10.

9. "How Will Reagan Go Down in History?" *Gallup Report,* no. 277 (October 1988).

10. "The President's News Conference," January 29, 1981, in *Public Papers of the Presidents of the United States: Ronald Reagan, 1981* (Washington, D.C.: U.S. Government Printing Office, 1982); "Remarks at the Annual Convention of the National Association of Evangelicals, Orlando, Florida," in *Public Papers of the Presidents of the United States: Ronald Reagan, 1983* (Washington, D.C.: U.S. Government Printing Office, 1984).

11. For a lucid account of the politics of the end of the cold war, see Don Oberdorfer, *From the Cold War to a New Era* (Baltimore, Md.: Johns Hopkins University Press, 1998).

12. I am indebted to Douglas Dillon for this account.

13. William C. Wohlforth, ed., *Witnesses to the End of the Cold War* (Baltimore, Md.: Johns Hopkins University Press, 1996), 105.

14. Cannon, *Reagan,* 137–138. Howard Gardner, *Frames of Mind: The Theory of Multiple Intelligences* (New York: Basic Books, 1983).

15. Wohlforth, *Witnesses to the End of the Cold War,* 103.

CHAPTER 11
George H. W. Bush

1. *Gallup Poll Monthly,* no. 306 (March 1991): 2.

2. The best biography of Bush is Herbert S. Parmet, *George Bush: The Life of a Lone Star Yankee* (New York: Scribner, 1997).

3. *Facts on File Yearbook: 1979* (New York: Facts on File, 1980), 326B1.

4. Unless otherwise indicated, quotations are from Herbert S. Parmet, *George Bush: The Life of a Lone Star Yankee* (New York: Scribner, 1997).

5. Toasts at the state dinner for Prime Minister Benazir Bhutto of Pakistan, June 6, 1989, in *Public Papers of the Presidents of the United States: George Bush, 1989* (Washington, D.C.: U.S. Government Printing Office, 1990), 686.

6. David Hoffman, "Bush Doubts Soviets Have Changed: Vice President Disagrees with Reagan's Assessment at Summit," *Washington Post,* June 8, 1988, A9, and David Broder, "Cold War 'Not Over,' Bush Warns: Slackening Buildup Called a Mistake," *Washington Post,* June 29, 1988, A14.

7. Jack F. Matlock, Jr., *Autopsy on an Empire: The American Ambassador's Account of the Collapse of the Soviet Union* (New York: Random House, 1995), 591.

8. *Facts on File Yearbook: 1990* (New York: Facts on File, 1991), 582A3.

9. "Inaugural Address," in *Public Papers of the Presidents of the United States: George Bush, 1989* (Washington, D.C.: U.S. Government Printing Office, 1990), 3–4.

10. Dan Goodgame, "Read My Hips: Bush's Flip-flops Add New Confusion to the Budget Battle and Raise Doubts About His Domestic Leadership," *Time,* October 22, 1990, 26–28.

11. *Gallup Poll Monthly,* no. 318 (March 1992): 43.

12. George Bush and Brent Scowcroft, *A World Transformed* (New York: Knopf, 1998).

13. The most influential statement of that thesis appears in Irving L. Janis, *Groupthink: Psychological Studies of Policy Decisions and Fiascoes* (Boston: Houghton Mifflin, 1982).

CHAPTER 12
Bill Clinton

1. For an excellent account of the prepresidential Clinton, see David Maraniss, *First in His Class: The Biography of Bill Clinton* (New York: Simon & Schuster, 1995). For a view of Clinton through the prism of psychoanalysis, see Stanley A. Renshon, *High Hopes: The Clinton Presidency and the Politics of Ambition* (New York: New York University Press, 1996).

2. Ernest Dumas, *The Clintons of Arkansas: An Introduction by Those Who Knew Them Best* (Fayetteville, Ark.: University of Arkansas Press, 1993), xvi.

3. Donald Baer, Matthew Cooper, and David Gergen, "Bill Clinton's Hidden Life," *U.S. News and World Report,* July 20, 1992.

4. For a fuller account of Clinton's actions to avoid the draft, see Maraniss, *First in His Class,* 167–205.

5. Dan Balz and Howard Kurtz, "Clinton Calls Tabloid Story of 12-Year Affair 'Not True,'" *Washington Post,* January 24, 1992; Jeffrey H. Birn-

baum, "Clinton Received a Vietnam Draft Deferment for an ROTC Program That He Never Joined," *Wall Street Journal,* February 6, 1992.

6. Howard Kurtz, "Clintons Agree to Do '60 Minutes,'" *Washington Post,* January 25, 1992.

7. R. W. Apple, Jr., "Clinton, Savoring Victory, Starts Sizing Up Job Ahead," *New York Times,* November 5, 1992. ABC-*Washington Post* poll finding supplied by the Roper Center, University of Connecticut.

8. Richard Lacayo, "A Moment of Silence," *Time,* May 8, 1995, 46.

9. Inaugural Address, January 20, 1997, in *Public Papers of the Presidents: William Jefferson Clinton, 1997* (Washington, D.C.: U.S. Government Printing Office, 1998).

10. The specifics are detailed in the referral of the independent counsel to the House of Representatives, popularly known as "The Starr Report." For a reprint with valuable added material, see *The Starr Report: The Findings of Independent Counsel Kenneth W. Starr on President Clinton and the Lewinsky Affair with Analysis by the Staff of the Washington Post* (New York: Public Affairs, 1998).

11. Tom Squiteri and Kevin Johnson, "Speech Boosts Clinton's Rating," *USA Today,* January 29, 1998. For a scholarly analysis, see John Zaller, "Monica Lewinsky's Contribution to Political Science," *P.S.* 31 (1998): 182–189.

12. "A Year of Grudging Compromises and Unfinished Business," *1999 CQ Almanac* (Washington, D.C.: Congressional Quarterly Press, 2000).

13. "Remarks at a Fundraiser for Mayor David Dinkins," New York City, September 26, 1993, in *Public Papers of the Presidents: William Jefferson Clinton, 1993* (Washington, D.C.: U.S. Government Printing Office, 1994).

14. Elizabeth Drew, *On the Edge: The Clinton Presidency* (New York: Simon & Schuster, 1994), 348.

15. Dick Morris, *Behind the Oval Office: Winning the Presidency in the Nineties* (New York: Random House, 1997); Robert Reich, *Locked in the Cabinet* (New York: Knopf, 1997); George Stephanopoulos, *All Too Human: A Political Education* (Boston: Little, Brown, 1999).

16. Maraniss, *First in His Class,* 138–139, 234–235.

CHAPTER 13

George W. Bush

1. The most balanced biography of George W. Bush is Bill Minutaglio, *First Son: George W. Bush and the Bush Family Dynasty* (New York: Times Books, 1999). See also Elizabeth Mitchell, *Revenge of the Bush Dynasty* (New York: Hyperion, 2000). During the 2000 presidential campaign there were a number of useful investigative reports on Bush's life. One of the best was the *Washington Post* series, "The Life and Times of George W. Bush," which appeared in six parts in July 2000. The account that follows draws on these sources.

2. George W. Bush, *A Charge to Keep: My Journey to the White House* (New York: HarperCollins, 1999), 182.

3. A manner that is engagingly captured in the 2002 HBO documentary *Journeys with George.*
4. Bush, *A Charge to Keep*, 180.
5. Minutaglio, *First Son*, 295–303.
6. Alan C. Miller and Judy Pasternak, "Records Show Bush's Focus on Big Picture," *Los Angeles Times*, August 2, 2000.
7. Bush, *A Charge to Keep*, 97.
8. For an official elaboration, see Marvin Olasky, *Compassionate Conservatism: What It Is, What It Does, and How It Can Transform America* (New York: Free Press, 2000).
9. Commission on Presidential Debates, "The Second 2000 Gore-Bush Presidential Debate: October 11, 2000," http://www.debates. org/pages/trans2000b.html.
10. George W. Bush, "Bush's Remarks on the End of the Race," *New York Times*, December 14, 2000.
11. Inaugural Address, January 20, 2001, in *Public Papers of the Presidents: George W. Bush, 2001*, vol. 1 (Washington, D.C.: U.S. Government Printing Office, 2002).
12. For a succinct summary of this event, see *Facts on File World News Digest Yearbook: 2001* (New York: Facts on File, 2002), 304.
13. David S. Broder, "The Reticent President," *Washington Post*, April 22, 2001.
14. Dana Milbank, "With Fanfare, Bush Signs Education Bill: President, Lawmakers Hit 3 States in 12 Hours to Tout Biggest Schools Change Since '65," *Washington Post*, January 9, 2002.
15. Office of the Press Secretary, "Remarks by the President after Two Planes Crash into World Trade Center," September 11, 2001, The White House, http://www.whitehouse.gov/news/releases/2001/09/20010911.html.
16. Office of the Press Secretary, "Statement by the President in His Address to the Nation," September 11, 2001, The White House, http://www.whitehouse.gov/news/releases/2001/09/20010911-16.html.
17. Office of the Press Secretary, "President Bush Salutes Heroes in New York," September 14, 2001, The White House, http://whitehouse.gov/news/releases/2001/09/20010914-9.html.
18. Leo Weiland, "Bush's New Image," *Frankfurter Allgemeine* (English Edition), October 20, 2001.
19. A list of the post–September 11 NSC meetings can be found in the index of Bob Woodward's *Bush at War* (New York: Simon & Schuster, 2002), 367. The exchange between Rumsfeld and Powell appears on page 49. Bush was also immersed in information during the Iraq war, receiving as much as three hours a day of briefings. Elisabeth Bumiller, "President, No Matter Where, Keeps Battlefield Close," *New York Times*, March 30, 2003. See also Judy Keene and Laurence McQullan, "Bush Dives into Details of Iraq Conflict," *USA Today*, March 21, 2003.

20. Office of the Press Secretary, "President Delivers State of the Union Address," January 29, 2002, The White House, http://www.whitehouse.gov/news/releases/2002/01/20020129-11.html.
21. Ibid.
22. Office of the Press Secretary, "President Bush Announces Major Combat Operations in Iraq Have Ended," May 1, 2003, The White House, http://www.whitehouse.gov/news/releases/2003/05/iraq/20030501-15.html.
23. John Meacham, "A Father's Words on Going to War," *Newsweek*, March 31, 2003, 43. The senior Bush also remarked that criticisms of Secretary of State Powell were part of what "burns me up," which suggests that he weighs in on the side of diplomatic options in global affairs.
24. Woodward, *Bush at War*, 177, 335–336, 345–349.
25. Dena Milbank and Thomas E. Ricks, "Powell and Joint Chiefs Nudged Bush Toward U.N.," *Washington Post*, September 4, 2003.
26. Dwight D. Eisenhower, Columbia University Oral History Interview, July 20, 1967, uncorrected transcript. The last sentence of the quotation was unaccountably omitted in the corrected final transcript. The classic discussion of the importance of rigorous debate in presidential advisory systems is Alexander L. George, "The Case for Multiple Advocacy in Making Foreign Policy," *American Political Science Review* 66 (1972): 751–785. It is possible that such a process would have saved the Bush administration from the embarrassment of including an assertion in Bush's 2003 State of the Union address about Iraq's alleged efforts to obtain uranium ore from Africa, which the Central Intelligence Agency had already established to be ungrounded.
27. Stephen Thomma, "Growing on the Job," *Miami Herald*, December 9, 2001.
28. Office of the Press Secretary, "President Bush, Prime Minister Blair Hold Press Availability," March 27, 2003, The White House, http://www.whitehouse.gov/news/releases/2003/03/20030327-3.html.
29. Woodward, *Bush at War*, 158.

CHAPTER 14
Lessons from the Modern Presidency

1. Arthur Schlesinger, Jr., "Rating the Presidents: Washington to Clinton," *Political Science Quarterly* 112 (1997): 179–190.
2. David Maraniss, *First in His Class: The Biography of Bill Clinton* (New York: Simon & Schuster, 1995), 280–281.
3. Eleanor Roosevelt, *This Is My Story* (New York: Harper, 1937), 167.
4. Dwight D. Eisenhower, Columbia University Oral History Interview, July 20, 1967, 103.
5. Chester L. Cooper, *Lost Crusade: America in Vietnam* (Greenwich, Conn.: Dodd, Mead, 1970), 223.

6. Richard E. Neustadt, *Presidential Power: The Politics of Leadership* (New York: Wiley, 1960).
7. See Chapter 4 and John P. Burke, Fred I. Greenstein, with Larry Berman and Richard Immerman, *How Presidents Test Reality* (New York: Russell Sage Foundation, 1988), chaps. 2–5, 32.
8. Richardson interview, Arts and Entertainment Network documentary: *Biography: Richard Nixon: Man and President* (New York, 1996).

FURTHER READING

CHAPTER 1

The Presidential Difference

The quotations that serve as this chapter's epigraph are assertions by distinguished political observers about the importance of the occupant of the Oval Office. The first is from Woodrow Wilson's *Constitutional Government in the United States* (New York: Columbia University Press, 1908), which was published two years before Wilson made the transition from academic student of politics to political practitioner, winning the governorship of New Jersey and going on to serve two terms in the White House.

Wilson's statement was a reversal of the position he had taken in his 1885 *Congressional Government* (New York: Meridian reprint, 1961), which appeared in the post-Civil War era of weak chief executives. In that book Wilson argued that it is in the nature of the American political system for Congress to be the dominant branch of government and the president to be a mere "executive in theory." By 1908, events had led Wilson to reconsider. Grover Cleveland (1885–89, 1893–97) had exercised firm, forceful presidential leadership. William McKinley (1897–1901) had been thrust to the fore by the Spanish-American War and other international developments. And Theodore Roosevelt (1901–9) was a whirlwind of presidential activism. Wilson's revised conclusion was that the president "is at liberty, both in law and conscience, to be as big a man as he can."

That judgment provided Wilson with the rationale for his own forceful presidential leadership. However, Wilson's immediate successors—Warren G. Harding, Calvin Coolidge, and Herbert Hoover—approached their responsibilities in the reactive spirit of the typical nineteenth-century chief executive. Then, during the long incumbency of Franklin D. Roosevelt, the president's responsibilities became permanently enlarged, leading the Columbia University professor and former Truman White House aide Richard E. Neustadt to amend Wilson's statement in his 1960 *Presidential Power: The Politics of Leadership* (New York: Wiley, 1960). Neustadt's assertion, which provides the chapter's second opening quotation, is: "But nowadays he can not be as small as he might like."

In seeking to identify the qualities that have served well and poorly in the

282

modern presidency, I have been influenced by two works referred to in the text of Chapter 1—Neustadt's *Presidential Power* and James David Barber's *The Presidential Character* (Englewood Cliffs, N.J.: Prentice Hall, 1972). Although many of those authors' insights are incorporated in the present analysis, there is no substitute for reading the originals, each of which warrants close attention.

Presidential Power and *The Presidential Character* are products of their times and their authors' previous experience. Neustadt was a Columbia University professor who came of age politically in the nation's capital in the 1930s, where his father was a mid-level official in the Roosevelt administration. During the Truman presidency, Neustadt worked in the Executive Office of the President, first in the Bureau of the Budget (now the Office of Management and Budget) and then in the White House. He wrote *Presidential Power* with the experience of the first three modern presidents at his disposal—Roosevelt, Truman, and Eisenhower.

Neustadt directs his attention to how the chief executive can put his stamp on public policy in the complex, easily stalemated American political system. Drawing upon case studies from the Truman and Eisenhower presidencies, Neustadt concluded that the president has three sources of influence:

> First are the bargaining advantages inherent in his job with which to persuade other men that what he wants of them is what their own responsibilities require them to do. Second are the expectations of those other men regarding his ability and will to use the various advantages they think he has. Third are those men's estimates of how his public views him and of how their publics may view him if they do what he wants (p. 179).

Neustadt presents a glowing account of Roosevelt's highly political leadership style, praising FDR for his sense of what it takes to enhance the president's power and for his method of maximizing the information and advice at his disposal by making his advisers compete for his attention. Neustadt's thesis is that Roosevelt provides the best model for effective presidential leadership. His corollaries are that his former boss, Harry Truman, sometimes approximated the political adeptness of FDR, but that Eisenhower was ill suited for effective presidential leadership, because he felt no compelling need to place his personal imprint on policy. Neustadt also faults Eisenhower for having imported a military-style staff system into the White House, cutting himself off from the richly varied political intelligence that made Roosevelt, and to a lesser degree Truman, the master of his own presidency.

As originally published, *Presidential Power* was an eight-chapter monograph that concluded with reflections on the prospects for presidential leadership in the 1960s. Neustadt expanded the book substantially in later printings, adding chapters on the post-1960 presidential experience, but the later versions retain the original text and leave the book's thesis unchanged. The final printing bears the title *Presidential Power and the Modern Presi-*

dency: The Politics of Leadership from Roosevelt to Reagan (New York: Free Press, 1990).

Presidential Power is written more in the manner of the humanities than the social sciences, but its argument can be restated with the specificity of a self-consciously empirical analysis. This translation has been accomplished by Peter W. Sperlich in his "Bargaining and Overload: An Essay on *Presidential Power.*" Sperlich identifies the variables implicit in Neustadt's account and sets Neustadt's formulation against the social science literature on the nature of leadership, arriving at two conclusions.

The first is that Neustadt overemphasizes presidential bargaining, ignoring "nonreciprocal" sources of influence, such as conscience, shared ideology, and personal commitment to the chief executive. The second is that Neustadt underemphasizes the role that loyal aides can play in presidential leadership. The result, according to Sperlich, is a prescription that overloads the president by insisting that he be personally responsible for the operations of his White House. Sperlich's essay appears in Aaron Wildavsky, ed., *The Presidency* (Boston: Little, Brown, 1969), and is reprinted in Wildavsky's *Perspectives on the Presidency* (Boston: Little, Brown, 1975).

In addition to clarifications such as Sperlich's, Neustadt's analysis needs to be modified to take account of historical knowledge that has emerged since 1960. Thus the merit of FDR's "competitive" approach to consulting with his advisers seems less obvious in the light of later presidential experience than it was to Neustadt. And there has been a transformation in scholarly assessments of Eisenhower, who is now known to have been a political sophisticate with a highly effective, but deliberately indirect, leadership style. For expansions on these assertions, see the chapters in this work on FDR and Eisenhower.

James David Barber is a psychologically oriented political scientist who did his doctoral work on political leadership at Yale in the 1950s. The personality classification he employs in *The Presidential Character* evolved from his 1965 book on the psychology of Connecticut state legislators, *The Lawmakers: Recruitment and Adaptation to Legislative Life* (New Haven, Conn.: Yale University Press, 1965).

The Presidential Character went to press in 1971 and was published the following year. It therefore could not take account of Nixon's political successes of 1972—his trips to China and the Soviet Union, removal of American combat forces from Vietnam, and reelection to a second term. Instead, it was informed by Barber's psychological sensitivities and the widespread concern with abuse of presidential power sparked by the U.S. military intervention in Vietnam of the 1960s.

Barber directs his attention to the emotional fitness of presidents for their responsibilities. He is disquieted by the danger posed to the nation by emotionally troubled presidents who become rigidly committed to their policies, persevering in counterproductive courses of action. Barber's examples of such action include Woodrow Wilson's stubborn refusal to accept modest compromises to win ratification of the Versailles Treaty and Lyndon Johnson's obsession with achieving victory in Vietnam, despite mounting evidence that the American military intervention was failing to accomplish its ill-defined purposes. Barber also presented an extensive analysis of Richard Nixon, whom he viewed as a prime candidate for a character-based political disaster.

Barber frames his book with an enumeration of five broad determinants of a president's White House performance. Two relate to the president's political context—his *power situation* (e.g., the partisan balance in Congress) and the contemporary *climate of expectations* (e.g., the state of public opinion). The remaining three relate to the president's inner characteristics. One is his *political style*—his habitual way of carrying out his job. The second is his *worldview*—his political beliefs and his more general conceptions of "social causality, human nature, and the central moral conflicts of the time." The third is the president's *character*, which in Barber's analytic scheme refers not to the president's moral probity, but to the deeper layers of personality that are molded early in childhood.

In practice Barber's almost exclusive emphasis is on character, which he analyzes in terms of whether the president is active or passive in his approach to his responsibilities and positive or negative in his feelings (affect) toward them. (Barber's four-fold classification scheme is summarized in Figure 1.) The presidents Barber places in the *active-positive* category are emotionally healthy problem solvers, who approach politics with a flexible emphasis on connecting means with ends. The nation is best served, in Barber's view, when its president has such a character. *Passive-positive* presidents are "compliant, other-directed" individuals, who participate in politics for the social satisfaction it provides, and *passive-negative* presidents serve out of a sense of duty. Neither of the passive types is a likely agent of constructive policymaking, according to Barber.

Finally there are the *active-negative* presidents. These are chief executives for whom political participation serves deep-seated emotional functions, helping them compensate for conscious or unconscious personal inadequacies. The actions of such emotionally flawed individuals have "a compulsive quality," Barber asserts. The active-negative presidents appear to be "trying to make up for something or to escape from anxiety into hard work." They "pour energy into the political system, but it is an energy distorted from

FIGURE 1. TYPES OF PRESIDENTIAL CHARACTER

LEVEL OF ACTIVITY

		ACTIVE	PASSIVE
AFFECT (FEELINGS) TOWARD ACTIVITY	POSITIVE	Active-positive	Passive-positive
	NEGATIVE	Active-negative	Passive-negative

within" (p. 9). Barber places Woodrow Wilson, Lyndon Johnson, and Richard Nixon in this category.

The Presidential Character was barely in print when the Watergate crisis began to unfold. There was much debate about how as shrewd and adept a politician as Richard Nixon could have allowed himself to engage in the actions that were in the process of undermining his presidency. This provided a ready audience for a book that thoughtfully examined Nixon's tangled psyche and speculated that his character flaws might bring his presidency to grief. *The Presidential Character* was favorably reviewed in popular and to a lesser extent learned periodicals. It also became a highly successful textbook in college presidency courses, and Barber himself became a widely read writer of op-ed essays on the political psychology of presidents and presidential candidates.

Barber added discussions of the presidents from Ford to George H. W. Bush to later editions of *The Presidential Character* (1977, 1985, and 1992). In the book's 1992 edition, he includes a section entitled "Beyond Character," in which he locates Presidents Carter and Bush. Carter has an active-positive character, Barber maintains, but his leadership was deficient because he lacked skill. Bush, he asserts, had both an active-positive character and a skilled political style, but his vision-free worldview impaired his performance. These qualifications do not alter the book's predominant emphasis, which continues to be on character.

The Presidential Character is trenchantly analyzed by Alexander L. George in his constructively critical review essay, "Assessing Presidential Character," *World Politics* 26 (January 1974): 234–282. George's essay is too complex for a brief summary, but it is required reading for those who seek to place the study of presidential personality on a firm intellectual footing. It is reprinted with a number of useful related discussions in George's book with Juliette L. George, *Presidential Personality and Performance* (New York: Westview Press, 1998). For a usefully complementary work, see Stanley A. Renshon, *The Psychological Assessment of Presidential Candidates* (New York: New York University Press, 1996).

My own assessment of Barber's analysis, which is consistent with George's, is that he performs an important service by highlighting the president's inner makeup, but his emphasis on the psychic depths is too limiting. Moreover, his effort to reduce personality to a handful of types ignores the complexity of human motivation. To take an obvious example, presidents and others are not always predominately positive or negative about their obligations—they may be subject to mood swings as was the case of Theodore Roosevelt and Lyndon Johnson.

The final edition of *The Presidential Character* was published before the Clinton presidency. The Clinton experience vindicates Barber's attention to the president's mental health, while highlighting the inadequacy of his taxonomy. The ever-smiling, hyperactive Clinton has all of the outward signs of an active-positive character. Yet his actions, particularly his astonishing recklessness in the Monica Lewinsky affair, reveal him to be as emotionally deficient as any classically active-negative president.

My approach to the problem of emotional fitness for the presidency is to eschew classifications and examine each president inductively. For this purpose

I employ "emotional intelligence" as shorthand for identifying presidents whose emotions enhance their leadership. Its antithesis, which might be called emotional obtuseness, provides a common denominator among presidents who are alike in not being masters of their own passions but as disparate on the surface as Bill Clinton and Richard Nixon. While I reject Barber's typology of presidential character, I fully agree with him about the importance of emotional fitness in the chief executive.

CHAPTER 2
Franklin D. Roosevelt

The body of writing about Franklin D. Roosevelt exceeds even that on Abraham Lincoln. For useful one-volume biographies, see Patrick J. Maney, *The Roosevelt Presence: A Biography of Franklin Delano Roosevelt* (New York: Twayne, 1992), and Frank B. Friedel, *Franklin D. Roosevelt: A Rendezvous with Destiny* (Boston: Little, Brown, 1990). Friedel is also the author of a major four-volume work that brings FDR from childhood through the first year of his presidency: *Franklin D. Roosevelt: The Apprenticeship, The Ordeal, The Triumph*, and *Launching the New Deal* (Boston: Little, Brown, 1952–1973). Another multivolume treatment is Kenneth S. Davis, *F.D.R.: The Beckoning of Destiny, 1882–1928* (New York: Putnam, 1971), *The New York Years, 1928–1933, The New Deal Years, 1933–1937*, and *Into the Storm, 1937–40* (New York: Random House, 1985, 1986, 1993).

Other biographical studies that provide insights into FDR's personality and leadership methods include James MacGregor Burns, *Roosevelt: The Lion and the Fox* (New York: Harcourt, Brace, 1956), and *Roosevelt: Soldier of Freedom: 1940–45* (New York: Harcourt Brace Jovanovich, 1970); Geoffrey C. Ward, *Before the Trumpet: Young Franklin Roosevelt, 1881–1905* and *A First-Class Temperament: The Emergence of Franklin Roosevelt* (New York: Harper & Row, 1985, 1989); and Arthur M. Schlesinger, Jr., *The Coming of the New Deal* (Boston: Houghton Mifflin, 1959). See also Doris Kearns Goodwin, *No Ordinary Time: Franklin and Eleanor Roosevelt: The Home Front in World War II* (New York: Simon & Schuster, 1994). A fascinating and original volume that uses Roosevelt's physical disability as a lens with which to examine his personality is Hugh Gregory Gallagher, *FDR's Magnificent Deception* (New York: Dodd, Mead, 1985).

FDR was a continuing source of fascination to his associates, many of whom produced valuable memoirs and diaries. Included are Raymond Moley, *After Seven Years* (New York: Harper Brothers, 1939), Frances Perkins, *The Roosevelt I Knew* (New York: Viking, 1946), Harold Ickes, *The Secret Diaries of Harold Ickes*, 3 vols. (New York: Simon & Schuster, 1953–1954), John M. Blum, *From the Morgenthau Diaries*, 3 vols. (Boston: Houghton Mifflin, 1959–1961), Samuel I. Rosenman, *Working with Roosevelt* (New York: Harper & Brothers, 1952), and Rexford Tugwell, *In Search of Roosevelt* (Cambridge, Mass.: Harvard University Press, 1972). Also see Robert Sherwood, *Roosevelt and Hopkins: An Intimate History* (New York: Harper, 1948). FDR also was a source of puzzlement and often frustration to Eleanor Roosevelt. For her memoirs, see *This Is My Story* (New York: Harper, 1937) and *This I Remember* (New York: Harper, 1947).

There is an extensive specialized literature on FDR. For a disparate set of useful works, see Leila A. Sussmann, *Dear FDR: A Study of Political Letter-Writing* (Totowa, N.J.: Bedminister Press, 1963), Halford R. Ryan, *Franklin D. Roosevelt's Rhetorical Presidency* (Westport, Conn.: Greenwood Press, 1988), Robert Eden, ed., *The New Deal and Its Legacy: Critique and Reappraisal* (Westport, Conn.: Greenwood Press, 1989), Sean J. Savage, *Roosevelt: The Party Leader, 1932–1945* (Lexington, Ky.: University Press of Kentucky, 1991), William E. Leuchtenburg, *The Supreme Court Reborn: The Constitutional Revolution in the Age of Roosevelt* (New York: Oxford University Press, 1995), Barbara Rearden Farnham, *Franklin Delono Roosevelt and the Munich Crisis* (Princeton, N.J.: Princeton University Press, 1997), and Verne W. Newton, ed., *FDR and the Holocaust* (New York: St. Martin's Press, 1996). The standard scholarly account of Roosevelt's foreign policy is Robert Dallek, *Franklin D. Roosevelt and American Foreign Policy, 1932–1945* (New York: Oxford University Press, 1979).

The bibliographical essay appended to Maney's *The Roosevelt Presidency* is an excellent guide for further exploration. Also see the many contributions to Otis L. Graham, Jr., and Meghan Robinson Wander, eds., *Franklin D. Roosevelt, His Life and Times: An Encyclopedic View* (Boston: G. K. Hall, 1985).

CHAPTER 3
Harry S. Truman

The most authoritative biography of Truman is Alonzo L. Hamby, *Man of the People: A Life of Harry S. Truman* (New York: Oxford University Press, 1995). See also the vividly written but less rigorous Pulitzer Prize-winning book by David McCullough, *Truman* (New York: Simon & Schuster, 1992). The most thorough examination of Truman's presidency is the excellent two-volume study by Robert J. Donovan, who covered the Truman presidency for the *New York Herald Tribune: Conflict and Crisis: The Presidency of Harry S. Truman, 1945–1948* (New York: Norton, 1977) and *Tumultuous Years: 1949–1953* (New York: Norton, 1982).

The first volume of Truman's memoirs, which focuses on his initial year in the White House, is entitled *Year of Decisions.* The second volume, which ranges across his presidency, is entitled *Years of Trial and Hope* (Garden City, N.Y.: Doubleday, 1955, 1956). Robert H. Ferrell has edited two collections of Truman's unpublished writings, including a number of the intemperate letters and speech drafts Truman confined to his files: *Off the Record: The Private Papers of Harry S. Truman* (New York: Harper & Row, 1980) and *The Autobiography of Harry S. Truman* (Boulder, Colo.: Colorado Associated University Press, 1980). See also Monte M. Poem, ed., *Strictly Personal and*

Confidential: The Unmailed Letters of Harry S. Truman (Boston: Little, Brown, 1982). There are few memoirs by Truman aides. The most important of them is Dean Acheson's *Present at the Creation: My Years in the State Department* (New York: Norton, 1969). Also see Ken Hechler's delightful *Working with Truman: A Personal Memoir of the White House Years* (New York: Putnam, 1982).

On the Truman White House, see Francis H. Heller, ed., *The Truman White House: The Administration of the Presidency: 1945–1953* (Lawrence, Kans.: Regents Press of Kansas, 1980). A valuable sense of Truman the man and his day-to-day operating style is provided by the journalist John Hersey, who was allowed to spend a number of days in Truman's presence, observing him in action throughout the day. Hersey's accounts originally appeared in the *New Yorker* and have been reprinted in his *Aspects of the Presidency* (New Haven, Conn.: Ticknor & Fields, 1980).

The most sharply contested issues in the literature on Truman relate to the origins of the cold war. There are too many writings on that topic to do justice to the range of their positions in a brief note. One of the most influential of the works that takes Truman to task for not being sufficiently accommodating to the Soviet Union is Gar Alperovitz, *Atomic Diplomacy: Hiroshima and Potsdam* (New York: Vintage Books, 1967). A highly influential work that views Truman's actions as largely a function of the circumstances he faced is John Lewis Gaddis, *The United States and the Origins of the Cold War: 1941–1947* (New York: Columbia University Press, 1972). For authoritative brief essays on many aspects of the Truman experience, including issues bearing on the origins of the cold war, see Richard S. Kirkendall, ed., *The Harry S. Truman Encyclopedia* (Boston: G. K. Hall, 1989). For additional sources, see the bibliographical essay appended to Donald R. McCoy, *The Presidency of Harry S. Truman* (Lawrence, Kans.: University Press of Kansas, 1984), and Richard Dean Burns, *Harry S. Truman: A Bibliography of His Times and Presidency* (Wilmington, Del.: Scholarly Resources, 1984).

CHAPTER 4
Dwight D. Eisenhower

The most comprehensive scholarly account of the Eisenhower presidency is Stephen E. Ambrose, *Eisenhower: The President* (New York: Simon & Schuster, 1984). On Eisenhower's early years, military career, and rise to the presidency, see Ambrose's *Eisenhower: Soldier, General of the Army, President-Elect, 1890–1952* (New York: Simon & Schuster, 1983). Also see Herbert S. Parmet, *Eisenhower and the American Crusades* (New York: Macmillan, 1972). For Eisenhower's own rather impersonal account of his presidency, see *The White House Years: Mandate for Change, 1953–1956* and *Waging Peace: 1957–1961* (Garden City, N.Y.: Doubleday, 1963, 1965). More of a sense of the man is conveyed in Eisenhower's wry, anecdotal *At Ease: Stories I Tell to Friends* (Garden City, N.Y.: Doubleday, 1967). Also see Robert H. Ferrell, ed., *The Eisenhower Diaries* (New York: Norton, 1981).

Memoirs of the Eisenhower presidency include Sherman Adams, *Firsthand Report: The Story of the Eisenhower Administration* (New York: Harper, 1961), Ezra Taft Benson, *Cross Fire: The Eight Years with Eisenhower* (Garden City, N.Y.: Doubleday, 1962), Herbert Brownell and John P. Burke, *Advising Ike: The Memoirs of Attorney General Herbert Brownell* (Lawrence, Kans.: University Press of Kansas, 1993), Nathaniel R. Howard, ed., *The Basic Papers of George M. Humphrey* (Cleveland, Ohio: Western Reserve Historical Society, 1965), and Henry Cabot Lodge, *As It Was: An Inside View of Power and Politics in the 1950s and 1960s* (New York: Norton, 1976).

Specialized works include Fred I. Greenstein, *The Hidden-Hand Presidency: Eisenhower as Leader* (New York: Basic Books, 1982), Robert Bowie and Richard Immerman, *Waging Peace: How Eisenhower Shaped an Enduring Cold War Strategy* (New York: Oxford University Press, 1998), Meena Bose, *Shaping and Signaling Presidential Policy: The National Security Decision Making of Eisenhower and Kennedy* (College Station, Tex.: Texas A&M Press, 1998), Robert A. Divine, *The Sputnik Challenge: Eisenhower's Response to the Soviet Satellite* (New York: Oxford University Press, 1993), Iwan W. Morgan, *Eisenhower Versus "the Spenders": The Eisenhower Administration, the Democrats and the Budget, 1953–1960* (New York: St. Martin's Press, 1990), and John W. Sloan, *Eisenhower and the Management of Prosperity* (Lawrence, Kans.: University Press of Kansas, 1991). For additional sources, see the bibliographical essay appended to Chester J. Pach, Jr., and Elmo Richardson, *The Presidency of Dwight D. Eisenhower,* rev. ed. (Lawrence, Kans.: University Press of Kansas, 1991).

CHAPTER 5
John F. Kennedy

The most important scholarly biography of Kennedy is Herbert C. Parmet, *Jack: The Struggles of John F. Kennedy* and *JFK: The Presidency of John F. Kennedy* (New York: Dial Press, 1980, 1983). A penetrating work that appeared before Kennedy reached the White House is James MacGregor Burns, *John Kennedy: A Political Profile* (New York: Harcourt, Brace, 1960), written with the cooperation of Kennedy and his associates, but about which they were less than enthusiastic. On their objections to the book, see Michael Beschloss, *"John Kennedy: A Political Profile* Revisited," in *Essays in Honor of James MacGregor Burns* (Englewood Cliffs, N.J.: Prentice Hall, 1989), ed. Michael R. Beschloss and Thomas E. Cronin, 66–74. A work that distills many of the negative claims about Kennedy of his numerous critics is Thomas C. Reeves, *A Question of Character: A Life of John F. Kennedy* (New York: Free Press, 1991).

Two years after Kennedy's death, two of his aides published laudatory but still valuable works: Arthur M. Schlesinger, Jr., *A Thousand Days: John F. Kennedy in the White House* (Boston: Houghton Mifflin, 1965), and Theodore Sorensen, *Kennedy* (New York: Harper & Row, 1965). One of the most valuable of the specialized works on Kennedy and his presidency is Michael Beschloss's richly documented account of the Kennedy-Khrushchev relationship: *The Crisis Years: Kennedy and Khrushchev, 1960–1963* (New York: HarperCollins, 1991). Another exceptionally important work is Ernest R. May and Philip D. Zelikow, *The Kennedy Tapes: Inside the White House During the Cuban Missile Crisis* (Cambridge, Mass.: Harvard University Press, 1997).

Also see Jim Heath, *John F. Kennedy and the Business Community* (Chicago: University of Chicago Press, 1969), Carl M. Brauer, *John F. Kennedy and the Second Reconstruction* (New York: Columbia University Press, 1977), William J. Rust, *Kennedy in Vietnam* (New York: Scribner's, 1985), Montague Kern et al., *The Kennedy Crises: The Press, the Presidency, and Foreign Policy* (Chapel Hill, N.C.: University of North Carolina Press, 1983), and Meena Bose, *Shaping and Signaling Presidential Policy: The National Security Decision Making of Eisenhower and Kennedy* (College Station, Tex.: Texas A&M Press, 1998). For a review of the Kennedy literature, see the bibliographical essay appended to James N. Giglio, *The Presidency of John F. Kennedy* (Lawrence, Kans.: University Press of Kansas, 1991).

CHAPTER 6

Lyndon B. Johnson

As of the late 1990s, the definitive scholarly biography of Johnson is the two-volume study by Robert Dallek: *Lone Star Rising: Lyndon Johnson and His Times, 1908–1960* and *Flawed Giant: Lyndon Johnson and His Times, 1961–1973* (New York: Oxford University Press, 1991, 1998). Just as Dallek's second volume went into production, the Johnson Library in Austin, Texas, embarked on a program of releasing thousands of hours of Johnson's secretly recorded telephone conversations. These amply confirm the image of a larger-than-life LBJ in the memoirs of Johnson's aides and the journalistic accounts of him; they also contain important new information. For transcripts of the initially released tapes, see Michael R. Beschloss, ed., *Taking Charge: The Johnson White House Tapes, 1963–1964* (New York: Simon & Schuster, 1997).

After leaving the White House, Johnson assembled a team of writers at his Texas ranch for the production of his memoirs—a not deeply informative but nevertheless valuable work: Lyndon Baines Johnson, *Vantage Point: Perspectives on the Presidency, 1963–1969* (New York: Holt, Rinehart & Winston, 1971). Various of Johnson's former aides provide a rich sense of their former boss in their memoirs. Among the most informative are Joseph A. Califano, Jr., *The Triumph and Tragedy of Lyndon Johnson: The White House Years* (New York: Simon & Schuster, 1991), Harry McPherson, *A Political Education* (Boston: Little, Brown, 1972), George Reedy, *Lyndon B. Johnson: A Memoir* (New York: Andrews & McMeel, 1982), and Jack Valenti, *A Very Human President* (New York: Norton, 1975).

There is a huge literature on Johnson and Vietnam. I have relied particularly on John Burke and Fred I. Greenstein, with Larry Berman and Richard Immerman, *How Presidents Test Reality: Decisions on Vietnam, 1954 and 1965* (New York: Russell Sage Foundation, 1988), and Larry Berman, *Planning* a *Tragedy: The Americanization of the War in Vietnam* (New York: Norton, 1982). For a valuable work that places the domestic enactments of the Johnson years in the context of the politics of domestic policymaking in the two previous presidencies, see James Sundquist, *Politics and Policy: The Eisenhower, Kennedy, and Johnson Years* (Washington, D.C.: Brookings Institution, 1968).

For reviews of the literature on Johnson, see Robert A. Divine, ed., *The Johnson Years,* Vol. 1: *Foreign Policy, the Great Society and the White House;* Vol. 2: *Vietnam, the Environment and Science;* Vol. 3: *LBJ at Home and Abroad* (Lawrence, Kans.: University Press of Kansas, 1987, 1987, 1994). See also the bibliographical essay appended to Vaughn Davis Bornet, *The Presidency of Lyndon B. Johnson* (Lawrence, Kans.: University Press of Kansas, 1983).

CHAPTER 7

Richard M. Nixon

The most comprehensive biography of Nixon is Stephen E. Ambrose's three-volume *Nixon: The Education of a Politician: 1913–1962; The Triumph of a Politician: 1962–1972; Ruin and Recovery: 1973–1990* (New York: Simon & Schuster, 1987, 1989, 1991). The quantity of biographical writing on Nixon is enormous, but much of it is polemical. There have been many attempts to use the insights of clinical psychology to take Nixon's measure, but they tend to reduce him to a catalogue of psychopathology, paying little attention to his strengths. One of the more careful of such works is Fawn Brodie, *Richard Nixon: The Shaping of His Character* (New York: Norton, 1981). One of the more instructive of the partisan biographies is that of Jonathan Aitken, a British conservative who sympathizes with Nixon but approaches him in an analytic spirit: *Nixon: A Life* (Washington, D.C.: Regnery, 1993). For an overview of the Nixon presidency, see Melvin Small, *The Presidency of Richard Nixon* (Lawrence, Kans.: University Press of Kansas, 1999).

Nixon wrote three autobiographies, each with a different emphasis: *Six Crises* (Garden City, N.Y.: Doubleday, 1962), *RN: The Memoirs of Richard Nixon* (New York: Grosset & Dunlap, 1978), and *In the Arena: A Memoir of Victory, Defeat and Renewal* (New York: Simon & Schuster, 1990). Nixon's presidential memoirs make for a fascinating comparison with the memoirs of his principal foreign policy subordinate, Henry Kissinger, *White House Years* and *Years of Upheaval* (Boston: Little, Brown, 1979, 1982), in that each of them comments on his perceptions of the other. Of the many memoirs of Nixon's former associates, the following are particularly insightful: John Ehrlichman, *Witness to Power: The Nixon Years* (New York: Simon & Schuster, 1982), Leonard Garment, *Crazy Rhythm: My Journal from Brooklyn, Jazz, and Wall Street to Nixon's White House, Watergate, and Beyond . . .* (New York: Times Books, 1997), and William Safire, *Before the Fall: An Insider's View of the Pre-Watergate White House* (New York: Da Capo Press, 1975). Also see Gerald S. Strober and Deborah H. Strober, *Nixon: An Oral History of His Presidency* (New York: HarperCollins, 1994).

An important exception to the proposition that most writers on Nixon have an ax to grind is A. James Reichley, who has written a perceptive and dispassionate account of the leadership and policies in the Nixon and Ford presidencies: *Conservatives in an Age of Change: The Nixon and Ford Administrations* (Washington, D.C.: Brookings Institution, 1981). Specialized studies of the Nixon administration include Vincent J. Burke and Vee Burke, *Nixon's Good Deed: Welfare Reform* (New York: Columbia University Press, 1974), Daniel P. Moynihan, *The Politics of Guaranteed Income: The Nixon Administration and the Family Assistance Plan* (New York: Random House, 1973), Richard P. Nathan, *The Administrative Presidency* (New York: Wiley, 1983), Raymond L. Garthoff, *Détente and Confrontation: American-Soviet Relations from Nixon to Reagan* (Washington, D.C.: Brookings Institution, 1985), and Richard C. Thornton, *The Nixon-Kissinger Years: Reshaping American Foreign Policy* (New York: Paragon House, 1989). For an overview and reassessment of Nixon's domestic and foreign policies, see Joan Hoff, *Nixon Reconsidered* (New York: Basic Books, 1994). For a review of the literature on Nixon, see the bibliographical essay appended to Melvin Small, *The Presidency of Richard Nixon*.

CHAPTER 8

Gerald R. Ford

There is no adequate biography of Gerald Ford, but there are excellent discussions of the Ford presidency and Ford's leadership by John Robert Greene, *The Presidency of Gerald R. Ford* (Lawrence, Kans.: University Press of Kansas, 1995), and James Cannon, *Time and Chance: Gerald Ford's Appointment with History* (New York: HarperCollins, 1994). There also are excellent discussions of the Ford presidency and Ford's leadership style by a pair of his former aides: A. James Reichley, *Conservatives in an Age of Change: The Nixon and Ford Administrations* (Washington, D.C.: Brookings Institution, 1981), and Roger B. Porter, "A Healing Presidency," in *Leadership in the Modern Presidency,* ed. Fred I. Greenstein (Cambridge, Mass.: Harvard University Press, 1988), 199–227.

Ford's own account appears in his *A Time to Heal: The Autobiography of Gerald R. Ford* (New York: Harper & Row, 1979). This is complemented by several memoirs of his aides, notably Robert T. Hartmann, *Palace Politics: An Inside Account of the Ford Years* (New York: McGraw-Hill, 1980), Ron Nessen, *It Sure Looks Different from the Inside* (Chicago: Playboy Press, 1978), and Henry Kissinger, *Years of Renewal* (New York: Simon & Schuster, 1999). For six days in March 1975, the journalist John Hersey was allowed to observe Ford in action for the entirety of his work day. Hersey's account, which appears in his *Aspects of the Presidency* (New Haven, Conn.: Ticknor & Fields, 1980), provides a valuable sense of the man and his political style.

For a study of an organizational innovation of the Ford presidency that warrants the attention of future presidents, see Roger B. Porter, *Presidential Decision Making: The Economic Policy Board* (New York: Cambridge University Press, 1980). Another instructive specialized study is Mark J. Rozell, *The Press and the Ford Presidency* (Ann Arbor, Mich.: University of Michigan Press, 1992). Other literature on Ford and his presidency is reviewed in the bibliographical essay appended to Greene's *The Presidency of Gerald R. Ford.*

CHAPTER 9
Jimmy Carter

Betty Glad provides a penetrating analysis of Carter's complex personality in her *Jimmy Carter: In Search of the Great White House* (New York: Norton, 1980). A later, more comprehensive biography is Peter G. Bourne's *Jimmy Carter: A Comprehensive Biography from Plains to Post-Presidency* (New York: Scribner, 1997). For a compact account of the Carter presidency, see Burton I. Kaufman, *The Presidency of James Earl Carter, Jr.* (Lawrence, Kans.: University Press of Kansas, 1993). Two prominent political scientists have written book-length studies of Carter's highly distinctive approach to presidential leadership: Erwin Hargrove, *Jimmy Carter as President: Leadership and the Politics of Public Good* (Baton Rouge, La.: Louisiana State University Press, 1988), and Charles O. Jones, *The Trusteeship Presidency: Jimmy Carter and the United States Congress* (Baton Rouge, La.: Louisiana State University Press, 1988).

Carter's campaign autobiography is *Why Not the Best?* (Nashville, Tenn.: Broadman Press, 1975). His account of his presidency is *Keeping Faith: Memoirs of a President* (New York: Bantam Books, 1982). The presidential memoirs of Carter's aides include Zbigniew Brzezinski, *Power and Principle: Memoirs of the National Security Advisor, 1977–81* (New York: Farrar, Straus, Giroux, 1983, rev. ed. 1985), Cyrus Vance, *Hard Choices: Critical Years in America's Foreign Policy* (New York: Simon & Schuster, 1983), and Joseph A. Califano, Jr., *Governing America: An Insider's Report from the White House and the Cabinet* (New York: Simon & Schuster, 1981).

There have been numerous accounts of specific aspects of the Carter presidency, including William B. Quant, *Camp David: Peace Making and Politics* (Washington, D.C.: Brookings Institution, 1986), Alexander Moens, *Foreign Policy Under Carter: Testing Multiple Advocacy Decision Making* (Boulder, Colo.: Westview Press, 1990), George D. Moffett III, *The Limits of Victory: The Ratification of the Panama Canal Treaties* (Ithaca, N.Y.: Cornell University Press, 1985), and Laurence E. Lynn, Jr., and D. F. Whitman, *The President as Policy Maker: Jimmy Carter and Welfare Reform* (Philadelphia, Pa.: Temple University Press, 1982). For brief accounts of various of Carter's domestic policies, see Gary M. Fink and Hugh David Graham, eds., *The Carter Presidency: Policy Choices in the Post-New Deal Era* (Lawrence, Kans.: University Press of Kansas, 1998). For a critique of Carter's attempt to put morality to the fore in foreign policy, see Gaddis Smith, *Morality, Reason, and Power: American Diplomacy in the Carter Years* (New York: Hill and Wang, 1986).

In his *The Press and the Carter Presidency* (Boulder, Colo.: Westview Press,

1989), Mark J. Rozell provides an excellent account of how Carter fared with the nation's newspapers. For a favorable reassessment of the Carter presidency, see John Dumbrell, *The Carter Presidency: A Re-Evaluation* (Manchester, U.K.: Manchester University Press, 1995). On Carter's postpresidential years, see Douglas Brinkley, *The Unfinished Presidency: Jimmy Carter's Journey Beyond the White House* (New York: Viking, 1998). There is a useful review of writings on the Carter presidency in the bibliographical essay appended to Kaufman, *The Presidency of James Earl Carter, Jr.*

CHAPTER 10
Ronald Reagan

The most authoritative Reagan biographer is Lou Cannon, a journalist who covered Reagan's governorship and presidency. Cannon's *Reagan* (New York: G. P. Putnam's Sons, 1982) takes his life into his first presidential year. *President Reagan: The Role of a Lifetime* (New York: Simon & Schuster, 1991) completes the story. For a balanced short work, see William E. Pemberton, *Exit with Honor: The Life and Presidency of Ronald Reagan* (Armonk, N.Y.: M. E. Sharpe, 1997). For an eccentric, uneven, but intermittently insightful biography that views Reagan through the eyes of a number of fictional observers, see Edmund Morris, *Dutch: A Memoir* (New York: Random House, 1999).

Reagan's first autobiography, coauthored with Richard C. Humbler, is entitled *Where Is the Rest of Me?* (New York: Duell, Sloan and Pearce, 1965). Its title is taken from a scene in the film *King's Row,* in which the character played by Reagan utters that cry when he awakes after surgery to discover that his legs have been amputated. Reagan used it as his title out of a conviction that by entering politics, he had met an unfulfilled need, making his life more complete. The book is breezy and unpretentious, conveying an engaging sense of the man. It contrasts with Reagan's second autobiography, *An American Life* (New York: Simon & Schuster, 1990), which is bland and uninformative.

Well before the Reagan presidency ended, memoirs of his former aides had begun to appear, including Michael K. Deaver, *Behind the Scenes* (New York: Morrow, 1987), Donald T. Regan, *For the Record: From Wall Street to Washington* (New York: Harcourt Brace Jovanovich, 1988), David A. Stockman, *The Triumph of Politics: How the Reagan Revolution Failed* (New York: Harper & Row, 1986), and Larry Speakes, *Speaking Out: Inside the Reagan White House* (New York: Scribner's, 1988). Later memoirs include Marlin Fitzwater, *Call the Briefing! Bush and Reagan, Sam and Helen: A Decade with Presidents and the Press* (New York: Times Books, 1995), and George P. Shultz, *Turmoil and Triumph: My Years as Secretary of State* (New York: Scribner's, 1993). The memoir that sheds the most light on Reagan's leadership style is Martin Anderson, *Revolution* (New York: Harcourt Brace Jovanovich, 1988). (Anderson was Reagan's first domestic policy adviser.)

Specialized studies include William K. Muir, Jr., *The Bully Pulpit: The Presidential Leadership of Ronald Reagan* (San Francisco: Institute for Contemporary Affairs Press, 1992), John W. Sloan, *The Reagan Effect: Economics and Presidential Leadership* (Lawrence, Kans.: University Press of Kansas, 1999), Daniel Wirls, *Buildup: The Politics of Defense in the Reagan Era* (Ithaca, N.Y.: Cornell University Press, 1992), Theodore Draper, *A Very Thin Line: The Iran-Contra Affairs* (New York: Hill and Wang, 1991), and Coral Bell, ed., *The Reagan Paradox: American Foreign Policy in the 1980s* (New Brunswick, N.J.: Rutgers University Press, 1989).

There is a rich literature on Reagan and the end of the cold war, including Don Oberdorfer, *From the Cold War to a New Era* (Baltimore, Md.: Johns Hopkins University Press, 1998), Jack Matlock, *Autopsy of an Empire: The American Ambassador's Account of the Collapse of the Soviet Union* (New York: Random House, 1995), and William C. Wohlforth, ed., *Witnesses to the End of the Cold War* (Baltimore, Md.: Johns Hopkins University Press, 1996).

For overviews and assessments of the Reagan experience, see Larry Berman, ed., *Looking Back at the Reagan Legacy* (Baltimore, Md.: Johns Hopkins University Press, 1990), Sidney Blumenthal and Thomas Byrne Edsall, eds., *The Reagan Legacy* (New York: Pantheon Books, 1988), and John L. Palmer, ed., *Perspectives on the Reagan Years* (Washington, D.C.: Urban Institute Press, 1986).

CHAPTER 11
George H. W. Bush

The first scholarly biography of George H. W. Bush is Herbert S. Parmet, *George Bush: The Life of a Lone Star Yankee* (New York: Scribner, 1997). For a thoughtful account of the Bush presidency, see David Mervin, *George Bush and the Guardianship Presidency* (New York: St. Martin's Press, 1996).

Other than Roosevelt and Kennedy, who died in office, Bush is the only modern chief executive not to have written a memoir of his presidency. His campaign autobiography, written in collaboration with Victor Gold, is *Looking Forward* (Garden City, N.Y.: Doubleday, 1987). Bush and his national security adviser coauthored a volume analyzing a number of his administration's foreign policy decisions: George Bush and Brent Scowcroft, *A World Transformed* (New York: Knopf, 1998). In 1999, he unexpectedly came forth with an often instructive collection of passages from his copius personal correspondence, with added selections from his personal diary. George Bush, *All the Best: My Life in Letters and Other Writings* (New York: Scribner, 1999).

The most important memoir of Bush's presidency is that of his former secretary of state: James A. Baker III, *The Politics of Diplomacy: Revolution, War and Peace, 1989–1993* (New York: Putnam's, 1995). Also see Marlin Fitzwater, *Call the Briefing! Bush and Reagan, Sam and Helen: A Decade with Presidents and the Press* (New York: Times Books, 1995), and Dan Quayle, *Standing Firm* (New York: HarperCollins, 1994).

Two of the most useful of the many studies of the Gulf War are Lawrence Freedman and Efraim Karsh, *The Gulf Conflict, 1990–1991: Diplomacy and*

War in the New World Order (Princeton, N.J.: Princeton University Press, 1993), and Jean Edward Smith, *George Bush's War* (New York: Henry Holt, 1992). The literature on the role of the Bush administration in the endgame of the cold war includes the following noteworthy reconstructions: Michael R. Beschloss and Strobe Talbott, *At the Highest Levels: The Inside Story of the End of the Cold War* (Boston: Little, Brown, 1993), and Don Oberdorfer, *From the Cold War to a New Era* (Baltimore, Md.: Johns Hopkins University Press, 1998). Also see Jack F. Matlock, Jr., *Autopsy on an Empire: The American Ambassador's Account of the Collapse of the Soviet Union* (New York: Random House, 1995).

By the late 1990s, the less sensitive portions of the inner record of the Bush presidency were becoming available to scholars, but little archive-based research had yet been published. For an early examination of a wide range of Bush's policies on the basis of the public record, see the contributions to Colin Campbell and Bert A. Rockman, eds., *The Bush Presidency: First Appraisals* (Chatham, N.J.: Chatham House Publishers, 1991).

CHAPTER 12
Bill Clinton

David Maraniss's *First in His Class: The Biography of Bill Clinton* (New York: Simon & Schuster, 1995) is an outstanding journalistic account of Clinton's life up to the point of the 1992 election, although it does not closely examine his governorship. For a brief biography of Clinton that covers much of his first term, see Martin Walker, *The President We Deserve: Bill Clinton, His Rise, Falls, and Comebacks* (New York: Crown Publishers, 1996). For a psychoanalytic perspective on Clinton, see Stanley A. Renshon, *High Hopes: The Clinton Presidency and the Politics of Ambition* (New York: New York University Press, 1996).

For memoirs of members of the Clinton administration, see Dick Morris, *Behind the Oval Office: Winning the Presidency in the Nineties* (New York: Random House, 1997), Michael Waldman, *POTUS Speaks: Finding the Words That Defined the Clinton Presidency* (New York: Simon & Schuster, 2000), Robert Reich, *Locked in the Cabinet* (New York: Knopf, 1997), and George Stephanopoulos, *All Too Human: A Political Education* (Boston: Little Brown, 1999). For a wide array of instructive exit interviews with Clinton aides, see the website for the ABC News Nightline and PBS Frontline joint *Clinton Years* specials at ABCNews.com.

The loose organization of the Clinton presidency made for easy access by journalists. The result is a number of detailed "inside-story" accounts, including Elizabeth Drew, *On the Edge: The Clinton Presidency* (New York: Simon & Schuster, 1994) and *Showdown: The Struggle Between the Gingrich Congress and the Clinton White House* (New York: Simon & Schuster, 1996), Bob Woodward, *The Agenda: Inside the Clinton White House* (New York: Simon & Schuster, 1994), and Haynes Johnson and David Broder, *The System: The American Way of Politics at the Breaking Point* (Boston: Little, Brown, 1996). The last of these focuses on the failure of Clinton's health program and is complemented by Jacob S. Hacker's excellent scholarly analysis, *The Road to*

Nowhere: The Genesis of President Clinton's Plan for Health Security (Princeton, N.J.: Princeton University Press). For details of the Lewinsky affair, see *The Starr Report: The Findings of Independent Counsel Kenneth W. Starr on President Clinton on the Lewinsky Affair with Analysis by the Staff of the Washington Post* (New York: Public Affairs, 1998).

William G. Hyland, *Clinton's World: Remaking American Foreign Policy* (Westport, Conn.: Praeger, 1999), is an in-depth analysis of Clinton's foreign policy. The speeches of Clinton's first secretary of state are reprinted in Warren Christopher, *In the Stream of History: Shaping Foreign Policy for a New Era* (Stanford, Calif.: Stanford University Press, 1998). For an early effort by presidential scholars to come to terms with the Clinton presidency, see Colin Campbell and Bert A. Rockman, eds., *The Clinton Presidency: First Appraisals* (Chatham, N.J.: Chatham House, 1996).

CHAPTER 13
George W. Bush

For a balanced biography of George W. Bush based on careful journalistic legwork, see Bill Minutaglio, *First Son: George W. Bush and the Bush Family Dynasty* (New York: Times Books, 1999). Most other efforts are marred by their pro- or anti-Bush biases, but also see Elizabeth Mitchell, *Revenge of the Bush Dynasty* (New York: Hyperion, 2000) and the July 2000 *Washington Post* series, "The Life and Times of George W. Bush." Also note Bush's own *A Charge to Keep: My Journey to the White House* (New York: HarperCollins, 1999), written with the assistance of his long-time communications director Karen Hughes, a bland, but occasionally informative, campaign autobiography. For a quasi-official account of the rationale of Bush's domestic policies see Marvin Olasky, *Compassionate Conservatism: What It Is, What It Does, and How It Can Transform America* (New York: The Free Press, 2000).

The first and, as of 2003, only memoir of the Bush presidency is that of David Frum, a speech writer who helped coin the "axis of evil" phrase in Bush's 2002 State of the Union address: *The Right Man: The Surprise Presidency of George W. Bush* (New York: Random House, 2002). The prominent journalist Bob Woodward draws on inside-the-administration sources to provide a valuable account of the Bush administration's decision making in the wake of the events of September 11, 2001, in *Bush at War* (New York: Simon and Schuster, 2002). Woodward's book is largely devoid of analysis, but its excellent index partially compensates for that shortcoming, making it possible, for example, to search out the passages in which Woodward quotes his interviews with Bush, who proves to have a well-articulated view of the requirements of effective presidential leadership.

Although there has been much opposition on the part of academics to Bush's policies, his leadership style, the events he has presided over, and the content of his policies have provided scholars with much to contemplate. Valuable analyses of the Bush presidency by academics are to be found in Gary Gregg and Mark Rozell, eds., *Considering the Bush Presidency* (New York: Oxford University Press, 2003); Colin Campbell and Bert A. Rockman, eds., *The George W. Bush Administration: First*

Appraisals (New York: Chatham House, 2003); and Fred I. Greenstein, ed., *The Presidency of George W. Bush: An Early Appraisal* (Baltimore, Md.: Johns Hopkins University Press, 2003). For a pair of works that present Bush's leadership methods as exemplary for others in leadership positions, see Donald F. Kettle, *Team Bush: Leadership Lessons from the Bush White House* (New York: McGraw-Hill, 2003) and the hyperbolically titled *The Leadership Genius of George W. Bush: 10 Commonsense Lessons from the Commander in Chief* by Carolyn B. Thompson and James W. Ware (New York: Wiley, 2003).

As is the case of any ongoing administration, the Bush presidency also needs to be studied by drawing on contemporary journalism and such official sources as the president's addresses and unscripted public utterances. For a valuable source on the latter see the White House's official website (www.whitehouse.gov).

CHAPTER 14
Lessons from the Modern Presidency

The striking image of the executive branch of government as a chameleon that takes its color from the president's personality, which serves as this chapter's epigraph, is taken from an essay contributed by Clark Clifford to former Eisenhower speechwriter Emmet John Hughes's *The Living Presidency* (New York: Coward, McCann and Geoghegan, 1973), 315. Clifford, who was a Washington insider *par excellence*, began his political career as a key aide in Truman's first-term White House. He went on to become a leading Washington attorney and behind-the-scenes maker and shaker, providing political counsel to Presidents Kennedy and Johnson and serving as Johnson's secretary of defense. Clifford's essay in the Hughes volume is accompanied by essays based on their own experiences as presidential aides by Sherman Adams, Benjamin V. Cohen, Abe Fortas, Bryce N. Harlow, David E. Lilienthal, Samuel I. Rosenman, and Theodore C. Sorensen.

There is a rich and varied literature on the modern presidency, which can only be touched upon here. As I note in chapter one and the essay appended to it, the two most influential works on the qualities that serve well and poorly in the Oval Office are Neustadt's *Presidential Power*, which was published in 1960 and Barber's *The Presidential Character*, which was published in 1972. A fascinating and instructive recent book that also addresses this topic is Erwin C. Hargrove, *The President as Leader: Appealing to the Better Angels of Our Nature* (Lawrence, Kans.: University Press of Kansas, 1998).

There are several one-volume studies of the presidency, which precede the publication of Neustadt's classic, all of which still bear attention. These include Pendleton Herring, *Presidential Leadership: The Political Relations of Congress and the Chief Executive* (New York: Rinehart, 1940), Harold Joseph Laski, *The American Presidency: An Interpretation* (New York: Harper and Brothers, 1940), Edward S. Corwin, *The President, Office and Powers, 1787-1957: History and Analysis of Practice and Opinion*, 4th ed. (New York: New York University Press, 1957), and Clinton L. Rossiter, *The American Presidency*, 2d ed. (New York: Harcourt Brace, 1960).

More recent one volume analyses include Larry Berman, *The New American Presidency* (Boston: Little, Brown, 1987), Thomas E. Cronin and Michael A. Genovese, *The Paradoxes of the American Presidency* (New York: Oxford University Press, 1998), George C. Edwards III and Stephen J. Wayne, *Presidential Leadership: Politics and Policy Making*, 4th ed. (New York: St. Martin's, 1997), Charles O. Jones, *The Presidency in a Separated System* (Washington, D.C.: Brookings Institution, 1994), and James P. Pfiffner, *The Modern Presidency*, 2d ed. (New York: St. Martin's, 1998). For an interesting comparison of executive leadership at the national and state levels in the United States, see Joseph E. Kallenbach, *The American Chief Executive: The Presidency and the Governorship* (New York: Harper & Row, 1966).

The all-important relationship between the president and the public is examined in Richard A. Brody, *Assessing the President: The Media, Elite Opinion, and Public Support* (Stanford, Calif.: Stanford University Press, 1999), Jeffrey E. Cohen, *Presidential Responsiveness and Public Policy-Making: The Public and the Politics that Presidents Choose* (Ann Arbor, Mich.: University of Michigan Press, 1997), Samuel Kernell, *Going Public: New Strategies of Presidential Leadership*, 2d ed. (Washington, D.C.: CQ Press, 1993), and John E. Mueller, *War, Presidents, and Public Opinion*, (New York: Wiley, 1973).

Of the many analyses of the organization of the presidency, the following warrant particular attention: John P. Burke, *The Institutional Presidency* (Baltimore, Md.: Johns Hopkins University Press, 1992), Alexander L. George, *Presidential Decisionmaking in Foreign Policy: The Effective Use of Advice and Information* (Boulder, Colo.: Westview Press, 1979), Stephen Hess, *Organizing the Presidency*, rev. ed. (Washington, D.C.: Brookings Institution, 1988), Richard Tanner Johnson, *Managing the White House: An Intimate Study of the Presidency* (New York: Harper & Row, 1974), Charles E. Walcott and Karen M. Hult, *Governing the White House: From Hoover Through LBJ* (Lawrence, Kans.: University Press of Kansas, 1995), and Shirley Anne Warshaw, *The Domestic Presidency: Policy Making in the White House* (Boston: Allyn & Bacon, 1997), Thomas J. Weko, *The Politicizing Presidency: The White House Personnel Office, 1948-1994* (Lawrence, Kans.: University Press of Kansas, 1995). Also see Irving L. Janis, *Groupthink: A Psychological Study of Foreign Policy Decisions and Fiascoes* (Boston: Houghton Mifflin, 1982).

The relationship between the presidency and Congress is explored in Kenneth E. Collier, *Between the Branches: The White House Office of Legislative Affairs* (Pittsburgh, Pa.: University of Pittsburgh Press, 1997), George C. Edwards III, *At the Margins: Presidential Leadership and Congress* (New Haven, Conn.: Yale University Press, 1989), Louis Fisher, *The Politics of Shared Power: Congress and the Executive*, 4th ed. (College Station, Tex.: Texas A&M Press, 1998), Mark A. Peterson, *Legislating Together: The White House and Capitol Hill from Eisenhower to Reagan* (Cambridge, Mass.: Harvard University Press, 1990), and Richard A. Watson, *Presidential Vetoes and Public Policy* (Lawrence, Kans.: University Press of Kansas, 1993). The standard account of the presidency and the Supreme Court is Henry Abraham, *Justices, Presidents, and Senators: A History of Supreme Court Appointments from Washington to Clinton*, rev. ed. (Lanham, Md.: Rowman & Littlefield, 1999).

For a mixed bag of other studies that warrant attention, see Peri E. Arnold, *Making the Managerial Presidency: Comprehensive Reorganization Planning, 1905-1996*, 2d ed. rev. (Lawrence, Kans.: University Press of Kansas, 1998), Charles O. Jones, *Passages to the Presidency: From Campaigning to Governing* (Washington, D.C.: Brookings Institution, 1998), William E. Leuchtenburg, *In the Shadow of FDR: From Harry Truman to Bill Clinton*, rev. ed. (Ithaca, N.Y.: Cornell University Press, 1993), Theodore Lowi, *The Personal President: Power Invested, Promise Unfulfilled* (Ithaca, N.Y.: Cornell University Press, 1985), Robert K. Murray and Tim H. Blessing, *Greatness in the White House: Rating the Presidents from George Washington Through Ronald Reagan* (University Park, Pa.: Pennsylvania University Press, 1994), James P. Pfiffner, *The Strategic Presidency*, 2d ed. (Lawrence, Kans.: University Press of Kansas, 1996), Arthur Schlesinger, Jr., *The Imperial Presidency*, (New York: Houghton Mifflin, 1973), and Stephen Skowronek, *The Politics Presidents Make: Leadership from John Adams to George Bush* (Cambridge, Mass.: Harvard University Press, 1993).

On the study of the presidency, see George C. Edwards III and Stephen J. Wayne, *Studying the Presidency* (Knoxville, Tenn.: University of Tennessee Press, 1982) and George C. Edwards III, John H. Kessel, and Bert A. Rockman, eds., *Researching the Presidency: Vital Questions, New Approaches* (Pittsburgh, Pa.: University of Pittsburgh Press, 1994).

There are a variety of collections of writings on the presidency and presidential leadership, including Fred I. Greenstein, ed., *Leadership in the Modern Presidency* (Cambridge, Mass.: Harvard University Press, 1988), Michael Nelson, ed., *The Presidency and the Political System*, 4th ed. (Washington, D.C.: CQ Press, 1995), Aaron Wildavsky, ed., *The Presidency* (Boston: Little, Brown, 1969), and Aaron Wildavsky, ed., *Perspectives on the Presidency* (Boston: Little, Brown, 1975). For a valuable work, which is not widely consulted because it is lodged in library reference rooms, see Henry F. Graff, ed., *The Presidents: A Reference History*, 2d ed. (New York: Scribner, 1996). This volume contains overviews by leading authorities on each of the chief executives from George Washington to Bill Clinton. It contains a useful appendix consisting of background on each of the presidencies, which is the basis of the factual addendum to this volume. Another important reference work is Leonard W. Levy and Louis Fisher, eds., *Encyclopedia of the Presidency* (New York: Simon & Schuster, 1993), 4 vols.

ACKNOWLEDGMENTS

I have incurred a very large number of intellectual debts in the course of writing this book. I would like to acknowledge the following for commenting on it in manuscript: R. Douglas Arnold, Sharon Barrios, Larry Berman, Meena Bose, John P. Burke, James MacGregor Burns, Reggie Feiner Cohen, Michael Comiskey, Robert A. Dahl, Douglas Dillon, Alexander L. George, Andrew J. Goodpaster, Gordon D. Griffin, Alonzo L. Hamby, Erwin Hargrove, Hugh Heclo, Pendleton Herring, Stephen Hess, Richard Immerman, Robert Jervis, Stanley Kelley, Jr., John H. Kessel, Stanley Lebergott, Patrick J. Maney, Thomas E. Mann, James McCullough, Paul L. Miles, William K. Muir, Jr., Richard P. Nathan, Don Oberdorfer, Arnold Offner, James P. Pfiffner, Nelson W. Polsby, Roger Porter, Michael Rothschild, and Harold H. Saunders.

Special thanks go to the indefatigable Helaine Randerson, who repeatedly gave drafts of the manuscript the benefit of her keen editorial eye and processed it for publication. I also want to express my appreciation to a truly gifted editor who played an important part in hatching this project, the late Martin Kessler. Kessler originally contracted for it when he was president of Basic Books, and he brought it with him when he moved to The Free Press. His premature death deprives the publishing world of an editor of surpassing imagination and creativity.

In the nearly three decades in which I have been studying the modern presidency, I have had the good fortune of having instructive meetings with Gerald Ford, Jimmy Carter, George H. W. Bush, and Bill Clinton.

Many years earlier, I took part in a meeting with former President Harry Truman, in the course of a visit he made to the Yale campus in 1958.

I have also had many discussions with former and present presidential associates. The following were especially informative: Sherman Adams, James A. Baker III, Robert R. Bowie, Herbert Brownell, McGeorge Bundy, William Bundy, Alexander P. Butterfield, Joseph A. Califano, Jr., Frank Carlucci, Richard Cheney, Clark M. Clifford, Thomas G. Corcoran, C. Douglas Dillon, John D. Ehrlichman, John S.D. Eisenhower, Milton S. Eisenhower, Leonard Garment, Andrew J. Goodpaster, H. R. Haldeman, Bryce N. Harlow, Roger W. Jones, Nicholas D. Katzenbach, David E. Lilienthal, Jack Matlock, Michael D. McCurry, Harry C. McPherson, Jr., Charles S. Murphy, George Reedy, Walt W. Rostow, James H. Rowe, Jr., Donald Rumsfeld, Dean Rusk, Harold H. Saunders, Arthur M. Schlesinger, Jr., Brent Scowcroft, George P. Shultz, Theodore C. Sorensen, Jack Valenti, Jack Watson, and Ann Whitman. These discussions were as valuable for the intangible impressions they provide of the ambiances of particular presidencies as for light they shed on particular episodes. They are much appreciated.

The preparation of this book was supported by grants from the Christian Johnson Endeavor Foundation, the Dillon Fund, the John J. Sherrerd and Oliver Langenberg funds of the Center of International Studies, Princeton University, and the Lynde and Harry Bradley Foundation.

INDEX